The Art of Public Strategy

The Art of Public Strategy

Mobilizing power and knowledge for the common good

Geoff Mulgan

OXFORD
UNIVERSITY PRESS

OXFORD

UNIVERSITY PRESS

Great Clarendon Street, Oxford OX2 6DP

Oxford University Press is a department of the University of Oxford.
It furthers the University's objective of excellence in research, scholarship,
and education by publishing worldwide in

Oxford New York

Auckland Cape Town Dar es Salaam Hong Kong Karachi
Kuala Lumpur Madrid Melbourne Mexico City Nairobi
New Delhi Shanghai Taipei Toronto

With offices in

Argentina Austria Brazil Chile Czech Republic France Greece
Guatemala Hungary Italy Japan Poland Portugal Singapore
South Korea Switzerland Thailand Turkey Ukraine Vietnam

Oxford is a registered trade mark of Oxford University Press
in the UK and in certain other countries

Published in the United States
by Oxford University Press Inc., New York

British Library Cataloguing in Publication Data

Data available

Library of Congress Cataloging in Publication Data

Data available

Typeset by SPI Publisher Services, Pondicherry, India
Printed in Great Britain
on acid-free paper by
CPI Antony Rowe, Chippenham, Wiltshire

ISBN 978–0–19–928964–6

1 3 5 7 9 10 8 6 4 2

Acknowledgements

MANY colleagues and friends have contributed to the ideas presented in this book. I'm particularly grateful to my collaborators in the Prime Minister's Strategy Unit, including Stephen Aldridge, Jamie Rentoul, and Catriona Laing, as well as other colleagues in and around the UK government including Jeremy Heywood, Andrew Turnbull, Gus O'Donnell, and John Birt. I've been lucky in being able to work for politicians who took strategy seriously—in particular, Prime Ministers Tony Blair, Gordon Brown, and Kevin Rudd. Other collaborators in Australia have also been a great source of support and inspiration, including ANZSOG's Allan Fels and John Alford; Terry Moran and Peter Shergold, successive heads of the Australian Public Service; Glyn Davis, the vice chancellor of Melbourne University; and the many colleagues who helped my period as 'thinker in residence' in Adelaide, including South Australia's Premier Mike Rann.

Others who have helped my thinking include Roberto Mangabeira Unger, strategic affairs minister for Brazil and one of the world's most consistently creative intellectuals; the lively thinkers around the party schools and universities in China, including Yu Ke Ping and Cui Zhiyuan; Eddie Teo, Tan Chin Nam, and others in Singapore; Wim Donk and Michiel Schwartz in the Netherlands; Bo Ekman in Sweden; Pekka Himmanen in Finland; and Diogo Vasconcelos in Portugal. From the university world, I've learned much from Mark Moore at Harvard, Rosabeth Moss Kanter at Harvard Business School, Manuel Castells at the University of Southern California, and Jack DeGioia, President of Georgetown, and in the UK from Peter Hennessy at Queen Mary and Westfield, Christopher Hood and Vernon Bogdanor at Oxford, John Bennington at Warwick and Gerry Stoker at Manchester. Sean Lusk at the UK National School of Government in the UK provided helpful comments on an early draft. David Musson and Matthew Derbyshire at OUP provided a series of invaluable steers and suggestions. Finally I would like to thank my family and my current colleagues at the Young Foundation for their patience in allowing me the time to put my thinking down on paper.

Contents

PART III   253

15. Separating the Urgent and the Important:
    Strategy as a Public Good   255

List of Figures

List of Tables

List of Boxes

Abbreviations

BEPA	Bureau of European Policy Advisers
CASS	Chinese Academy of Social Science
CDMs	Clean Development Mechanisms
CERN	European Centre for Nuclear Research
CMT	Common Measurement Tool
COMPSTAT	New York's police data system
DALY	disability adjusted life year
DARPA	Defense Advanced Research Projects Agency
ENA	École nationale d'administration, France
EQ	emotional intelligence
FEMA	Federal Emergency Management Agency, USA
IMF	International Monetary Fund
IPPC	Intergovernmental Panel on Climate Change
NDRC	National Development Reform Commission, China
NEPP	Netherlands National Environment Policy Plan
NGO	non-governmental organization
NICE	National Institute for Clinical Excellence
NIJ	National Institute of Justice, USA
OECD	Organization for Economic Cooperation and Development
OED	Operations Evaluation Department, World Bank
OU	Open University
PEST	political, economic, sociocultural, technological
PESTLE	PEST plus legal and environmental
PFI	Private Finance Initiative
PISA	OECD Programme for International Student Assessment
QALY	quality adjusted life year
R&D	research and development
RCTs	randomized control trials
SITRA	Finnish technology agency
STEEP	an arrangement of factors similar to PESTLE
TOWS	a variant of SWOT—strengths, weaknesses, opportunities, and threats
WHO	World Health Organization

Note on the Author

DR GEOFF MULGAN CBE worked in the UK Prime Minister's office and Cabinet Office between 1997 and 2004 in a variety of roles including head of policy, and director of the Government's Strategy Unit. He is now director of the Young Foundation in London; visiting professor at LSE, UCL, and the University of Melbourne; and visiting Fellow at the Australia New Zealand School of Government and at the UK National School of Government. He also works as a part-time adviser to Prime Minister Kevin Rudd in Australia and Prime Minister Gordon Brown in the UK. He was founder and director of Demos, a think tank rated by *The Economist* magazine when he left as the UK's most influential. He has been a broadcaster, consultant, investment executive, newspaper columnist, and academic. His publications include *Good and Bad Power: The Ideals and Betrayals of Government* (Penguin, 2006); *Connexity* (Harvard Business Press, 1998), *Life after Politics* (eds) (HarperCollins, 1997), *Politics in an Anti-political Age* (Polity, 1994), *Communication and Control: Networks and the New Economies of Communication* (Polity, 1991). He was ranked in 2004 as one of the UK's top 100 public intellectuals, and has lectured in over thirty countries, including to governments in Russia, China, Japan, France, Finland, Sweden, Germany, the Netherlands, Canada, Australia, Singapore, the Czech Republic, Romania, and Spain. He has also served as thinker in residence for the government of South Australia, and as an expert adviser to the European Commission. He sits on many boards including the Design Council, the Work Foundation, the Health Innovation Council, and Involve. He has been profiled in several books including *The New Alchemists* by Charles Handy (HarperCollins, 1998), and *Visionaries* by Jay Walljasper (Utne Books, 2001).

Introduction: From Tangled Knots to Virtuous Circles

THIS is a book about how governments think and act. Governments can be brutal and stupid. But the best have helped their citizens to live longer, safer, richer, and freer lives. They have achieved their successes by being strategic—knowing where they want to go and how to get there.

Being strategic is neither natural nor easy for governments. Most opt for mediocrity and the lines of least resistance. Some trust in intuition (with all the virtues and vices it's known to bring).[1] Some—like Indira Gandhi and Ronald Reagan—rely on astrologers. And more than a few just use ideology to guide them.

Moreover, all governments face pressures to be tactical rather than strategic. The cut and thrust of competitive politics easily obscures long-term goals: good strategy is helped openness, and mobilizing many minds, but politicians like secrecy, and taking their opponents surprise. For ministers and bureaucrats with a brief tenure in any job there are strong incentives to fudge difficult choices, and little pressure to learn from mistakes. The future may literally be undervalued: governments apply discount rates to future benefits and the effective 'political discount rate' can be much higher still, especially in the run-up to elections.

Yet far-sighted politicians and committed public servants have helped many societies face up to both their problems and their potential. James Tobin, one of the greatest economists of the later twentieth century wrote that it was 'a bunch of planners—Truman, Churchill, Keynes, Marshall, Acheson, Monnet, Schuman, MacArthur in Japan—whose vision made possible the prosperous post-war world'.[2] France and Germany in the 1950s, and Malaysia, South Korea, and Spain in the 1990s, were all role models, channelling public aspirations while also achieving a fit between their societies' capacities to act and the environments they were acting in. Other nations have shown how the right strategy can turn impossible aspirations into reality. Finland began the 1990s with its GDP declining by 7 per cent in a single year but ended it as a technological powerhouse. Estonia in the same decade transformed itself from being 'bankrupt, polluted and decaying' (according to the OECD) to become the EU's most competitive economy. On the other side of Europe Ireland used a sophisticated consensus about economic policy (forged by its National Economic and Social Council), and highly entrepreneurial development agencies (led by Forfas), to make the most of EU membership and overtake the UK in GDP per head. Other nations have been highly strategic in working their way back from dictatorship or civil war: outstanding examples include Chile's patient work to become a modern social democracy under President Lagos, and Rwanda's more recent efforts to become a mercantile hub under President Kagame.

Many exemplary cities have also shown that good strategy pays off. Singapore transformed itself from a backwater into one of the world's great economic hubs. Hugely ambitious city states like Dubai and Abu Dhabi, as well as hungry city governments within nations, like Barcelona, Bogota, or Shanghai, have achieved extraordinary momentum. Below the radar of high politics innumerable ministers and officials have carefully diagnosed problems and designed solutions with evidence and experience to guide them rather than hunch or anecdote, on issues as varied as cutting carbon emissions or reducing mortality rates.

Although their individual stories were often messy, the governments and public agencies which achieved these successes acted in line with what Adam Smith described as the most useful virtue: the prudence that brings together superior reason (which 'discern[s] the remote consequences of all our actions') and self-command.[3] They acted fast, but steadily, in line with Aldus Manutius' famous prescription: 'festina lente', hurry slowly.[4]

What should strategies aim to achieve? Governments pursue many goals, from national prowess and GDP growth to well-being, usually trying to grow some things and shrink others. Past states wanted to grow their territory, crops, gold, and armies. Today the most valuable things which democratic governments want to grow are intangible: like trust, happiness, knowledge, capabilities, norms, or confident institutions. These grow in very different ways to agriculture or warfare. Trust creates trust, whether in markets or civil societies. Knowledge breeds new knowledge. And confident institutions achieve the growth and societal success that in turn strengthens the confidence of institutions. Much of modern strategy is about setting these virtuous circles in motion, whether through investments and programmes or by creating the right laws, regulations and institutions.

The things that most need to be shrunk are 'bads', some physical, like pollution, and others less tangible, like social exclusion or mutual hatreds. These are often wound up in tangled knots of irreconcilable interest as well as malign habits of thought and behaviour. The job of untangling them takes many forms: painstaking negotiation (as in the case of Northern Ireland, or the position of the Maoris in New Zealand), frontal assault (as with Norway's and Spain's legislation requiring companies to have at least 40 per cent women on their boards[5]), sophisticated, multi-dimensional actions (as in many fields of social policy, from teenage pregnancy to youth crime) and finding ways for problems to be outgrown as well as solved. Sometimes the goods and bads are intertwined. Life expectancy is rising at a remarkable rate in many countries (nearly 0.3 years each year in the UK), which appears to be an unmitigated good. But disability-free life expectancy is scarcely rising at all, and many countries are struggling with a rising incidence of chronic disease and dementia for which their health systems are unprepared.

There is no single formula for organizing strategy in public organizations. It can be led by specialized strategy teams and units, task forces and commissions; it can grow out of the discussions and collaborations of networks that cut across departments; it can have its roots in political parties, or in the civil service.[6] It can be open and inclusive, tapping into the collective intelligence of a society, or it can be closed and tightly controlled.

But all successful governments have created spaces for thought, learning, and reflection to resist the tyranny of the immediate, and any government or public agency that takes its responsibilities seriously needs structures and processes to do these things. Otherwise the competing forces that can be found within government, including party tacticians, media and public relations experts, cynics, and time-servers, are even more likely to sacrifice the future for the present. The costs of strategy need not be high, but the benefits can be, focusing energies where they matter, and refreshing governments that otherwise go stale.

Effective strategies need wide engagement and ownership. But they also have to be led from the very top. Leaders can't do this on their own. They need help from strategy teams to do the detailed work of analysis and planning and to keep track of implementation. At their best these teams become skilled in spotting threats and opportunities, and diagnosing which policies are likely to fail. They can be as valuable for killing ill-conceived ideas, and 'iatrogenic' policies which cause more problems than they cure, as they are for opening up creative possibilities. To be useful it's vital that they aren't a separate cadre, cut off from everyday life and actions, and immersed in a world of desiccated charts. They need to be well integrated with the daily practice of governments, to be streetwise as well as analytical, with their ears to the ground, and enriched by a continual flow of people in and out of strategy teams (including practitioners) so that the strategists acquire good judgements of what will work and the practitioners learn how to see the bigger picture.[7] They need to be an interface with the intelligence of every part of their society. And their work needs to be shared: strategies that are seen to belong only to ministers, or the board, or the strategy unit, are doomed to fail, as are strategies that are dominated by just one function (for example, finance or IT).

How should strategy be done? Again, there is no single answer: there are as many ways to be strategic as there are to be tactical. But all strategy involves setting priorities—being rigorous about what matters most, and directing energies to tasks which can be accomplished. A remarkable number of governments dissipate their energies, trying to please everyone, or tilt at windmills, engaging in struggles they have no prospect of winning. To focus their energies and get results governments need to pay systematic attention to:

- **Purposes**—*why* they should act in the first place: defining the compelling purposes which arise from the gaps between public needs, aspirations and fears and current realities.
- **Environments**—*where* they are seeking to achieve their goals, the contexts (present and future) for action and the capacities they have to get things done. It is from the interaction of these two that governments and agencies then define their chosen:
- **Directions**—*what* they want to achieve: the goals and outcomes that are desirable and achievable (which in the military take the form of the 'commander's intent' which is written at the top of any order), as well as their relative priorities and sequencing. These in turn define:
- **Actions**—*how* they are to achieve their goals, with detailed strategies, policies, laws and programmes, as well as inspirational leadership to persuade others to commit to the cause. Together these aim to create public value,[8] but since all actions have unexpected results, strategy also depends critically on:
- **Learning**—systems for understanding not just *which* actions did or didn't work but also whether there's a need to rethink purposes, analyses and chosen directions.[9]

This model contrasts with the traditional view of a linear progress from political commitments through policies to implementation (see Fig. 1.1). It implies an iterative, experimental, and adaptive view of how real governments

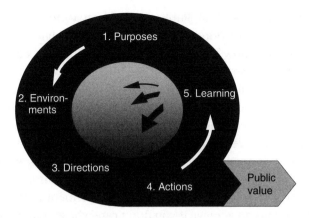

Figure 1.1. Development of effective strategy

work, with positive feedback reinforcing processes of change. And it puts knowledge at the heart of government—knowledge about why some schools systems work better than others, why some economies grow faster than others, or why some communities trust each other more than others.

That knowledge constantly evolves. During periods of rapid change governments have to learn quickly from their environment, relying on networks as much as hierarchies, and tapping dispersed learning as well as the assumptions of the centre (as Abraham Lincoln once wrote, the 'dogmas of the quiet past are inadequate to the stormy present'). They also have to learn to learn, and to experiment, even if that sometimes means failing. The instinct of most bureaucracies is to respond to failure with more rules and tighter controls. But lasting improvements come from innovation and the discovery, or adaptation, of new knowledge. As the great political scientist Aaron Wildavsky once wrote, 'error must be the engine of change. Without error there would be one best way to achieve our objectives, which would themselves remain unaltered and alterable. The original sin, after all, was to eat of the tree of knowledge so as to distinguish between good and evil. However great our desire, however grand our design, we ordinary mortals can only play at being God.'[10] What differentiates good strategists is not that they never make mistakes, but that they learn quickly from their mistakes, and that they learn deeply when the world responds in surprising ways.[11]

The circle also serves as a metaphor for the political context in which public actions take place. Democracy is a circle in which power and sovereignty come from the people, are temporarily vested in governments, and then come back to the people in the form, hopefully, of wise decisions and the conditions that make it easier to live good lives. These processes can be uneven and irrational. Public strategists have to learn how to ride unpredictable waves of hopes and fears; how to navigate minefields of public anxiety; and how to make the most of unforeseen events. Indeed their ability to do so smartly is one of the ingredients that makes real live democracies work. But for governments to act, and learn, effectively these circles need to be wide and inclusive, drawing on the intelligence of as many parts of society as possible, no mean challenge for traditions which have emphasized secrecy, closed decision-making, and contained elites. President Harry Truman once remarked that 'it's amazing what you can achieve if you don't care who gets the credit', and this is good advice for anyone wanting to promote ideas. But the complement to this is that it's amazing what you can achieve if you don't care whose ideas you draw on.

Autocrats assume that public engagement gets in the way of good strategy, but experience suggests otherwise. Norway is the only oil-rich nation which has successfully invested its proceeds to prepare for future needs without corruption or the enrichment of a small elite, in part because it went through a sustained and very open discussion about what should be done. Democracies are usually better at tapping into relevant knowledge, and they're less prone to corruption and self-delusion. They're also better placed to make use of the new technologies which make large-scale public dialogue much more feasible than it was in the twentieth century. Technologies allowing for social networking and collaboration are rapidly becoming more common-place, and easy to use, and can bring together wider circles to work both on the design of strategies and on their implementation. Official data can be made available for others to use, match, and mine and thousands of minds can be mobilized to share insights and solve problems. Indeed a common theme in this book is that many of the best strategies are simple—they provide a framework within which smart, responsive and responsible people and units can work things out for themselves, supported by rapid feedback, and easy communication. Overelaborate strategies that attempt to prepare for every eventuality are much more likely to fail.

In some respects this circular view of how government works isn't new. In democracies it is never enough for leaders to have good ideas, or the will to act. Power doesn't emanate from them; it passes through them and they also depend on the climate of opinion and the pressure that's put on them. Robert Caro's voluminous biography of Lyndon Johnson tells the story of the President being visited by a feminist delegation in the 1960s. Johnson listened patiently to their submission, and quizzed them about its details before saying: 'Well, you have convinced me that I should do it. Now go out and make me do it.' The women were outraged, believing that if they had convinced him, the most powerful man on earth, that must surely be enough. The President asked them why he should take the flak for actions that would be unpopular with many. They needed to create such a clamour that he could, with some (false) appearance of ill grace, respond. Public opinion is indeed all-important to democratic governments, the ultimate currency on which power is based. Leaders have to learn both to lead and challenge opinion and to follow it, ever sensitive to the up-swell of movements from civil society. No strategy today is complete without an account of how opinion will be moved, and how enemies will be defeated and allies mobilized,[12] and that's particularly true when governments are trying to influence public behaviour.

Causation: What Makes Things Happen?

Strategy translates wishes into results by mobilizing power and knowledge. Public strategy has achieved many unlikely successes, but few as unambiguous as the successful eradication of smallpox in the 1960s and 1970s, the first and only case of its kind, which provides a preview of many of the themes I address later on.[13] Smallpox had been a cruel and efficient killer all over the world: 100 million died as a result of warfare in the twentieth century; 300 million died of smallpox, which is highly contagious as well as untreatable. There were nearly 15 million cases as recently as the late 1960s, when the World Health Organization (WHO) committed itself to eradicating the disease, and gave the task to an unusually imaginative official, Donald Henderson.[14] At first the many public agencies involved in the field believed that the primary goal was mass vaccination. Vaccination appealed to governments because it was very visible, measurable and appeared to offer a direct link between inputs and outputs. Large-scale programmes could be planned, taking advantage of freeze dried vaccines which had been developed by the Lister Institute in London, and a jet injector that could do over 1,000 vaccinations an hour which had been developed by the US National Communicable Disease Center.

Yet on their own these programmes didn't work. They were too inflexible to contain new outbreaks, which demanded rapid surveillance and containment led by teams that could quickly spot incidences of smallpox, and innovate their own methods fitted to local customs, such as registers to track rumours and smallpox recognition cards.

The programmes that succeeded were founded on medical knowledge about the disease, but also depended on how operational information was gathered, shared, and then used. The central idea was 'ring immunization'—rapid action to immunize everyone in the vicinity of an outbreak. Strict rules for data collection, and action, were imposed by the WHO. For example, there was a rule that containment of any outbreak had to start within 48 hours of its discovery—motivating the data collectors that their information would be quickly put to use. In India every case of rashes or fevers was recorded and monitored and treated as smallpox unless proven otherwise. In some areas new cases prompted extensive room to room searches as well as rapid actions, for example, to vaccinate everyone within a one mile radius of an initial case. For the people working in the field, training involved simulations and real village-level exercises, usually run by junior staff rather than high ranking clinicians. Resources were then allocated according to strict rules—villages with recent outbreaks, for example, received a standard complement of petrol, vaccines, staff, and a jeep. At the same time there was constant evaluation of how different teams were faring, with the findings shared between the largely independent national programmes. In 1977 the last case of smallpox was found in Somalia, prompting the then director general of the WHO, Dr Mahler, to describe the programme's success as a 'triumph of management not medicine'.

Smallpox turned out to be easier to eliminate than other diseases, like polio, which lies dormant for long periods. But there are many striking features of the smallpox programme which give useful pointers to effective public strategy. It began as a classic top–down programme but evolved into something much more complex, as new ideas emerged from local teams, and as the many thousands of people working on smallpox eradication around the world became a community of learning. It made use of governments' ability to act on a large scale, and with standardized tools, but wasn't limited to this style of action. It began with medical knowledge but ended up drawing on many other kinds of knowledge, some formal (from administrators, sociologists, and anthropologists) and some informal. It combined very rigorous and standardized protocols and targets, along with considerable flexibility, rule breaking, and flouting of hierarchy. Above all it was a programme with a clear goal, and one that was inspiring enough to quicken the pulse of everyone working towards it.

In this case the WHO built up an accurate picture of causation, of the kind that any strategy has to rest on. Public institutions have to use many different kinds of knowledge (political, social science, statistical, public opinion . . .) to make sense of cause and effect: how a law, a programme, or a service will change some behaviours. In some respects public policy is similar to medicine, with diagnoses, assessments, and decisions that draw on established knowledge but are made in conditions of uncertainty, and which have to be followed up with careful observation of results.

Yet causation in public policy is more ambiguous than in other fields. There are a few fields where public agencies' actions are founded on reasonably secure knowledge about causes and effects. That foundation may be social science (for example, the knowledge that an interest rate rise will lead to changes in investment or savings, or that a reduction in overall levels of drinking will also lead to a reduction in problem drinking). It may be administrative experience (for example, that reducing the speed limit persuades drivers to drive more slowly). Yet much of the business of government rests on less solid foundations than this, dealing with issues where there are many interacting causes, some proximate and some ultimate, where there are competing claims for credit, and where governments' actions are more like improvisation than following a reliable music score.

Take a prominent example like the fall in crime in New York in the 1990s. It may have been caused by clever new policing tactics (the claim made by Commissioner William Bratton), by demographics (fewer 'crimogenic' young men), by the abortion reforms of the early 1970s (which meant fewer poor young men becoming criminals fifteen years later) or by subtler factors like younger brothers reacting against their older siblings (the conclusion of a large-scale ethnographic study). Which explanation is right is obviously crucial for any strategists who want to sustain the fall in crime.

It's also notorious that many apparently simple problems turn out to be symptoms rather than causes. In most western cities homelessness is not a problem of lack of homes, but rather of other traumas, from mental illness and family breakdown to drug addiction, that drive people onto the streets. Traffic congestion may appear to be the result of insufficient roads, but it might also be a result of inadequate public transport. As a rule it's always better to deal with upstream causes rather than downstream symptoms. But there are exceptions. Mental illness is a good example. Seventy years ago there was no mental disorder for which any treatment worked better than no treatment. Today many disorders can be treated, and a few even cured. But because psychology's understanding of the deep causes of many mental illnesses remains tentative and contested, interventions which focus on symptoms are often more effective than ones that purport to deal with underlying causes.

Knowledge and Power

Knowledge and power are at the centre of the approach to strategy which I advocate. I argue that governments need to cultivate a rigorous understanding of the nature of the fields that are being influenced: how stable, complex, or chaotic they are; how much is known about causes and effects; how much power government has to act, whether alone or in concert with others. Where government has both power and knowledge it can act in much more directive ways than when it has only one, or neither. When knowledge is widely distributed governments need to cultivate humility, and when power is widely distributed they need to be collaborators not commanders. The practical tools outlined later on encourage policy makers to think hard about the degree of power and knowledge they have in responding to threats and opportunities. They may have no choice but to act decisively—but if they're acting without firm knowledge they need to be quick to adjust and to listen to their environment. A high proportion of the mistakes made by governments come from overestimating the extent of their power and knowledge. The smallpox strategy was a good example of how to mobilize different kinds of knowledge to make up for the limitations of the WHO, and of how to mobilize different kinds of power too. The failed strategies to eliminate hookworm, or for that matter polio, demonstrated the limited power and knowledge of the agencies in charge.

The relationship between knowledge and action is the theoretical heart of the book, which presents government as about reflexive power and reflexive knowledge: power whose primary purpose is its own reproduction, through legitimacy and trust, and knowledge that includes knowledge of its own limits and so seeks to create knowledge for others. History and political science are full of examples of how to use power to create power, whether through persuasion and co-option, 'divide and rule', or judo moves that use enemies' energy to undermine them. There is less literature on how to use knowledge, and many of the tools are relatively new. For the strategists these include the analytic tools of systems thinking or logical modelling which make explicit the connections between things, how systems work and what effect different interventions may have. As teenagers learn about the feedback loops that shape the climate or water, these methods of thinking are becoming more mainstream, but they are still rare amongst civil servants.

There are many new methods for handling disparate kinds of knowledge such as user and frontline voices and formal evidence, from data on public opinion to the latest findings from genomics. Alongside the well established methods of pilots and pathfinders, expert commissions and task forces, others aim to tap society's collective intelligence, through open processes that allow for commentary and discussion on everything from background research to policy recommendations and laws; strategic audits and other methods for taking stock of what is and isn't working; futures, foresight, and benchmark exercises to set goals over longer time horizons (like the Oregon benchmarks programme); open contests and tenders for advice and research (of the kind being pioneered by the US Social Science Research Council); large-scale expert collaboratives (like the International Panel on Climate Change); collaboratives linking different places experimenting in parallel and sharing data and experience (such as the Clinton Global Initiative's work on climate change); and 'innovation accelerators' linking public agencies, entrepreneurs, and users to test out new ideas.[15]

These new models are evolving rapidly, taking advantage of an era of abundant information, and a far wider range of easily accessible sources of insight than was available for governments in the past. They embody the idea that no one is as clever as everyone, and that wider circles tend to be wiser than small ones.[16]

Theory and Experience

This book draws on the extensive literature on public management, government, and strategy. But I've also drawn on a long experience of many different kinds of public action. When I first left full-time education, after a spell selling encyclopaedias door to door, the combination of luck and the need to pay off debts pushed me into city government in London, working on the arts and helping to produce what may have been the world's first creative industries strategy.[17] Later I worked on regeneration and job creation in a city then suffering from mass unemployment, and a widespread (and, it transpired, misplaced) fatalism about whether anything could be done about it. In the late 1980s I worked in the European Commission in Brussels, focused on high technology and regulation at a time when Europe was confidently (and, as it turned out, mistakenly) laying the foundations for a super-state. In the 1990s I worked as a political adviser first in parliament (for a politician, Gordon Brown, who later became Prime Minister), then in a small NGO which spent much of its time working with frontline practitioners, and then in the office of Brown's colleague, Tony Blair, who became Prime Minister first, including a period as head of his policy team. In parallel, in the 2000s, I became a civil servant and set up and ran the government's Strategy Unit (part of the Cabinet Office) as well as helping to set up strategy teams in government departments.

In many of those roles I was lucky to have bosses who were genuinely interested in finding the right answers rather than just the expedient ones. My roles also allowed me to move back and forth between high-level macro policy and the very micro realities of job centres and community organizations. In the Cabinet Office I built up a large team working on strategy—including at its peak some 140 people in the main unit and a series of strategy teams dotted around departments. Our work was deliberately carried out without fanfare, and below the radar of media commentary; but it had a substantial impact on issues as varied as energy and climate change, poverty and post-conflict reconstruction.

To carry out our work we had to devise our own methods, since there was very little written material available on how strategy should be done in the public sector. The strategy manuals developed to guide business were of little use. Nor was there much available on the strategic use of money, technologies, people, or the law. In response, we developed our own tools and shared them on the web.[18] Parts of this book derive from that experience; others from more recent work with governments around the world, from Australia and New Zealand to China, Japan, Canada, Denmark, and Sweden, including as an adviser to two other serving Prime Ministers.[19]

In every government strategy is both important and frustrating. Strategists constantly struggle for time and attention in competition with the latest crisis, speech, or factional battle. The governments they work in combine rigid hierarchy and barely disguised chaos, apparent novelty and underlying stagnation. Nor are they always rational: as Keynes once commented in relation to markets, 'there is nothing so disastrous as a rational investment policy in an irrational world', and smart strategists have to be as attuned to apparently irrational motives as they are to facts and trends. Strategists also face the subtler challenge that no one near the heart of governments can easily judge just how much impact their work is having. I saw many published strategies that were implemented in ways that ignored their most important insights. Even when things happen according to plan it's rarely easy to judge which actions achieved which results. One remedy is active listening. When I worked in government I spent at least one day each week out and about, talking to people in schools and prisons, hospitals and welfare offices and community centres in as informal and honest a way as possible. Often that meant travelling incognito to avoid the welcoming party of senior officials. I learned never to fully believe anything I was told by departments and agencies until I had 'triangulated it' by confirming its accuracy with my own eyes (and on many occasions what was believed at head office turned out to be fiction on the ground).

Every government feels unique. The all-powerful district office in India is a world away from the ministry offices with papers piled high in Tokyo or the high-tech confidence of Singapore, or the cool efficiency of Scandinavia, or the boisterous energy—and hype—of American states and cities, or the meagre hospitals of rural China. Countries like Singapore that are dominated by a single political party can afford to think about strategy in very different ways to those like the USA where strategy is far more about competitive, and often short-term, electoral politics. Yet all share many common patterns. For example, most tiers of government have similar prejudices: the ones above are seen as out of touch and pointlessly interfering, the ones below as amateurish and prone to corruption. Everywhere there are well-intentioned officials trying to make sense of the wishes of flailing politicians, and principled politicians driven to distraction by incompetent and complacent civil servants. Every government mixes up the dramatic poetry of crises and spin, and the day to day prose of legislation, budgets, and programme management even if the cultures of government are very different in big countries like the USA or Russia, which operate to a soundtrack heavy with a sense of their own historic destiny, and the much more agile, and humble, cultures of government in small countries like Ireland and Finland. And in every public sector there are many who simply want to make their societies better without much prospect of glory or monetary reward (interestingly, in the UK, the Blair years saw a marked rise in public service commitment—by 2007 65 per cent of public servants under 35 said that it was important to them that their work was useful to society, compared to 14 per cent in the private sector).[20]

The dull realities of public administration provide plenty of fuel for cynics who believe that any long-termism, and any commitment to values, is a luxury that's made unreachable by the day to day cut and thrust of politics, the contradictory nature of public opinion, and the malign influence of interests. But my experience has left me with a cautiously confident view of the potential of government. Governments always risk failure, futility, and unintended consequences. Many become overloaded with tasks which they have no realistic prospect of carrying out. But good government is at heart about our collective freedom—our ability to exercise sovereignty together in ways that also enhance our individual freedom and sovereignty to be different. That this matters should not be in dispute, despite several decades when it was fashionable to decry the contribution of government to human well-being. Every serious analysis has found that the quality of governance is a decisive contributor to human well-being. There is a vast gulf between the life chances of people living in the best governed places like Switzerland or Norway and the worst governed in benighted places like North Korea or parts of West Africa.[21] At many times it's become a conventional wisdom that governments can do little good and much bad. But this view is not only at odds with the facts: it also hurts everyone's interests when it becomes entrenched, and none more than the weak and vulnerable.

Quality matters more than size: indeed, within a wide range, the size of government has little if any impact on growth rates or GDP rates—contrary to the widely accepted claims made in the 1970s and 1980s. Taxes which are too high will at some point choke off enterprise (though it's worth recalling that in the United States, the wealthiest saw their tax rates rise from 24 per cent in the 1920s to 91 per cent by the 1950s, which by many measures was the country's golden era of enterprise: the figure is now down to 35 per cent). What matters more than the size of government is whether public spending is devoted to productive uses, and whether it is used efficiently and without corruption.[22] Indeed recent research emphasizes the benefits of social spending rather than its costs,[23] and most of the countries which do best in rankings of global competitiveness are also relatively high spenders: their advantage comes from high levels of human and organizational capital. A recent World Bank study analysed why the same person can earn five to ten times more when he or she leaves a poor country to work in a rich one. Their answers focused on the value of the skills around them and the quality of institutions, including governance in all its forms and the rule of law. The study estimated that 80 per cent of the wealth of developed countries and 60 per cent of the wealth of poorer countries is of this intangible type: 'human capital and the value of institutions ... constitute the largest share of wealth in virtually all countries'. According to their regression analyses institutions account for 57 per cent of intangible capital, education for 36 per cent (Switzerland scored top).[24]

How to Read this Book

Many governments have been content just to be there: slowly administering their societies, suspicious of change and reform, and at worst tending to predatory behaviour and oppression. Even some of the better civil services see themselves as shock absorbers—sources of stability amidst the fluid and uncertain world around them—and many governments live in an eternal present of media commentary and opinion polls. This book is an aid to focusing on the things that really matter, providing societies with what they really need and having the courage to avoid being blown off course by events.

The book can be read in one go, dipped into, or used as a practical guide. Part I sets out the background to public strategy. Chapter 2 defines public strategy and looks at its character, and how it's different from strategy in business and the military. I also look at why strategies fail, and the common patterns of error that afflict governments. Chapter 3 analyses the supply and demand for public action, the historical context that has shaped modern government and the legacy of recent reforms. Chapter 4 then sets out the model of strategy and the steps that need to be taken by anyone wanting to shape an effective strategy with a good chance of being implemented. In Part II I dig in more detail into the major issues facing contemporary governments Chapter 5 addresses where strategy should be organized within government, and how it fits with other functions such as political management and communications. Chapter 6 investigates the nature of the knowledge that strategy rests on and Chapter 7 looks at how to turn plans into actions, including the virtues and vices of targets. Chapter 8 addresses the challenges of innovating and taking positive risks in the public sector and Chapter 9 addresses the parallel challenge of handling negative risks and remaining resilient. Chapter 10 focuses on how to act across organizational boundaries ('joined-up government'). Chapter 11 looks at the growing importance of behaviour and culture change as goals of strategy and Chapter 12 at the importance of trust as an overt goal of strategy. Chapter 13 addresses measurement—and how to judge success. Chapter 14 is about leadership, and its relationship to strategy. Finally, in Part III, Chapter 15 pulls the threads together and sets out some conclusions.

By the end I hope the reader will understand the relevance of three very ancient comments from Chinese sages, about fish. The first is that 'the fish discovers the water last': it takes hard work to understand accurately the world in which you live. The second is that 'only dead fish go with the tide': better to make your own fashions than be a slave to others' ideas. The third, which comes from Lao Tsu, tells us that 'governing a great country is like cooking a small fish: don't overdo it.'

PART I

PART I

What is Public Strategy?

LET's start with definitions. Public strategy is the systematic use of public resources and powers, by public agencies, to achieve public goals. The word 'public' means concerning the people as well as referring to the formal authority of states. Strategy comes from the Greek 'strategos', a general, a word which brought together 'stratos', the idea of something which is spread out (an army or multitude), with 'agos' the idea of leadership. So what we're concerned with here is how the sprawling mass of public agencies, laws, services, embassies, armies, and laboratories that make up a modern state can be led in the same direction and serve a public interest that lies well beyond the state.

Strategy isn't always either possible or relevant. It's easier when the environment is reasonably stable or predictable. Governments with very small majorities or in unstable coalitions; ministers and officials with short job tenures; and organizational cultures focused on tomorrow's news coverage, are unlikely to be very interested in strategy. They may feel more attuned to Groucho Marx's question: 'what's posterity ever done for me?'[1] or to the comment of the ruler who corresponded with Machiavelli, and claimed to conduct his government 'day by day and arrange my affairs hour by hour; because the times are more powerful than our brains'. In other cases there may be the will to act strategically but no way of turning ideas into action: ministers feel that they're putting their foot down on the accelerator but all they can hear is the engine turning over with no forward movement. Meanwhile some public bodies become so consumed with their own processes that they lose sight of what they're for, ending up both goal-less and soul-less.

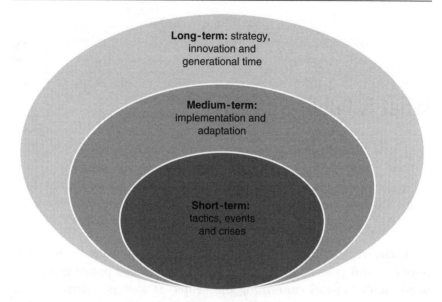

Figure 2.1.   Three horizons of decision-making

But competent and responsible organizations that are ready for the future manage to keep their values and principles in sight while focusing simultaneously on three different horizons of decision-making (Fig. 2.1):

- The short-term horizon of day to day crises and issues, from the pressures of media and politics, to problems like strikes or IT crashes. Getting these wrong can be fatal for a political leadership, or an individual executive.
- The medium-term horizon of existing policies and programmes— where performance and successful implementation are paramount, but most spending and programme delivery is already set.
- The longer-term horizon where new policies and strategic innovations become ever more critical to survival and success, including the 'generational horizon' of issues like pensions and climate change where governments increasingly have to look fifty years into the future.

During the mid-1990s I often taught at the Civil Service College and asked officials to describe the typical timescales of the plans and decisions they were involved in. The outlying agencies were often working over long time horizons, for example procuring defence systems that would not be delivered for another twenty years, or designing national curriculums for children who wouldn't leave school for almost as long. Yet the closer you came to the centre of power the shorter the time horizons were. The

Treasury was looking little more than a year ahead, perhaps understandably given Britain's history of economic volatility. The Prime Minister John Major's people were thinking from week to week, the price paid for a small majority and a band of disruptive rebels in his own party.

Some stability and consistency are essential preconditions for institutions to pay serious attention to the third horizon. Without them, the future is simply too unknown. But competent strategic organizations learn how to act and think in all of these horizons. Although leaders need to devote most of their time and energy to the first and second horizon, they also need to carve out significant slices for the long term and ensure that some of their staff are entirely insulated from immediate pressures (a reasonable ratio for the allocation of time and people is 50 : 30 : 20). Their core staff need to be able to work across these different horizons, connecting the long-term to the immediate. But around them there need to be specialists, working with the media, tracking implementation or planning for the long-term. These latter will include advisers and members of round tables, units, and teams within agencies, as well as more formal structures like the Commissariat de Plan and its successor the Centre d'Analyse Stratégique in France; BEPA in the European Commission; the Scientific Council (WRR) and the Social and Cultural Planning Bureau in the Netherlands; the UK's Strategy Unit; CASS and the NDRC in China; and SITRA in Finland, to name just a few. Their roles vary from defining the high strategy of geopolitics (building up alliances, or military preparedness), to strategy at the level of political economy (for example, establishing institutions which can negotiate income levels and social wages), to strategies at the level of public service systems (setting legal and regulatory frameworks, ensuring the right flow of trained staff, or the right sequence of reforms to build confidence and trust).

The best strategies are clear about what they're trying to achieve and how they'll do it. That's where their power to inspire comes from. They may be at heart very simple—and based on simple insights into the nature of things—like the idea of universal healthcare provided as of right, or the idea that key infrastructures could be opened up to competing companies, or the idea that drivers should pay for their use of roads. These may be imaginative leaps. They may be surprising combinations: some problems that in isolation are intractable in combination turn out to be tractable. The American jurist Oliver Wendell Holmes put it well: 'I don't give a fig for the simplicity this side of complexity but I would give my life for the simplicity the other side of complexity.' Developing strategies is partly a linear process, but also involves circling around issues until this simplicity is achieved, often with the help of intuition or subconscious thought as much as logical deduction. A common lesson of the practice of strategy is that too much elaboration and complexity actually leads to worse decisions. Indeed the best strategists draw on experience to cultivate a 'strategic intuition' which enables them to grasp the essentials of a situation in one go and to judge what will work in ways that can be supported, but never substituted, by analysis.

There is a vast literature on strategy. Throughout history rulers have wanted insights on how to win wars and how to survive against difficult odds. From Sun Tsu to Clausewitz, and Alfred Chandler to Michael Porter, this literature has been primarily about two domains: war (how to defeat the enemy), and business (how to achieve and sustain competitive advantage).[2] This literature offers many insights for the leaders of governments and public organizations. There are some common principles and factors to be borne in mind in every field: the behaviours and mentalities of competitors; the critical resources; the morale and motivation of real and metaphorical foot soldiers; perceptions as well as realities. The very large literature on change within organizations is intended to be universal in its implications, and has provided many insights into the often highly political dynamic whereby early enthusiasts persuade resisters. It also emphasizes the importance of early actions (and early wins) in building confidence and stakeholders in change, something that is very familiar to social movements and civil society. In all fields, too, there are severe limits to the ability of any organization to understand the world it is operating in. Facts may be distorted; analyses may be confused; events intervene; and strategies evolve as they bump against the real world. But, equally, in all fields, as Seneca wrote two millennia ago, 'There are no fair winds for those who don't know where they are heading'.[3]

Despite these similarities, the challenges public agencies face are often radically different than in other fields. Strategy for public organizations is not just about achieving competitive advantage (though competition with other jurisdictions for territory and resources can often be crucially important). Public organizations face very different constraints (including public opinion, political factions, or tax-raising capacity) than businesses or armies. They can make use of very different tools (including law, tax, and regulation). They generally have more goals at their disposal and have to deal with more complexity and ambiguity, reflecting the wider range of stakeholders they have to satisfy, not least because electorates rarely speak with a single voice. They are more likely to want to shape environments as well as responding to them, and they generally work with a wider mix of motivations—including more intrinsic motivations (curing people, teaching them, protecting them) as well as self-interest.

These differences are partly reflected in the much smaller emerging literature on strategy in public organizations,[4] and a very large, and over-lapping, literature on management and administration in the public sector.[5] There is also a literature proposing various different tools for strategy, including qualitative methods and methods which seek to put numbers on as many variables as possible.[6]

A recurrent question in much of this literature is whether strategic methods are universally applicable across sectors. My view is that although some of the questions are universal the answers are not: smart strategies are very specific to their contexts. As James Q. Wilson pointed out in his classic book *Bureaucracy*, the essential qualities needed to run a good prison are very different from those needed in an excellent school or an excellent hospital. The details of a strategy to create jobs will be very different from those for cutting crime.[7] Some public services, such as postal services or benefits payments, are large-scale retail and distribution industries with many close parallels in the private sector. Others, such as policing or public health, operate at the intersection of public behaviour, strong professions, and profound asymmetries of power and knowledge. In some services the public's primary concern for reliability is best delivered by high levels of integration and coordination (for example, in crisis management or transport), while in others improvement is most likely where there is decentralization and user empowerment.

These differences can easily be obscured. The major consulting organizations advocate using the same methods for strategy in any kind of public or private organization.[8] Some similar methods can indeed work well for second-order issues, such as organizational design, introducing technologies, or the detailed planning of implementation, sequencing, and interdependencies. Consultants and advisers can become adept at applying generic methods for breaking issues down into their component parts, and systematically piecing together implementation plans. These methods have long been the bread and butter of competent administration, but public organizations all too often let their skills atrophy. But such generic methods are less useful in fields where knowledge is all-important (such as medicine) and they provide few insights for the more central tasks of government including legitimation, public value, and, for politicians, how to win re-election. At worst, the indiscriminate use of generic methods from the private sector can do harm, generating paper efficiencies that are experienced by the public as worse service, or doing away with public engagement and democracy in the name of cutting waste.[9] Generic methods are equally unhelpful in guiding the core business of military organizations: they can help with improving logistics or recruitment, but not with winning wars.

One of the most important areas of difference between business strategy and public strategy is time. In business the future is discounted according to consistent and precise measures that arise in the market. Discount rates measure the opportunity cost of capital, defining how much less $100 in five years' time is worth compared to today, and this in turn drives investment decisions. This 'exponential discount rate' provides a very rigorous way to make decisions about the future. It also, notoriously, drives long-term values down close to zero: from the perspective of today's market an asset that won't be realized for fifty years is almost worthless (a 5 per cent discount rate values $100 in fifty years' time at $7.69). No wonder action on climate change is so hard. In the public realm, by contrast, very different views of future value are used, even though many finance ministries apply standard discount rates to projects like airports and roads. Some theorists describe public decisions as closer to 'hyperbolic' discounting, where the discount rate steadily falls, and then levels off. Seen through another lens, many public decisions are taken more through the lens of stewardship or guardianship, where the priority is to leave behind a more useful set of assets than you inherit (this is also the strict definition of sustainability), rather than automatically favouring consumption now over consumption in the future. As a rule strong social bonds tend to reduce or even eliminate discount rates (which is why parents are quite happy to leave large bequests to their children, and tight-knit communities automatically restrain current consumption in the interests of the future). As I will show, real governments apply a range of different approaches to time and discounting, some very similar to business and some radically different.[10]

Another subtler difference is that governments have no choice but to be more engaged in design than businesses or NGOs. It is simply not possible for governments to treat every event and every situation as unique. Instead generalizations are embodied in laws, programmes, principles, and protocols: indeed the power to apply general rules serves almost as a definition of the state (and as Alfred North Whitehead put it, civilizations advance by 'extending the number of operations we can perform without thinking of them'). These rules still leave space for discretion and judgement, and generally more discretion is allowed in times of crisis or when events move fast. But it is impossible to be strategic without some element of standardization, generalization, and routinization, and without some sense of the design principles that are needed, for example, to reshape industries to become zero waste or low carbon, or to make public services more personalized, richer in information and feedback, or better at tackling underlying causes rather than symptoms. Herbert Simon once wrote that 'the intellectual activity that produces material artifacts is no different fundamentally from the one that prescribes remedies for a sick patient or the one that devises a new sales plan for a company or a social welfare policy for a state... in large part, the proper study of mankind is the science of design, not only as the professional component of a technical education but as a core discipline for every educated person.'[11] In a democracy that skill in design needs to reside not just in the bureaucrats and politicians but also in the commentators and citizens who judge, reward, and punish.[12]

There is, however, one less obvious respect in which business thinking can provide insights into public strategy. In business, strategic thinking often begins with organizational capabilities and then looks for how they be used in different ways to create as much value as possible. It is entirely legitimate for, say, a company focused on cables and wires to remake itself as a mobile phone company (as Nokia did). Public strategy has traditionally begun the other way around, with goals: it then designs organizations and programmes to meet them and treats any additional capacity as a threat to focus. It's often seen as illegitimate for bureaucrats to seek new roles. But both politicians and officials often act as entrepreneurs, looking for new demands in a dialogue with the public in which goals are not fixed.

Performance and Strategy

Figure 2.2 is a recent ranking produced by the World Bank covering government effectiveness. It's striking that most of the front-runners are not only good at current performance but have also taken strategy seriously. Denmark, which comes top, is a particularly interesting example. The Danish public expect a lot of their government, and pay a lot for it (as measured by the public sector's share of GDP). But they also get much for their money: Denmark generally comes near the top of international rankings for GDP and employment rates as well as social and environmental outcomes. Denmark also stands out for having pursued a sustained and effective strategy in response to the economic shocks of the 1980s that helped to preserve its very high levels of social provision.

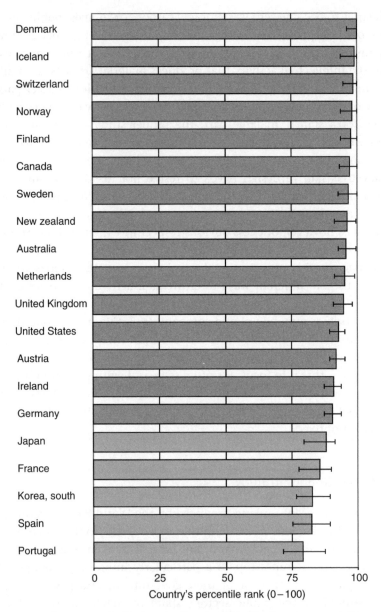

Figure 2.2. Government effectiveness by country. The bars represent the overall position and the lines at the end represent margins of error. *Source*: World Bank.

In the words of a recent Danish 'Handbook for Prime Ministers': 'the overriding goal has been to make Denmark one of the most competitive economies in the world. This has been achieved by tough economic control and by coordinating policies all the way down to the most insignificant detail in the fields of employment, the labour market and education'. Cross-party consensus has been critical to this, and has meant that a broadly similar strategy has been adhered to over more than two decades, alongside a broad consensus in other areas from care for children to environmental improvement.

Other countries in this list have also worked hard to be strategic. Finland has already been mentioned; Switzerland has long required senior civil servants to learn formal strategy methods; Norway has been one of the wisest countries in making use of windfall gains from natural resources, as well as being boldly radical in fields as varied as gender equality and the environment, while the Netherlands has done more than any other country to embed futures thinking into its decision-making. Before its current travails, Iceland presented itself as a laboratory for the world, a nation where the future would arrive first. Other impressive examples of strategies directed to high-level goals include:

- Singapore's strategy to become a leading economic power, executed between the 1960s and the present day within the constraints of a quasi-democratic city state;
- Egypt's strategy to cut child mortality;
- Cuba's strategy to improve public health, which enabled it to achieve mortality rates much lower than wealthier societies;
- Germany's strategy to rebuild the old East Germany, which despite problems ranks as one of the most successful acts of integration in history;
- France's strategy to influence the European Union which for a long period worked amazingly well, casting Europe's governance in a French mould;
- the US strategy to contain the USSR which succeeded beyond expectations when the Cold War ended with the Soviet Union's collapse;
- the US strategy to make the dollar the pivotal currency of the global economy;
- Lebanon's strategy to rebuild the economy in the wake of civil war, a much less even story, not least because of continued interference by its two powerful neighbours, Israel and Syria;
- China's strategy for long-term economic growth, that has so far broken every record in economic history, or its one child policy which cut population growth by some 400 million;

- New Zealand's strategy to achieve a fairer deal with its indigenous Maori population;
- Uganda's strategy to cut HIV/AIDS;
- the policies pursued by many other countries to raise birthrates, including France's policy of providing child benefit for second children (and since 2005 an extra grant for third children), and Singapore's more ambitious plans to raise the birthrate amongst graduates (including state-supported dating agencies); and
- Iceland's strategies for reshaping the labour market, involving school-children in work as well as members of extended families.

Many other examples could be cited, but this list gives a sense of the sheer variety of high-level strategies that governments have pursued. These high-level objectives tend to be so all-consuming that few governments can pursue more than two or three at any one time. In other cases the objective may be more limited, for example:

- building up the science base in Australia as part of an economic strategy to shift Australia's comparative advantage away from minerals and mining to human capital;
- raising employment rates in Denmark;
- dealing with urban migration in coastal China, or official corruption;
- cultivating a meritocratic civil service in Mexico;
- France's strategies to create high-speed rail networks; and
- the widespread adoption of parenting programmes to cut crime (which in the US have been shown to be three times as cost effective as the 'three strikes' programme).[13]

Bad Strategies

The strategies listed above broadly worked. But some of the most visible strategies of recent years have been disasters, and disasters are always instructive. Indeed, most people learn more from their own failures than they do from successes. When Japan's Emperor famously told his people as the Second World War came to an end that 'the war situation has developed not necessarily to Japan's advantage,' he was responding to a self-imposed disaster with the typical air of denial that afflicts those in power. Yet ironically, this turned out to be the beginning of a period of unprecedented prosperity and freedom, and the government he ruled over learned quickly and transformed itself completely. One of the most prominent recent disasters was Russia's reform programme in the 1990s. This was shaped by a group of economists from Harvard (notably Jeffrey Sachs and Andrei Shleifer) and others at the World Bank and IMF, and backed by the US government with very large sums of money. Its central idea was shock therapy—that the right mix of shocks could move an economy at a stroke from planned communism to market capitalism. The strategy combined the introduction of market prices, slashing public spending, and privatization of public assets. The programme was designed to set in motion a period of rapid economic growth. Instead it led to a roughly 50 per cent cut in Russia's GDP, almost unprecedented in peacetime in any major economy. Poverty rose from some 10 per cent to at least 25 per cent, and almost every social indicator worsened. The country was left with much stronger organized crime, and powerful oligarchs. In 1998 the rouble fell by 70 per cent. The strategy combined a fundamentally flawed view of how people work (its only intellectual model was the raw individualism of neoclassical economics); misconceived policies and strategies; and disastrous implementation.

The Russian case is unusual in that it achieved precisely opposite effects to those intended. Japanese expansionism fell into the same category, as in some eyes, did the Iraq invasion of 2003: promoted to discourage terrorism and to provide a democratic power in the region as a counterweight to Iran and Syria. At the time of writing it had increased terrorism and brought Iran and to a lesser extent Syria into Iraq's governance as never before.

Failures are instructive because they remind us what makes a strategy good. These failures—from Japan's defeat in the Second World War to Russia's economic retreat in the 1990s—happened because of deeply flawed assumptions that were not adequately interrogated by those in power. Right from the start they were doomed because they were based on flawed observations and weak intelligence. There was inadequate planning for any path of events other than the one hoped for. And then, to compound the problems, they proved unable to learn quickly from mistakes.

Anti-strategy

The truly bad strategies, and the mediocre ones, have encouraged critics who claim that any strategies will be at best futile and at worst damaging. A variant of this argument was made several centuries ago by Pandolfo Petrucci the Lord of Siena whom Machiavelli quotes as saying that wise government should be organized moment to moment because of the unpredictability of the times. The modern variant of this argument is that the environment is so unpredictable, so full of unknown unknowns as well as known ones that any planning is foolish (as the old saying goes, life is what happens while you're making other plans). Since no plan will survive its first encounters with reality, the best stance is to improvise and adjust. According to this view strategy and planning provide a comforting appearance of rationality but are not functional.[14] They are a symptom of humanity's fear of losing control and of 'being cast into the abyss' rather than a cure for it.

For other critics, strategy exemplifies the mistaken belief that thought and action can be separated. This belief in its modern guise is most closely associated with Frederick Taylor, who broke the workings of factories down into their component parts, and believed in a rigid division of labour in which thought was monopolized by professionals and managers broken down into cadres of specialists; some for finance, some for marketing, and some for strategy. This approach is associated in recent decades with the work of such figures as Michael Porter who have advocated a highly detached and formalized model of strategy-making in which the only useful knowledge can be codified, abstracted, and turned into models. As critics like Henry Mintzberg point out, these models rarely work well in practice. They exaggerate the solidity and relevance of the data, undervalue frontline experience, and prove slow to adapt when things go wrong. Another common vice is that they tend to reinforce hierarchy, encouraging strategists to blame implementers when things go wrong, or to devise ever more elaborate methods to constrain their autonomy.[15] It's claimed that 90 per cent of strategic plans in business are never implemented and that 70 per cent of change projects fail. Perhaps this is not surprising since in a 2005 survey of 1,400 chief executives 91 per cent said that increasing complexity required new skills and tools, but only 5 per cent believed that they had these skills.

At one extreme bad strategies reflect the hubris of leaders who believe that they can plan systems which are in fact far too complex for any planner to grasp. At another extreme they become empty exercises which give the appearance of coherence even where there is none. There are important insights in many of these critiques of strategy. The twentieth century was replete with grandiose and ineffective plans and strategies, from the Soviet economy to the US military, and from businesses like Ford and IBM, to Nikita Khruschev's extraordinary plans for turning virgin lands into fertile farms, with far-fetched targets, inflated rhetoric at every turn, and for a time imaginary successes before the strategy ended up with dust bowls. Visions may, after all, be 'things you have before you get locked away', as one minister once commented to me. But none of these are arguments against strategy as such. They are rather arguments for better strategies that are humbler, wiser, done for real, and more integrated with their systems and their environment.

Incrementalism

An equally old tradition of academic study of government has been suspicious of the very idea of strategy in government. Instead it has argued that most of the daily business of government is more like incremental adjustment in response to the battles and compromises of organized interests, with little assessment of alternative options and no clear boundaries between means and ends. The classic exposition of this case was written by the political scientist Charles Lindblom in 1959. He described government as 'muddling through', with clear goals and strategies the rare exception.[16]

Muddling through is indeed common in most governments (and in some businesses), and is entirely rational if you don't know where you want to go, or why, or how. Muddling through can even be designed into the DNA of government: the German constitution favours iterative adaptation over bold leadership for obvious historical reasons, and America's still reflects its founders' fears of too imperial a presidency. In others muddling through results from fractured authority, internal competition, or simply no one taking responsibility for the future. In benign times this may not matter too much: Italy managed reasonably well for much of the post-war period with very weak governments. But in more turbulent times the muddlers are likely to lose out to the nations that can act quickly and decisively.

The distinction between incrementalism and strategy can be misleading. All real strategies have to adapt and change, and are made up of many increments, and it's never wise to be locked into a strategy. 'Management by groping along', and the habit of acting fast so as to learn quickly, can be a rational response to uncertainty and can sometimes add up to a strategy.[17] Even in the rare cases where a government develops a fully thought-through reform agenda—such as in New Zealand, or to a lesser extent Spain or Britain in the 1980s—policies have to constantly adjust to the prevailing patterns of power, to setbacks and events. Margaret Thatcher's

Conservatives had no idea at the end of the 1970s how important privatization would become to their purpose and image. When at roughly the same time France's socialists came to power for the first time in a generation the initial strategy was fully implemented in some fields (such as regional devolution), and comprehensively scrapped in others (such as industrial policy). Conversely, however, even the most committed incrementalists sometimes have to become strategic, responding to bigger forces—as West Germany did when it took over the former East Germany in one of the boldest moves of recent history.

In other fields, too, incrementalism can be very radical. The 'statistical process control' methods developed by William Edwards Deming for Japanese industry, and executed most successfully by Toyota, combined relentless measurement, constant assessment, and mobilizing the intelligence of all levels to drive improvement. These methods have turned out to work well in rethinking flows in the public sector too—from hospitals to transport, taxation and welfare payments to prisons, and their cumulative impact can be profound.

Predictable Mistakes

History is full of examples of governments that misjudged the future, like the 1822 Parliamentary Committee on Trade which advised King George IV that the idea of a steam engine was useless and the result of 'a distempered imagination', or the Royal Commission, a century later in 1930, which advised that Britain would never need the continental innovation of motorways. The future is never easy to discern; radical change is improbable and unsettling because it means the destruction of contemporary habits and interests. There will always be some eminent experts who can be relied on to be utterly wrong.[18]

In the British television series *Yes Minister*, a senior civil servant comments that one thing shared in common by many of the world's leaders is that they were all imprisoned by the British. Undoubtedly the police who arrested them, and the judges who sentenced them, had no idea that before long they would have to pay them respect as heads of state and heads of government. All large organizations tend to make similar types of mistake. Power brings with it predictable kinds of myopia. Governments share the systematic biases that are built into human nature: the confirmation bias that leads us to look for evidence that confirms what we already believe, and ignore evidence that challenges it; the narrative fallacy that leads us to connect disparate events into single narratives, and to prefer stories over truths.

Governments' mistakes are predictable: they fall into common patterns. As Robert McNamara acknowledged at the end of a long career (from Ford to the Pentagon to the World Bank), governments' biggest failings are generally those of empathy—the inability to think into the minds of others, particularly enemies. This is the commonest error in diplomacy. Diplomats and leaders simply fail to understand that people living in different countries think differently, and have different cultural references. Within nations, too, lack of empathy explains a large proportion of errors, in particular failure to understand the resentments that powerless people feel towards the rational plans of the powerful, whether they are slum clearances and vasectomies in India or poll taxes in Britain.

A second common pattern of error comes from the psychology of investment: governments find it much harder to end policies and programmes that have had significant past investment. Once a department or agency has spent years devising plans, commissioning consultants, and making public announcements, it is not easy to look rigorously at whether it is still worth proceeding. Many governments have gone ahead with programmes even when there is strong evidence that they are unlikely to succeed, or that the costs will be far higher than originally envisaged (the UK's Millennium Dome was a particularly visible example of this, a costly white elephant that went ahead more because of momentum than because of any great demand or enthusiasm). This is why smart institutions make use of independent advisers to take a fresh look at big programmes and projects—as if they were starting from scratch. Wise leaders recognize that it is better to take the short-term flak for stopping a project that no longer makes sense than it is to take the long-term flak for going ahead.

The third common pattern is wishful thinking. Many strategies assume either that their operating environment will remain constant or that existing trends will continue in a straight line. They may do. But more often history takes twists and turns. A particularly common type of wishful thinking is profligacy, which afflicts governments that put their faith in high rates of economic growth, as well as financial sectors which in every generation repeat the same mistakes of overstretch, soft credit, and weak controls. A good protection against mistakes is to test strategies against alternative scenarios—bad as well as good, for example in the business cycle. Periods of growth tend to encourage even apparently

hard-headed investors to forget that economies move in cycles. Governments are just as poor at preparing for downturns and recessions.

The fourth more subtle common error is the failure to understand
runaway and dynamic processes. Most of the things that governments
deal with change in reasonably incremental ways, and in slow straight
lines. Demography, for example, is reasonably predictable: the great majority of the people who will be alive in ten years' time are already
alive today. But one of the strange features of the world is that dynamics
can run much further than appears likely or common sense. Stock markets
tend to rise further than appears logical—and then they fall further
too. Epidemics can spread in an exponential way—again, more dramatically than the human mind is designed to expect. Many governments
simply did not believe the predictions made for the spread of AIDS in
the mid-1980s because they seemed implausible. New phenomena like the
Internet, and new patterns of behaviour like text messaging, have also
spread at a pace that defies normal human experience. This is why it
is useful to immerse decision makers in simulations that help them to
understand dynamic, cumulative processes.

A fifth error, shared with most people in their own lives, is the failure to
understand that normal probability patterns mean that extremes are
likely. Any phenomenon that is distributed in a normal curve will be
found in extreme forms. So highly unlikely events are still likely to occur
sometimes. A one in a million possibility could happen well over sixty
times in a nation of 60 million people. A variant of this is the difficulty
governments have in understanding patterns of extreme evil. History
tells us that almost any population is capable of extreme evil in the right
conditions. Populations are equally capable of extreme good, of generosity
and self-sacrifice. But governments tend to assume that people will operate in a more predictable middle zone.

A sixth pattern of error is to continue with assumptions that happen
to be wrong. This was well described in David Halberstam's book on the
'best and the brightest' who filled the higher reaches of John Kennedy's
administration.[19] They tended to be affected by 'groupthink'—shared
perspectives on the world that squeezed out sceptics. Apparently rational
chains of analysis might easily miss out the factors that to others were
blindingly obvious. Kennedy's administration almost led the world into
a Third World War during the Cuba missile crisis because the narrow group
with which he was surrounded, mainly men in their forties, and mainly
from Harvard, saw the world in a particular way and left insufficient scope
for internal argument and diversity to challenge assumptions. Almost

every public organization suffers from a version of this weakness—and finds it painful to dismantle its own world view even when it is clearly leading to failure. This is why it's so vital for leaders to have around them people confident enough to tell them when they're wrong.

Finally there are the errors which come from wanting to avoid difficult or cognitively challenging trade-offs. The human brain works very hard to sustain a meaningful world view, even against the evidence. Today's most obvious example is the question of whether 'people, planet, and profit' can be aligned: there are very good reasons for wanting to believe that they can be. But it's possible that they can't, and past civilisations disappeared because of a failure to face up to profound incompatibilities between existing ways of life and the demands of the future.

These patterns of error are common.[20] The failures they lead to are experienced as strange and incomprehensible. But they are to a fair degree predictable, the consequences of common patterns of human psychology, like the desire to be accepted within a group, which then become amplified in the context of government.[21] They can amplify other common causes of failure—like the malign influence of old ideologies or old intellectual paradigms.[22] Understanding these patterns of failure is at least a partial protection against succumbing to them.

In politicized climates we can add to this list the failures that come from ignoring truths that are simply too difficult to absorb. George W. Bush's resistance to the 'inconvenient truths' of climate change was a very visible example in the 2000s. Two decades before, when Britain's Central Policy Review Staff in the 1980s prepared a report looking at demographic change and pointed out that current pensions policies were simply not sustainable, its leak to the press forced Mrs Thatcher to disavow them. Not long afterwards they were closed down.

Airing future possibilities creates present headaches. It may highlight the flaws and deficiencies of current policies. It may remind voters that they are bored of their rulers. It is equally risky to act now in the name of the future. According to hard-nosed political analysts governments never back prevention over cure. Why spend scarce resources on actions that will benefit your successors, probably from a different party? Why antagonize the powerful interests that currently provide cures? I've often heard world-weary officials offer variants of this argument, and remember a very senior Treasury official telling me in the mid-1990s why no government would ever invest significant sums of money into support for young children, however strong the evidence for the long-term payback. Yet on many occasions governments have acted more responsibly. A classic instance was the Headstart programme in the US which survived many changes of administration. In the UK the similar Surestart programme was strongly promoted by the Treasury only a couple of years after my cynical interlocutor made his comment, and directed very substantial sums of money to young children on the promise of benefits in fifteen to twenty years' time.

How does this happen? Partly because people want to do the right thing; partly because of a climate of opinion; partly because the sheer weight of evidence becomes impossible to ignore.

Public Action: The Dynamics
of Supply and Demand

THE ultimate purpose of strategy in a democracy is to meet public wants and needs, refracted through politicians' more immediate need to win elections. All governments have to navigate the relationship between their limited ability to provide or act, and the demands of their citizens. Their best policy may be to do less and cut taxes (like Estonia's Mart Laar who introduced a 26 per cent flat tax for both income and business[1]). Or it may be to introduce new programmes and services, whether on a large scale like the universal childcare introduced for 3-year-olds in the UK in the 2000s, or on a smaller scale like 'Fixer-Sven', a free public service in Sweden that helps over-75 year-olds with risky jobs (and claims to have saved money by cutting injuries associated with falls).

The relationship between supply and demand can be mapped as a diagram (see Fig. 3.1). The supply curve captures what governments can achieve with varying levels of resources and power. With 100 per cent of GDP they might be able to provide outstanding infrastructures, top-quality healthcare on demand and tertiary education for anyone who wants it (though in time, of course, the economy might disappear). With 20 per cent of GDP their offer is bound to be much more limited, perhaps little more than 'safety net' public services and basic defence and policing. This supply curve is a very rough approximation because the different services provided by a state are not easily interchangeable, and for convenience we're mixing up the ones which are paid for with money and the ones that are paid for with freedoms.

The demand curve roughly captures what prices in taxation the public would be willing to pay for different quantities of public provision (Oliver Wendell Holmes described taxes as 'the price I pay for civilization' but it is a negotiable price). Again this is a very rough approximation because public

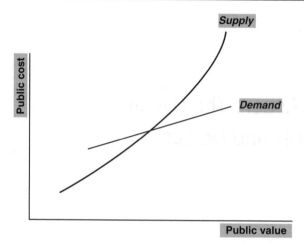

Figure 3.1. The relationship between supply and demand

demands can be contradictory and they are certainly non-transitive. Nor do real publics get much chance to find out what they would really get for different levels of taxation (though the discerning traveller in a continent like Europe, or moving across the different US states, can make a broad assessment).

In some situations a rough equilibrium can survive for many decades as the public get the mix of services and welfare they want at a price they consider reasonable. At other times the situation is unstable. When Charles Dickens's father was sent to debtors' prison he said to him that if a man had 20 pounds a year and spent 19 pounds 19 shillings and sixpence he would be happy; but a shilling spent the other way would make him wretched.[2] When expectations and demands exceed capacities the result is distrust and a sense of failure. When capacities exceed expectations the public are broadly satisfied and governments remain legitimate (see Fig. 3.2).

This framework for thinking about supply and demand provides a useful simplification and it's not so far from the arguments at election time as parties promise either to spend more or less, or to change the balance of public spending. In the long run the terms of trade can change. Governments can push their supply curve to the right with new knowledge and techniques which allow them to do more for the same or less (for example, there is strong evidence of good returns for investment in programmes of parenting skills, well-conceived mentoring, or cognitive behavioural therapy). Conversely what William Baumol called 'cost disease'—the tendency for the costs of providing labour-intensive education, health, or art galleries, to rise relative to the rest of the economy—can push supply curves to the left.[3]

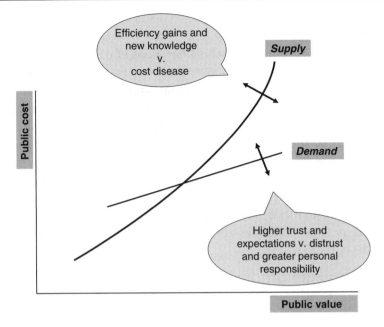

Figure 3.2. Public value/public cost negotiation

Many governments also seek to influence the public's demand curve, reducing expectations so that they are more in line with reality, or encouraging people to take more responsibility for their own risks. Politicians can make speeches about the problems of affording pensions or healthcare; or about the virtues of introducing charges for previously free services. Hypothecation of tax can also influence demand: people may be willing to pay more if they can see exactly where their taxes are going.

These negotiations between supply and demand involve entrepreneurship, albeit within limits that are set by everything from global markets to technology and public opinion. But because they involve entrepreneurship, overly rigid definitions of what governments should or shouldn't do turn out to work better in theory than in practice. Many theories have attempted to show where governments are most likely to add value, and where they are most likely to destroy it. These generally explain governments' roles in terms of market failure. According to mainstream economics, competitive markets are the normal way of delivering goods and services. Governments come in, and are most likely to add value, where markets fail, for reasons including: inadequate information, or asymmetric information; externalities—where private actions load costs onto others, for example the costs of pollution, or infectious disease; public goods where consumption by one person does not reduce what is available for others (like defence, or new knowledge) or where the good is non-excludable (like policing); and where questions of equity are paramount.

According to one school of thought governments should only act where there is clear evidence of market failure, and less risk of government failure[4] (which is most likely when governments' knowledge is missing distorted, or when agencies or intermediaries are captured or diverted: Joseph Stiglitz, for example, cites the lax regulation of the American Environmental Protection Agency as an example of capture by special interests).[5] Any attempts to supply beyond these areas would lead to failure and waste. Yet experience shows that the entrepreneurial character of democratic politics has undercut the theory—if political entrepreneurs successfully offer electorates new services it matters little if the theoreti-cians deem them wrong.

Innovation in Tools

Under the regime of Enver Hoxha schoolchildren began each day by pro-claiming their love for him, for the communist party, for Albania, and for their mothers (in that order). Spies were on hand to spot any hint of disrespect. Exhortation, fear, and command—the preferred tools of the Albanian state before 1989—remain common methods for governing nations in some parts of the world. But most use more benign tools, and most are more honest about the limits of their power and knowledge (Hox-ha's state was one of the least successful of modern times judged by any measure other than its ability to survive). At the other end of the spectrum from Albania, New Zealand's government in 2007 went so far as to briefly launch an online 'wiki' for the public to make suggestions on revising its police legislation, a tentative step towards open source government that is about as far removed from the totalitarian police state as one could imagine.

In many countries the last few decades have brought an immense amount of change to government and governance, under the shifting banners of public management reform, transformation, re-engineering, and modern-ization driven both by politicians and by dynamic bureaucratic leaders. A glut of acronyms has washed across public organizations—from TQM and NPM to JUG and RIGO. Most have tried to make government more efficient and better informed, with more precise goals, faster feedback, and more measurement. They have improved the supply of government—but also reshaped how people demand what government provides. This innov-ation in tools have affected every field of government action.

Some new tools have changed how governments describe, observe and judge the world around them. It's well known that most of the day to day errors in government start off as errors of observation—failing to see important realities, screening out uncomfortable facts, or simply misreading the world. Doctors are estimated to misdiagnose at least 15 per cent of cases. There are no comparable data for governments but the figure is likely to be much higher, and this has justified new methods for measuring everything from public satisfaction to the results of hospital operations.

Some of the newer tools exist to help judgements. The most glaring errors of all come when governments lose their moral compass, or confuse ends and means, and here too there has been constant innovation, from codes of conduct, Truth Commissions, and financial rewards for good rulers[6] to the growing use of arm's length bodies (like the committees of central banks or utility regulators) that make their decisions in public, a shift which is premised on the hope that their judgements will be sounder.

Finally there are the new tools of policy and implementation—ranging from providing birth control pills for cats (in Denmark) to compulsory parenting classes for parents of misbehaving children (in Britain), and smart cards for public transport systems (in Hong Kong) to regulations (in Germany) requiring power companies to buy surplus electricity from residential windmills or solar-powered homes. In later chapters, I look in more detail at these new tools and their virtues and vices.

The Presence of the Past and the Four Duties of Government

Governments are usually creatures of continuity. Most schools that try to impart knowledge would be immediately recognizable to a teacher from 100 years ago. Similarly many of the procedures and buildings of government would be recognizable to a civil servant or minister of a century or more past. Parliamentary debates, cabinets, white papers, laws, programmes, initiatives, files and papers, minutes and memorandums, budgets, and treaties continue to be the bread and butter of administrative life.

Some very ancient methods remain in use. By 2,500 years ago most modern forms of government already existed: dictatorships and democracy, militaristic states, theocracies, and paranoid empires. Their tools included permanent bureaucracies with laws, decrees, and records, and like contemporary governments they worried about how to get the right balance between taxation and prosperity, freedom, and security. Through many thousands of years some of the fundamental duties of government have also changed surprisingly little. From ancient Sumeria and Rome to contemporary Asia or Latin America governments have sought legitimacy through pursuing four broad sets of duties which continue to be the tests by which governments are judged.

The first is their duty to protect the community from threats, in particular the threats of invasion, civil war, and natural disasters such as floods and famines. This is the heart of any state's contract with its people. If it fails to protect them it soon loses legitimacy. The second duty is to promote public welfare, through cultivating a thriving economy and providing care for the sick and poor. Although we think of the welfare state as a modern invention, it had many antecedents—from the rationing of grain in ancient Sumeria to public jobs programmes in ancient Rome. The third duty is to enforce justice, punishing crimes and resolving disputes, and the fourth is to promote truth, helping the community to understand the world around it, whether through religion or more recently through science.

Governments have often pursued other ends, from glory and conquest, to self-enrichment, revenge, and exploitation. But their claims to obedience and loyalty have largely centred on these four sets of goals, and these goals have been the ones demanded of governments by the people they claimed to serve. They also define the main goals for strategy in the modern world. Protection remains paramount: indeed, governments' ability to address dangerous risks is as prominent as ever in the era of terrorism, climate change, and a greater preponderance of natural disasters, as well as partially man-made ones like avian flu. When governments fail in this their legitimacy is irredeemably scarred, as the Bush administration discovered over Hurricane Katrina. Some of the paranoid habits of cold war military planners are now spreading around domestic policy. This is where government comes up against both known and unknown unknowns, the infinite number of threats that could explode into crises. Welfare has become even more important than in the past, thanks to democracy, and the failure to care for people can be as damaging to legitimacy as failures of protection. Justice too has widened its spread, to encompass everything from the claims of gay couples for legal recognition and the claims of indigenous peoples to the rights of children.

The search for better ways to carry out these varied duties stretches back throughout history. Ancient China produced many handbooks for rulers (from Confucius and Mencius to the Legalists). Ancient India's Kautilya and Plato and Aristotle in Greece all set out models of good governance and discussed problems that are easily recognizable today. Much past statecraft was concerned with security: how to conduct wars (or avoid them), forge alliances, and prevent usurpers. But the traditions of thinking about government are much richer than this. Many emphasize the risks that rulers will only serve themselves, losing sight of their duties and slipping into excessive oppression. Some focus on the close relationship between the character of rulers—their own 'self-governance'—and their ability to govern well, and many present service to the public as a pragmatic necessity for rulers seeking to retain power (Samuel Finer's *History of Government* in three volumes provides by far the best overview of the structures and ideas of governments from Sumeria to modern times).

Every ambitious state throughout history has sought to do much more than to preserve peace and prosperity: it has also tried to influence how people think and behave. The less moral states have done this with malign means and for malign ends (for example encouraging young men to hate). The better ones have used more virtuous means in the name of more virtuous ends (for example trying to encourage habits of learning, personal hygiene, or respect for the law).[7] At various points during the nineteenth and twentieth centuries liberalism came to see these influences on behaviour as illegitimate: freedom should mean the freedom to make your own mistakes and to shape your own beliefs. But in the early twenty-first century the need to influence beliefs and behaviour is at the forefront of many governments' thinking. Climate change is the starkest example: given that there is little prospect of technology advancing quickly enough to cut the CO_2 emissions from air travel and (to a lesser extent) energy within the next two decades, the only alternatives have to involve changing behaviour.

There are many other fields which pose similar challenges. Obesity is one: according to the WHO there are 300 million obese people worldwide, and analysts predict that by the middle of the next decade 20 per cent of US health spending will go on obesity and obesity-related diseases. Singapore is one of the few countries which has bucked the trend, with a firmly illiberal approach: its National Healthy Lifestyle Program, begun in 1992, tests schoolchildren for weight and fitness and puts those who fail on group running and aerobics programmes.[8] Many other countries are now trying to reshape their 'obesogenic' environments (the Mississippi Legislature has even considered a bill to ban restaurants from serving obese customers). Smoking is an even clearer example, where the freedom to choose has quickly lost ground to bans and prohibitive taxes.

The Three Drivers of Change: Democracy, Knowledge, and Connections

Democracy: More Constraints and More Demands

By modern standards past governments barely impinged on people's daily lives. Apart from the occasional visit by a tax collector, the rhythms of life were set much more by the seasons and nature than by decisions taken in a distant capital. Three mutually reinforcing trends dramatically accelerated the evolution of government. Each of the three has raised the prominence of a public good which has also turned out to support private prosperity.[9] The first is the spread of democracy, a public good which has turned out to be the best insurance against famine and oppression. The second is the growth of knowledge, most of it commonly owned. The third is the rise of connections, which has created a set of positive externalities since the value of any network grows in proportion to the square of the numbers of nodes it has. The spread of these three clusters of public goods, and their interactions, explains much about governance today.

Democracy is the most unlikely victor of the modern era. Written off as a failed historical curiosity until the late eighteenth century, it also looked vulnerable in the 1930s and 1940s. Yet it turned out to be a contagious idea, and its spread from England, Switzerland, and the USA, to many other nation states in Europe and later around the world, has now gone so far that well over 100 nations define themselves as democracies. Even the exceptions have experimented with elections and some of the trappings of constitutional government. Democratization is far from always being a one-way street, and many countries have 'de-democratized': indeed some have talked of a global 'democratic recession' that's followed the great wave of democratization of the 1990s. But when democracy has taken root it has oriented governments' capacities much closer to public needs and demands, rather than the needs and demands of rulers.

Table 3.1 (drawn from work by Charles Tilly) distinguishes states by their level of capacity and their degree of democracy. For most of human history all states were in the bottom left-hand quadrant. Over the last century and a half democracy has evolved in tandem with growing capacity and brought the mass of the public into the domain of public strategy, although there are nations which combine high levels of democracy with lower capacity (like Jamaica), as well as a smaller number that combine high capacity with low levels of democracy (like Kazakhstan).

As democracy takes root people gain in confidence in making demands of the state, and this in turn forces states to attend to the practical things

Table 3.1. *State capacity and level of democracy*

	Democracy Low	Democracy High
State Capacity High	Kazakhstan, Iran	Norway, Japan
State Capacity Low	Somalia, Congo	Jamaica, Belgium

Source: Charles Tilly, *Democracy* (Cambridge: Cambridge University Press, 2007).

that they need. Democracies spend 25–50 per cent more on public goods and services than autocracies, and pollution controls are twice as high in democracies as autocracies once the effects of income are excluded.[10] Strong environmental policies turn out not to be caused by, or associated with, higher income as was once thought: rather they are encouraged by democracy, and the claims of the relatively poor for cleaner air and water.[11] Evidence from Africa shows a similar story: as democracy spreads, governments spend proportionately more on primary education while spending roughly the same as non-democratic societies on the university education that benefits the elite.[12] In China, which has recently experimented with elections for very local government, the evidence points in a similar direction. Research by Beijing University's Yao Yang showed that where local elections were held public spending rose by 20 per cent while spending on 'administrative costs' (which often included perks for local officials) fell by 18 per cent.[13]

Democracies also tend to tax progressively. A good mark of autocracies is that the rich pay few or no taxes: the burden falls on the powerless. In democracies the marginal rates on income and wealth can rise as high as 80 per cent or 90 per cent, and substantial sums are redistributed from the rich to the middle or the poor (which, according to economic theory, should increase net happiness since a dollar for a poor person is worth much more than it is for a millionaire).

Democracy is often captured, corrupted, or compromised. But these correlations help to explain why studies of happiness find very strong correlations between democracy and life satisfaction: people thrive from having the experience of power, and they also benefit from policies that reflect their interests. Contrary to widespread assumptions, there are also strong relationships between government and civic activism: according to one recent survey, 'bigger government is associated—although probably not causally—with a higher degree of active citizenship.'[14] Yet despite these advances, in the most mature democracies many worry that it is in crisis. In 1997 the Norwegian parliament launched a five-year study on

'Power and Democracy in Norway' which concluded that 'the parliamentary chain of government is weakened in every link'. Sweden in the same year commissioned a Commission on Swedish Democracy, and Finland later launched a Citizen Participation Programme which proposed regular 'general checkups' for the health of democracy.

Elected representatives make claims to authority, and mandates, that often crumble on closer examination. They may have won fewer votes than opponents (like George W. Bush), or won the support of only a small minority of the total electorate (like Tony Blair). They may have won support more because of hostility to the other side than because of any great enthusiasm for their programme. Under pressure from civic and social movements, reformers in many countries have therefore sought to deepen democracy, or even to democratize democracy: passing more power to citizens and consumers; finding ways to engage them more in decisions; and making government more open and transparent. A panoply of methods have grown up to give meaning to the goal of 'empowerment', including ombudsmen, guarantees, and charters; rights of redress; rights of choice; rights to information; online petitions and citizens' juries; easier access to services through call centres and contact centres; and attempts to smooth 'service journeys' (how citizens experience being treated for a disease, for example). It's no longer acceptable for elected politicians to claim that they are the only legitimate channel for accountability: instead as democracies mature they create multiple channels of accountability, some very formal and some informal.

Democracy, along with pressures from civil society, has also radically changed the environment for governments by institutionalizing higher ethical standards. There are still plenty of cases of financial corruption, particularly where large contracts or planning consents are being given, and there is no shortage of corruption around party funding—giving special treatment to favoured tycoons or businesses and covering up mistakes (typically when scandals unfold the cover-ups turn out to be more serious than the original mistakes). The best sign of how ethically problematic these are is the effort made to keep them secret (though those involved typically overestimate their ability to keep them confidential). But most democracies have institutionalized higher standards. Many methods have been used to discourage unethical behaviour, to strengthen the virtuous, and frighten the wicked. There are ethical training courses in civil service training colleges, whether through formal pedagogy, teaching people how to reason ethically, or the use of case studies. Codes of conduct and laws provide formal rules that are regularly reviewed and updated to manage the boundaries, sometimes enforced by regulators and commissioners able to make quasi-judicial rulings and punish infractions. Parliamentary committees take evidence and report on both specific cases and patterns of wrongdoing, with their findings amplified by the media.

Ethics and effectiveness were once seen as mutually exclusive alternatives. Governments could either be virtuous—or they could get the trains to run on time. Advocates for reversing democracy often claim that this will make the state more effective. Yet the rankings of government effectiveness correlate pretty closely with the rankings of corruption prepared by bodies like Transparency International, and truly predatory states govern very badly. Cambodia is one of the contemporary world's extreme examples of a system that has lost touch with any duty of humble service: with 343 ministers, 849 generals, 30,000 officers, and 50,000 NCOs (for 15,000 soldiers), and pervasive corruption.

In the strong democracies there are now more restraints on what governments can do than in the past. These blocks and restrictions have come from constitutions guaranteeing a greater balance of powers, from powerful judiciaries and second chambers; auditors and inspectors scrutinizing what agencies do; international organizations providing a running commentary, sometimes critical; and more open global markets for money and goods. The restraints are reinforced by active and independent media, and sometimes bolstered by public rights to information as well as by robust political argument. These have all transformed the environment for politicians and officials alike. They are no longer figures of uncontested power, like the governors in imperial China or Prefects in France. Yet, as we shall see, despite these constraints their capacity to act has generally grown, not shrunk.

Knowledge

That capacity to act depends on knowledge (see Box 3.1). In most developed societies the proportion of the population with formal qualifications has gone from a minority to the majority within a generation. A half of each new age cohort is now sent to higher education, and governments are obsessed with their comparative performance, whether measured through school results (in the OECD PISA programme), attracting in foreign students or vocational qualifications.

Governments are also voracious for knowledge for themselves. They've always depended on spies, merchants, and ambassadors because their power over others depended greatly on their relative speed and accuracy of information, but the modern era brought a revolution in the sheer volume of knowledge available to government and in the techniques with which it could be used—from the statistical methods (derived from the German *Staat*) that provide the fuel for modern governments to the stark rationality of the cameralists in Germany or the utilitarians in Britain.[15] Improvements in public knowledge made it possible for the first time for governments to improve public health, educate whole populations, or run universal pension systems, and these explain much of the growth in the size of states. In 1870 national states typically absorbed around 11 per cent of GDP in developed countries; by the mid-1930s that level had more than doubled, before another surge of growth in the 1950s–1980s took the averages up to 28 per cent in 1960 and 43 per cent in 1990, pulled forward by public demand for welfare and services. The biggest growth took place during the major wars, yet after the wars levels of spending never returned to the previous status quo. In Britain, for example, civil service numbers grew from about 30,000 in 1850, to 50,000 in 1890, to some 730,000 in the mid-1970s, and then down to under half a million today. The period after the Second World War saw the high-point of confidence in the state's knowledge of how to solve problems. This was the era when many countries nationalized industries, expanded regulation and planning, and introduced new systems of social insurance and universal benefits. Punchcards and computers spread alongside professions like planning and social work, and techniques for such things as the measurement of national income and accounts.

Confidence in states' capacity to know has waxed and waned, but their tools and techniques have continued to advance, and today states make use of everything from supercomputers to predict the weather to DNA databases for criminals and iris scanners to verify the identity of ordinary citizens. Knowledge has also become one of the vital resources to be distributed by states. In another era the most important resources were financial, or physical things like food and housing. Increasingly, human capital is the resource that matters most. This was the insight of the American GI Bill in 1944, which provided for college or vocational education for returning Second World War veterans, and of new rights to places at university and in further education. Entitlements to learn are continuing to grow (for example with rising educational leaving ages), alongside other types of resource such as learning accounts, conditional support for families to allow children to learn (like Brazil's Bolsa Escola or Mexico's Oportunidades programme which was recently copied by Mayor Bloomberg in New York), financial assets (such as child trust funds) that can be used to pay for education, or rights to packages of time off and money for parents wanting to refresh their skills.

Governments have also felt impelled to compete in making their businesses smarter, and faster at developing and adopting technology, whether through tax relief for research and development (R&D), collaborative research programmes or subsidized consultancy. Some try to turn public knowledge into proprietary knowledge in the hope that this will ultimately lead to greater prosperity (though surprisingly few governments can demonstrate that the benefits have exceeded the costs). Every country seems to want to cultivate a strength in the four key converging domains of 'nano, bio, info and cogno',[16] and every government, like every business, aspires to shift its economy from quantity to quality, from things to knowledge. Some like Finland, Denmark, and Israel, have sharply increased spending on R&D. Not all are succeeding: despite official encouragement for a shift from quantity to quality, Chinese spending on R&D remains relatively low, and the ratio of prices of Chinese exports to EU exports (a rough mark of the value of knowledge and design embedded in products) remained stable at around 2.5–2.6 between the mid-1990s and mid-2000s, suggesting how far China is from becoming a high value producer.

Knowledge is becoming an influential lens for policy-making as issues that were once marginal have become central, from the regulation of stem cells and biotechnology to policies for higher education (see Box 3.1). New tools have come into widespread use: for example, designing regulations to promote innovation (such as stricter building regulations, or stretching goals for energy providers to use renewables), or reshaping public purchasing to promote innovations as well as value for money. Many countries are trying to match the dynamic circuits of knowledge that drove growth in California, linking public funding, universities, venture capital, and high technology business in ways that accelerate the speed with which new knowledge is put into practice. Few have yet succeeded, though industrial policies are now much more oriented to knowledge, for example helping industries made up of small producers to access up-to-date information about technology or export markets.

Governments' own knowledge is also being rethought. In fields as diverse as crime policy and pensions, governments draw on an increasingly global pool of knowledge and ideas, as well as investing in research, piloting, evaluation, and innovation. The methods of 'open coordination' (as in the EU) use greater transparency to guide policy, for example to encourage governments to keep public sector deficits under control.[17] Meanwhile the large data sets that are produced by governments can increasingly be linked together and interrogated—for example to see the patterns linking crime and consumption patterns, schools and congestion, air quality,

> **Box 3.1   New agendas around knowledge**
>
> Human capital policy, from higher education to early years
> R&D-led growth as key to economic policy
> Environments for knowledge—regulatory, spatial/milieux, fiscal
> Handling sensitive new knowledge (e.g. stem cells)
> Strategies for public and social innovation
> Evidence-based government
> Personal identity and security
> Intelligence services focused on corporate knowledge
> Use of large data sets and providing public data freely
> Sovereign investment and knowledge-rich firms

and diseases. In healthcare, as in manufacturing, the systematic tracking of data has turned out to show patterns, and predict events, that even the most brilliant experts would miss. It's also opening up a new relationship between the state and citizen, as very large public databases using anonymized information become available for citizens themselves to use, for example to see how a new treatment is working for others suffering from the same condition.

Not all of the trends are making knowledge more public. The USA has widened the scope for patent protection to include what many see as discoveries of nature (particularly in genetics). Europe has tightly protected commercial databases, and the World Trade Organization has tried vigorously to enforce intellectual property rights (often in a rather desperate battle with the burgeoning power of copying technologies). Personal data too is becoming more tightly protected. Germany has guaranteed its integrity under Article 1 of the Constitution, and there are growing civic movements to ensure that citizens own and control their personal data rather than big business or the big state (with much of the technological work being done under the prosaic banner of 'Vendor Relations Management').

Governments never had a monopoly of public goods but networked technologies make it even easier for citizens to create their own public knowledge goods. Hurricane Katrina was a striking harbinger of the future. While the government's FEMA turned out not to know what was going on, citizen action did. Within a few days online volunteers had processed 50,000 entries about displaced or missing people. They also helped to find temporary housing. The volunteer-created Peoplefinder database helped over 5,000 into new homes and achieved at almost zero cost what government might have spent millions on, helped by business (Salesforce) and charity (the Red Cross), but most importantly by thousands of enthusiastic citizens using relatively simple technology.[18]

Connectedness and the Dissolving Boundaries of International and Domestic Policy

The third great driver of change has been increasing connectedness, and the growth in flows of money, information, goods, and people that has tied the world much more closely together. Connectedness has widened people's opportunities and their wealth (the world market for goods has doubled in size every 8–9 years) but it's also created new tensions and resentments amongst the disconnected and the bypassed, as summarized in Box 3.2.

Most nation states were formed by war, and war and defence lay at their heart. Every state has had to balance its external priorities—protection and survival in a dangerous world—with its internal priorities of ensuring prosperity and the rule of law. Some of the challenges that follow are very old in nature even if their forms are very new.[19] The struggles over global economic power are again heating up: the USA accounts for 25 per cent of world GDP, and (through the dollar) 52 per cent of capital markets, 58 per cent of foreign exchange and 68 per cent of foreign reserves, a position that both the EU and China will contest. The struggle to control natural resources may be equally fierce. It has brought large US bases to the Gulf, as well as some 750,000 Chinese citizens to Africa. Old-fashioned spying wars have found new tools with the advent of

---

Box 3.2   New agendas of a connected world

Migration—legal and illegal—and asylum
Drugs flows
Organised crime
The spread of new contagious diseases (e.g. SARs, avian flu)
Competition for high value investment
Trade wars (e.g. farming subsidies)
Intellectual property wars (e.g. TRIPs)
International competition policy (EU v. US, Microsoft and Google)
Cities as key players
Nations as brands

cyber warfare, as Estonia discovered in 2007 when it faced severe attacks apparently originating in Russia.

Globalization makes many new things possible: like finding partners to share purchasing (something the world's biggest cities are doing to cut carbon emissions, with joint purchasing of such things as LED traffic lights); or outsourcing data management to distant countries (admittedly a risky venture when, as happened with UK driving data in 2007, the contractor in Iowa managed to lose millions of files). Some Norwegian cities have established care centres in Spain, and the British health service offers some patients the option of having their treatment and rehabilitation in Bangalore.

But a more connected world also puts immense pressures on governments to compete. Many have felt an imperative to compete for foreign investment, both as a source of capital and as a means of securing new skills. This has put some ceilings on marginal corporate tax levels, though, contrary to predictions, the overall take of tax on profits has risen over the last fifteen years. Regulation in some fields has become more difficult because of the need to harmonize rules—on accounting standards, intellectual property or e-commerce. New battlegrounds are taking shape over the regulation of monopolies (especially in the knowledge economy where a continuing struggle over competition policy has broken out between the EU and the USA over firms such as Microsoft, battles which are likely to become even more intense around biotech monopolies, or the extraordinary power of Google). Tax is another battleground thanks to multinational companies' use of transfer pricing and other methods to minimize their tax obligations. This was a major concern of the UN in the 1960s and 1970s—and some global companies continue to pay little if any net tax. Tax havens are one of the most common forms of tax avoidance—and may be becoming more common despite some countermeasures. The growth of e-commerce is also a concern to governments in their role as tax collectors since the Internet offers both anonymity and potentially untraceable purchases. It's possible that digitized software will make it easier in the long run to trace transactions—and some anticipate the wild west of the contemporary Internet will be succeeded by much more tightly controlled variants, partly because of commercial pressures to charge for uses and partly because of governments' desire for control. But no one can be certain.

Illegal immigration and refugees are another product of more open international borders. 12 million people are languishing in refugee camps. Meanwhile governments want to attract in the highly skilled and motivated (for example through points systems of the kind used by Australia), and deter the costly (New Zealand's government decided to give residence to immigrants only if they could show an acceptable standard of health, and in 2006 refused one economic migrant on grounds of obesity). Those facing the fastest ageing have no choice but to use migration to boost their work-force. Europe in particular has little prospect of sustaining economic growth and generous welfare provision without continuing flows of migrants. But the upsurge in numbers of refugees and asylum seekers, as well as legal migrants, in Europe in the 1990s and 2000s had profound impacts on the political climate, and in some countries became the public's number one concern. Finding ways to cope with much greater diversity has become one of Europe's most pressing strategic priorities. The USA, a nation of migrants, has not been immune to these pressures and increased fourfold its surveil-lance of borders in the 1990s, while also being riven by arguments about whether, or how, illegal migrants should be given a route to legalized status. At the global level, family reunion continues to be the major reason for migration; but recent years have seen a rise in migration for employment purposes, especially for temporary work. Each year 700,000 Chinese cross over into Siberia for agricultural work (a number which is almost certain to rise thanks to climate change) while the expansion of the EU brought well over half a million new migrants to the UK in the two years after 2004 (by 2008 a remarkable 42 per cent of London's workforce were foreign born).

Cross-border crime is yet another field where states have lost control while global institutions remain weak. But it's also a field where some states are at best complicit and at worst actively involved. The Swiss finance ministry in 1998 confirmed that the country was involved in money laundering of at least $500bn each year, and it's estimated that some $15–20bn leaves Russia each year (Prime Minister Putin has been estimated to have a personal wealth in the tens of billions). The IMF estimates global organized crime's turnover at over $2 trillion (the official estimate in the UK is between £19bn and £48bn), and the value of (legal) offshore accounts is estimated at around $5 trillion, growing by some $500bn each year. Organised crime still centres on drugs, but the fastest growing form of trafficking is in human cargo. At least 4 million people each year are trafficked, earning the traffickers between $5bn and $7bn.

Outranking all of these issues in some governments' minds is the threat of global terrorism, even if it has directly touched only a very small number. The anarchist terrorists of the late nineteenth century showed what impact a small group of committed individuals could have (none of the more recent groups has come close to matching their success in murdering heads of state), and in the 1970s a wave of terrorism arose from Palestine, alongside more domestic terrorism in countries including

Northern Ireland, Italy, Germany, and Spain. Thirty years later the attack on New York's Twin Towers unleashed a dramatic tightening of internal security, and a sharp shift in public spending towards security and security technologies (even though domestic terrorism continues to be much more deadly than international terrorism: Albert Abadie of Harvard estimated 1,536 reports of domestic terrorism worldwide in 2003 compared to 240 of international terrorism). Governments have attempted to respond with strategies that deal both with the causes of terrorism (from alienation of Western Muslim populations to conflicts in the Middle East) and with the symptoms (through human and signals intelligence). All governments have to strike a balance between civil liberties and the prerogatives of security: greater connectedness increases the likelihood that struggles in one part of the world will manifest themselves elsewhere.

Nearly all of these conflicts can be found in a band across the middle latitudes, from Central America, through the Middle East and central Asia. The more temperate nations to the north and the south generally have more stable and effective governance—from Chile to Canada, South Africa to Europe, Australia to Japan. These conflicts are becoming bound up not only with the traditional conflicts for power and influence between superpowers, but also with newer tensions between superpowers and global institutions. It remains unclear whether the great powers of this century will cede autonomy in the way that the USA did after 1945 ('no matter how great our strength we must deny ourselves the license to do always as we please', as President Harry Truman put it). But the behaviour of today's predominant powers, in particular the USA and China, has an enormous impact on the options for others, and on the scope for effective global cooperation.

The new geography of power and relative advantage that's come with globalisation has changed the nature of public strategy, diminishing the importance of military power and increasing the returns to strategies of attraction that pull in investment, research functions, or skilled people. Being attractive has become an overt goal of strategy, that's crystallized in branding and marketing strategies. China's government is a rare exception which followed Deng Xiaoping's slogan 'hide brightness, nourish obscurity', during its period of rising power. Yet, since the early 2000s, it too has become increasingly concerned with matching military and economic power with cultural influence. Within nations, cities, which now account for more than 50 per cent of the world's population, have grown in influence, with a few becoming the critical hubs for an interconnected global economy based on the combination of business services, design, corporate headquarters, the arts, media, and tourism.[20] In East Asia, for example, national strategies for growth now both compete and sometimes collide with the strategies of Seoul and Shanghai, Hong Kong and Tokyo, for pre-eminence as hubs. In Europe cities like Copenhagen, Malmö, and Stockholm compete to be the location for advanced business services, while everywhere cities and regions try to promote themselves as brands, marketing their virtues to investors, potential migrants, and tourists.

These cities have benefited from one of the more surprising corollaries of globalization: decentralization. Without the presence of military threats, decentralization has become more credible as a superior way to organize public agencies, services, and governance. Survey evidence also shows that public well-being correlates well with how local democracy is, and how much direct influence people feel they have on state power.[21] Switzerland remains a paramount example of radical decentralization, and regularly comes near the top of league tables of government effectiveness, a standing rebuke to believers in centralization and economies of scale. Over the last few decades many other countries have radically decentralized to bring government closer to the people.[22] In the early 1980s France passed power down to departments and some 36,000 communes, and introduced innovations like the 'contrat de ville' to rebalance the relationship between local and national government. In the late 1970s Sweden allowed local areas to opt out of parts of the welfare state and declare themselves free communes, running their own services. India introduced a triple devolution down to Panchayats (local councils for villages, areas, and regions)—and in legislation in the mid-2000s introduced remarkable new powers for local communities to sign off public spending controls for higher tiers—confirming that money allocated for bridges and schools had been properly spent. Even China has allowed local government to become more autonomous, albeit with periodic moves to recentralize control over tax and spending.[23] Latin America has been a particularly fertile laboratory for passing power down to communities, from famous examples like the participative budgeting programmes in Porto Alegre to neighbourhood empowerment in Curitiba. The question of the optimal scale for states remains unanswered, despite a substantial body of economic theory (making claims for economies and diseconomies of scale) and political theory (on subsidiarity). But, as examples from Iceland to Bhutan show, it's possible to run highly successful states at very small scales.

What of the very biggest scales? All of the new global issues described above have cast light on the strengths and weaknesses of global governance. Much of the architecture of the UN, IMF, and World Bank was created to deal with questions of economic stability or interstate warfare, not migration, drugs, or civil war and state failure.[24] Even on more traditional issues the world has been sluggish when it comes to translating intentions into actions. One authoritative recent report noted that since 2000 governments have

failed to bring into force the Comprehensive Nuclear Test-Ban treaty; failed to move forward the biological weapons convention; failed to agree on the necessary actions to give force and meaning to the Kyoto protocol; failed to avoid war in Iraq; failed to take more than half measures to reform the International Monetary Fund; failed to design a European Constitution that could convince voters; failed to break the stalemate in the Doha Round of the World Trade Organization.[25]

Yet there have been some relative successes, like the Montreal agreement which led to curbs on CFCs to protect the ozone layer;[26] and this turned out to cost barely a tenth of what had originally been forecast. The interventions in Bosnia and Kosovo were broadly successful, as were less visible interventions (like Macedonia) which prevented conflict and therefore never made it to the front pages. The European Union continues to operate with a modest staff of 25,000, and for all its many flaws has mostly succeeded in its goals, not least in the accession of new members in 2004 which represents one of the most startling successes of modern governance.

Perhaps the most interesting future territory for global action will be global public goods. These are where concerted collective action has the potential to deliver big collective benefits, but where, as with public goods within nations, there need to be institutions with the power to pay for them. One example is health. According to some estimates the global cost of a serious avian flu pandemic could be as much as $500bn (the SARs outbreak is judged to have cost $54bn). Yet the World Health Organization estimates the cost of developing vaccines and drugs to suppress an outbreak would be around $500m alongside another $1bn to fight the pandemic in poorer countries with underdeveloped public health systems. The investment would cost dramatically less than the cure. But at present there are few incentives for national governments to make these investments—and if some did, others could free-ride on their spending.[27] There are many other examples of this kind, from successful action to contain climate change to the common interest in financial stability and the common interest in preventing nuclear proliferation.

The three broad trends described above—the spread of democracy, the growth of knowledge, and the rise of connections—each of which involves the growing importance of a set of public goods, explain much of the dynamics of governance. They are tightly interwoven. Knowledge and connectedness go hand in hand, as China's intelligence agencies seek out technologies from Western companies, or state-owned investment organizations take stakes in innovative companies in other countries. Knowledge and democracy are interwoven too: Freedom of Information laws, for example, have spread to over 90 per cent of OECD countries compared to only five in 1970, and given fuel to a burgeoning global civil society.[28] The tensions and contradictions that accompany these trends also explain much: from the resentments of the disconnected, to the losses of those who can't survive in an economy based on knowledge, to the autocrats who have faced down democratic oppositions and survived.[29]

The Patterns of Reform

There are many ways for states to respond to democracy, knowledge, and connections. But there have been common themes, some the result of changes to the structure of demand and supply, some the result of shifting patterns of power, and some the result of fashion. The functions of states have moved upwards (to transnational bodies), downwards (to local government), and outwards (to the private sector and non-profit organizations), but in quite complex patterns that have often left the remaining public sectors just as large as before.

Markets, Efficiency, and the New Public Management

Economics has played its part in driving reform. Ever since the oil price shocks of the early 1970s the upwards drift of public spending as a share of GDP has halted, though it hasn't reversed. Because governments face profound upwards cost pressures, particularly in health and welfare, they have had to seek efficiencies—delivering more for less. The panoply of methods that have grown up over the last generation, including performance management, privatizations, contestability, and efficiency drives, were all responses to this situation, and to the assumption that public servants and agencies were not well-placed to know how best to use resources. Their spirit was in part democratic—strengthening the citizen and consumer relative to the bureaucrat and the professional—and in part a reflection of the growing power of business.

An influential body of ideas, sometimes labelled the new public management, profoundly affected the scope for public agencies to be strategic, sometimes helping them (by encouraging transparency and clarity) and sometimes hindering them (by fragmenting government and favouring short-term performance over long-term change). Much of the momentum for these ideas came from the oil crisis of the early 1970s, which prompted widespread anxieties about the fiscal crisis of the state. Government was presented as vulnerable to capture by interest groups and to power hungry bureaucrats wanting to expand their empires. Markets were seen as the answer, and so economic liberalization, the removal of exchange controls, the end of attempts to control prices and incomes were combined with privatization of utilities, trade union reform, and deregulation. In some cases these were combined with cutbacks to universal benefits and charges for public services. The trends were most marked in the Anglo-Saxon countries—New Zealand, the USA and the UK—but had a much wider influence through organizations like the OECD and IMF (the latter became a particularly vocal evangelist for neo-liberal policies).

The more serious reforms experimented with structures. Agencies were corporatized and then privatized. Some were turned into arm's length executive agencies, given quantitative targets to meet but kept out of the main civil service. Many functions were contracted out where there was good reason to suppose that government didn't have any real comparative advantage—for example maintaining buildings, cleaning streets, or even providing economic advice. Some functions were financed in novel ways using Public Finance Initiatives and Public Private Partnerships—sometimes with great success, and in other cases at exorbitant cost and with no obvious improvement in quality.[30]

Seen through one lens the reforms were part of a deliberate strategy to roll back government, and to destroy the faith in government that had become so strong in Europe after the Second World War and in North America after the New Deal. Certainly there were influential ideologues who thought in these terms.[31] For others the motives were more pragmatic: scepticism about the knowledge and capabilities of government and curiosity about the potential for other models to achieve more for less. Whatever their motivations (and, as always in history, there were many) these experiments blurred the boundaries of the state. Mayor Steve Goldsmith (later a senior adviser to George W. Bush) when he was in charge of Indianapolis argued that if the local Yellow Pages contained at least three entries for a service the city provided he would contract it out. New South Wales in the 1980s even invited the public to nominate public servants for dismissal on the grounds that their jobs were unnecessary.[32] Paul Light estimates the US federal government employs nine times as many shadow employees as direct ones (around 17 million compared to around 2 million non-military public servants).[33]

In their milder versions the reforms helped to improve public services—making them more focused and responsive. More rigorous measurement has been much resented, but in fields as diverse as warfare, medicine, and schooling it has brought to the surface much sharper understanding of what works and why. Performance management methods—embodied, for example, in the 1993 US Government Performance and Results Act—spread widely, promoted as a way to cut out corruption and improve efficiency, as well as better decision-making. In principle these—and the many forms of 'results-based management'—aimed to link budget allocations to outcomes achieved. By the early 2000s forty-seven US states had performance budgeting requirements, thirty-one of them enshrined in legislation. Their underlying idea, that agencies should be better incentivized to deliver outcomes, was sound. Input-based budget systems give few incentives for efficiency. Instead they encourage a 'use it or lose it' mentality. Failures can be rewarded with extra injections of money.

In countries scarred by corruption, greater transparency will tend to help good governance (though for the same reasons, this will be resisted: the director of Transparency International Romania complained that in her country 'everybody pays bribes—to doctors, teachers nurses and to officials—and institutions are not strong enough to deal with corruption').[34]

But overall the results of the many 'new public management' reforms fell far short of their promise. A recent survey of international comparisons of performance by Christopher Hood found that the countries which had done most to follow these routes remained generally poor performers. The UK, he noted, was 'in a position mostly in the middle to lower third of the top dozen or so developed countries'. The United States came last in his survey—ironically given its continuing influence in global public policy debates.

One factor was that the technicalities of reform proved difficult. No one has yet designed a budgeting system that successfully rewards performance. Everything depends on what counts as good, and sophisticated judgements need to be made about why a target has or has not been met, which will range from the state of the economy to the timescales of change, the soundness of the policy to the capacity of the implementing institutions. Equally difficult judgements need to be made about what should be done when targets aren't met: for example, whether services need more money, less, or the same. (I discuss the practical challenges of performance management in more detail in Chapter 7.)

Fracturing the state also brought problems as well as greater efficiency, and these sometimes came to light during crises. Hurricane Katrina revealed that Wal-Mart had a far superior logistical system than the US Government. The Hatfield rail crash in Britain in 2000 showed the limits of government power in the wake of liberalization when, for a few months after the crash, the private rail operators' fear of litigation led them to run the whole network at dramatically lower speeds. The fact that this led to more road traffic, and therefore almost certainly more fatalities than were risked on the railways (four had died in the crash itself), was irrelevant to them. But there was very little that government could do.

Bold claims were made for the potential of markets to transform public services and other areas of public action during the 1980s and 1990s. In some cases markets and quasi-markets have worked reasonably well—opening up routine parts of the state to competition, for example. But market-based solutions have underperformed relative to expectations. Pensions reform was perhaps the classic example. In some countries—including the UK—encouragement for highly competitive markets to promote personal pensions led to waves of mis-selling by private companies. In others, like Chile, the move from 'pay as you go' state pensions to funded pensions excluded large swathes of the population, as well as bringing extraordinarily high transactions costs that eliminated any efficiency gains a more marketized system could have brought. It was widely assumed that pensions supported by funds holding equities would somehow be more sustainable than tax-based pensions: yet in any one year both involve precisely the same economic transfer from today's workers to yesterday's workers.

Those countries which went furthest in marketization served as warnings to the rest. New Zealand's government long ago disowned its more radical market-based reforms of the 1980s and 1990s. Britain had more than its fair share of very visible failures, ranging from the botched rail privatization to the significant proportion of private finance initiatives which now look like poor value for money because of their high transaction costs and their failure to transfer risk. More extreme examples include the partial collapse of China's once impressive health system, which came about when market principles replaced collective provision, and Latin America's profoundly flawed privatizations in the 1990s whose failures paved the way for the sharp swing to the left in the 2000s.

For some countries it remains attractive to deliver welfare through the market, with individuals and families purchasing insurance against risk. But for others an inclusive welfare system remains the guarantee of a coherent society. In societies where there is much less absolute poverty the terms of the political deal that sustains universal pensions, or healthcare, has changed. The political commitment of the middle classes has become more important than ever, and with it the requirement that welfare should offer clear value for money, and support that's directly suited to them, not just to the poor: for example, childcare, eldercare, and rights to time as well as money. In many cases political settlements of this kind have stopped moves to marketization, helped by evidence that markets in social fields like health can be extremely inefficient (the USA for example spends twice as much per capita on health as the UK, but with generally worse outcomes, in part because of the vast transactions costs for accountants, lawyers, marketing people, and managers). The politics of redistribution is likely to shift further. According to the IMF, while income growth has been positive for all income groups over the last two decades, income inequality in middle-income and high-income countries has increased, and this is mainly explained by gains by the richest quintile at the expense of the middle, while the share of the poorest has remained relatively stable.

Markets have many virtues, and they have played an important role in making public sectors richer in information, and in feedback. But the assumption that they are a natural phenomenon, the default option for social organization, is wrong. When the state and law disappear healthy markets do not fill the space; instead something more like a state of nature emerges instead. Markets have to be shaped, constructed, and adapted, and although there are many ways in which this can be done, and many varieties of capitalism, these are all as much political and policy settlements as they are organic evolutions. Not all human activities respond directly to financial incentives. If you want teachers to teach or doctors to cure, rewards help but only up to a point. As a vast range of empirical observation shows, and contrary to a good deal of theory, people respond as much to social signals, and to what March and Olsen describe as the 'logic of appropriate behavior'.[35]

New Zealand has become an interesting example of how market-like incentives can work in both improving health outcomes and cutting health inequalities, so long as they are combined with many other types of tool. Its GPs lose income if patients seek care from a practice other than the one they're registered with. But the government has also invested heavily in population-wide programmes on diet and exercise, targeted at the most at-risk groups, and they have given the public a role in electing two-thirds of the members of health boards.

Similar arguments about getting the mix right are now working themselves out in environmental policy, where for several decades governments have sought to create tradable permits for 'bads' such as pollution or CO_2 emissions. A number of markets have been established, most ambitiously with the creation of CDMs (Clean Development Mechanisms) from the Kyoto treaty, and Europe's related introduction of a market for carbon emissions. Their founding idea, that industry would know better than governments where the most cost-effective cuts could be achieved, was sound, and markets look set to be part of any future approaches to climate change. But all of these markets have brought with them problems of pricing and policing. The EU greatly oversupplied carbon credits, leading to a collapse in the price of carbon. This problem is relatively soluble, but the IPCC found wide margins of error in measuring the baseline emissions which are vital for any market to work—60 per cent with oil, gas, and coal and 100 per cent for some agricultural processes. There are also heavy 'deadweight' effects (funding projects that would have happened anyway), 'rebound' effects (as money raised through CDMs is respent on carbon-emitting activities), and double counting. As a result most of the heavy lifting on environmental improvement has been achieved through regulation and standards rather than markets, and this will probably continue to be true in the future too.

Citizen-Centred and Systemic Government

Can we identify some of the themes that will succeed the reform drives of the late twentieth century? Prediction is always hazardous but many of the directions of change can already be found in the present. Some will amplify existing trends, such as the availability of much more information and feedback (whether through data, markets, or user voice). But others point in different directions. These harbingers of the future can be found where governments face the most intense pressures. One of these is the growing incidence of chronic illness. Worldwide chronic illness already accounts for some 46 per cent of the overall burden of disease and this is expected to increase to 56 per cent by 2020, partly the consequence of ageing and partly the consequence of improved healthcare keeping people alive for longer. In the USA more than three-quarters of hospital admissions are now for treatment of chronic conditions, as are 88 per cent of filled prescriptions and about 70 per cent of physician visits.[36] Mental illness is equally predominant, accounting for some 30 per cent of all GP consultations and 50 per cent of follow-up consultations. The World Health Organization predicts that depression will become the second most prevalent cause of ill health worldwide by 2020.[37] In the UK more than 900,000 now claim sickness and disability benefits for mental health conditions, a figure which is larger than the total of unemployed on the jobseeker's allowance. Measured in lost working hours, this is now the biggest category of illness in the world, and in some European countries the mortality rate from suicide exceeds that from road traffic accidents.

Yet chronic conditions are not easily administered or treated either through the traditional clinical lens of prescriptions and cures, or through a modern consumerist lens. Much of the care for people suffering from diseases is provided by families and friends, and is too expensive to be provided through formal structures by highly paid doctors and nurses. Much of the most important knowledge about how to handle these long-term conditions resides with other patients rather than doctors, one reason why so many powerful membership-based self-help and mutual help organizations have grown up in the last few decades. Doctors and hospitals continue to have a big role to play—but they will increasingly sit alongside self-care, much more use of technology to provide monitoring, as well as mutual support. The outcomes that matter will include the classic concerns of speed of response or mortality, but they will also include patient satisfaction and well-being.

Rather than seeing government through the lens of delivery—doing things to people—chronic disease is an example of an issue which has forced attention to shift to the quality of the relationship between citizens and state, and to services that are shaped around the individual's needs rather than being too standardized. The commitment to make services more personal can mean little more than having someone—a doctor or teacher—to talk to face to face. But it can potentially mean a different curriculum and programme for every pupil, and a radically different pattern of care for every patient, or at the very least a series of modular options navigated with the help of a personal coach or adviser. The simple, if potentially revolutionary, idea behind many recent reforms, is that the individual's experience should be paramount, not least in shaping services. Personal budgets have given people with disabilities control over how money is spent to meet their needs, turning on its head the assumptions of most twentieth-century services, and linking together direct power over money, new platforms (to show people what they can buy for their money), and new structures of advice. At one point these seemed very radical (since they threatened existing professionals) as well as dangerous (since they threatened to push costs out of control). Yet they have, so far, turned out to increase life satisfaction and to cut costs.

Some of these reforms are the latest stage in the long march of consumerism, which took several decades to take hold in the public sector.

In the UK, Michael Young promoted consumer bodies and rights in public services in the early 1950s yet it was only in the 1980s that the first formal guarantees began to appear (like the UK's Citizen's Charter) and the first formal targets (like Canada's consumer satisfaction targets for public agencies which are backed up by a standard measurement system—the Common Measurements Tool (CMT)).[38]

Giving consumers power—including the power to exit—can transform the culture of public services. But consumerism on its own is never enough. People often want to be involved in shaping services, not just choosing between them. How decisions are made affects how people think about them. The answer to the question 'why do people obey the law?', for example, is in part because they feel they have a role in making the law.[39] Open source methods that involve users in designing products and services (like Lego's 'Mindstorms User Panel' of 'leader users' who help create toy designs and test out prototypes) have become commonplace in business (having always been common in civil society) and are beginning to spread into the public sector. The Netherlands' 'Kafka Brigade' is a good example of how the public can share views about how public services can be improved, while the National Health Service Expert Patients Programme has gone a step further in giving patients the power to reshape services.[40] 'Peer-production' networks like Mozilla's 'Firefox' and the collaboratively produced encyclopedia *Wikipedia* are the (much larger-scale) equivalents of the cooperatives that paved the way for many modern public services in the nineteenth century, and point the way to a very different relationship between production and consumption which could transform public services (imagine for example, a more open-source school curriculum, or small business advice service).

Another limit of consumerism is that the outcomes that matter most often depend on changing the preferences and behaviours of citizens, rather than treating them as supreme. The same governments that talk the language of empowerment also use their power to make their citizens healthier, richer, or more secure. This takes them into the territory of co-production or co-creation, and a way of thinking about services that is different from the traditions of 'delivery' by all-powerful professionals, bureaucrats, and businesses to passive users. Instead they depend much more on the quality of relationships between teachers and pupils, doctors and patients, or between citizens and other citizens. This has led among other things to the rise of home schooling and parental engagement in learning, the proliferation of self-help groups in health, the return of micro-credit and mutual finance, and the rediscovery of older mutualist traditions which can be found in every country (see Ivan Illich).[41]

If one of the tendencies for public services has been to become more focused on the micro-level of individual needs, the other trend has been to become more interested in systems. Climate change has been a powerful factor, requiring policy makers to look at every area of human activity through the lens of carbon emissions. Social policy has become increasingly attuned to the complex feedback mechanisms that reinforce exclusion. In health, the World Health Organization has promoted the idea of 'health in all policies', looking in the round at the impact on health of everything from transport to stress.[42] Social networks play an important role in keeping people healthy, and so does nature: a recent review of the empirical evidence concluded that contact with nature has a positive impact on blood pressure, cholesterol, outlook on life, and stress,[43] and a fascinating study in which public housing residents in Chicago were randomly assigned to buildings with and without trees and grass nearby found that the second group procrastinated in facing their problems and assessed their issues as more severe, less soluble, and more long-standing than the residents living in greener surroundings.[44]

Viewed from the top down, the many methods for influencing behaviour include laws (such as smoking bans), incentives (such as carbon taxes), provision (for example of condoms), social marketing (of the kind used to cut car traffic in some cities), advertising (of the kind used for drink-driving), mobilizing endorsers and celebrities, new roles to promote change (such as street wardens or personal advisers), and contracts such as those used to persuade parents to read to their children. In some countries these are becoming fairly mainstream, and psychologists and sociologists are gaining as much weight within government as economists. Yet, viewed from the bottom up, what matters most is the energy of ordinary people organized in social movements to protect the environment, promote recycling or healthy living, and governments look like latecomers to much deeper-rooted processes of cultural change.

At its best politics tries to bridge the bottom–up and the top–down: starting with empathy and paying attention to the micro worlds of daily experience rather than seeing people through abstract categories. Networks are another place where the bottom–up and top–down perspectives intermingle and sometimes conflict. Networks are used by states for surveillance over citizens, and by citizens for 'sous'-veillance of states, showing up mistakes, or providing visible feedback on services. They can link previously separate databases tracking citizens' behaviour but they also make it easier for users to band together (for example to demand help with a health condition) and they can help to disintermediate (as for example when children in the care of the state are given control of their budgets so that they can buy their own care).

The Problem of Trust

Liberalization and decentralization were in part responses to distrust—the sense that government no longer served the people's best interests. Many societies have faced a vicious spiral that was well summarized by Joseph Nye, the former dean of the Harvard Kennedy School: 'If people believe that government is incompetent and cannot be trusted then they are less likely to provide resources. Without critical resources government cannot perform well, and if government cannot perform well people will become even more dissatisfied and distrustful'. In some cases, cuts in public spending in 1980s and 1990s influenced by neo-liberal ideas did do more damage to productive investment (education, infrastructure) than to re-medial public spending, thus undermining long-term economic growth.

So in the 1990s attention turned away from arguments about whether government should be big or small to a more sophisticated discussion of how its powers and resources should best be used, and how the right balance of supply and demand could be struck. Governments could be highly effective commanding 60 per cent of GDP or 30 per cent. Size mattered less than quality. Quality might be ensured by direct public provision or by creating more open markets for public goods. What mattered was success and a scale of government that fitted local political conditions. The critical issues for shaping trust are bound to vary: in South Africa success in cutting poverty has been decisive,[45] while in the USA the evidence points to economic management and addressing fears about crime as critical factors shaping public trust.[46] But the evidence from political science has consistently shown that the legitimacy and durability of all democratic systems depends on how much the public trust their governments to do what's right and fair as well as what's efficient.[47]

That requires them to pay close attention to what the public really want, rather than relying too much on theory or experts. Politicians have always been interested in this, and tools of growing sophistication have been used to make sense of the public's often inchoate wishes: from the 'Coopers Snoopers' used by the British government in the Second World War to survey the public, to Gallup and MORI, and more recently a battery of methods using focus groups, citizens juries, and deliberative polls. In

Chapter 13, I look at how this information is being used to make sense of public or social value. One of the many reasons this matters is the growing evidence of a gap between personal optimism and optimism about society as a whole. Across the EU, surveys show an average net personal positive of 29.2 per cent (i.e. people who are optimistic about their lives over the next five years minus those who are pessimistic) and a net collective optimism of 4.5 per cent. In the UK the figures are a remarkable 43 per cent and −7 per cent, a gap of 50 per cent. Since it is clearly not possible for everyone's lives to improve while the overall state of society is deteriorating, these figures tell us something profound about people's disconnection from politics and government, and the distorted lens through which collective issues are seen.[48]

The Rise of Well-being as a Primary Goal

For most of human history a primary concern of governments was to capture or protect territory. The military stood at the top of the social hierarchy, and had the first claim on taxes. Then in the twentieth century the centre of attention turned to the economy. Economic prowess came to be even more important than military prowess. League tables of armies were replaced by league tables of GDP or GDP per capita. Government strategists concerned themselves with growing export industries, avoiding downturns or attracting inward investment. But by the early twenty-first century it was becoming clear that economic growth would not provide a sufficient focus for policy makers in the future. One factor was shifting values: as many researchers had shown, once people's basic needs are met their attention turns to other things: the quality of life as well as the quantity of goods; the character of local environments; and so on.[49] Once famine and acute poverty are no longer serious threats, even subliminally, for most of the population, and when memories of acute shortage are more than two generations in the past, the focus of societal concern shifts—to questions of health, well-being, and thriving.

This shift has deep roots—in the US Constitution's commitment to the pursuit of happiness, and the English utilitarians' commitment to the greatest happiness of the greatest number. It has been reinforced more recently by evidence showing that once a certain level of prosperity has been reached, economic growth does not reliably lead to higher levels of happiness (this is known as the Easterlin paradox after the American economist Richard Easterlin). This evidence draws on the vast number of surveys now undertaken to measure happiness, such as the World Values Survey,[50] or the 916 surveys from forty-five countries that Ed Diener synthesized (and found people rated themselves around 7 on a scale of 0–10), or the truly global survey in 132 countries that Gallup conducted in 2005/6 (these surveys echo Aldous Huxley's forecast in his foreword to *Brave New World* that 'the most important Manhattan Projects of the future will be vast government-sponsored inquiries into what the politicians and participating scientists will call "the problem of happiness"').

This avalanche of data has produced a small industry of analysts. In most countries levels of reported happiness have risen over the last thirty years (Switzerland often tops the rankings), and standard deviations show that inequality of happiness has also reduced, even though large minorities can be unhappy (in the UK 8 per cent fall below 5 on a scale of 0–10). But during long periods when GDP has doubled or tripled the available data appear to show that happiness levels for much of the population have remained flat.[51] A more pessimistic picture is shown by other measures of welfare, like the Index of Sustainable Welfare developed by Daly and Cobb, which recorded a decline in most Western countries since the 1970s.

There are many possible explanations for stagnating happiness: habituation (people become accustomed to greater prosperity) or the particular characteristics of consumerist societies where people are much more aware of the relative income of people richer than themselves. Some nations (such as Denmark) have seen happiness rise quite sharply while others (such as Belgium) have seen declines. The factors seem to have more to do with levels of social trust and the quality of governance than they do with income. Status is another factor that is clearly important. In the world's most extensive long-run survey of health, carried out in the British civil service, top officials enjoyed life expectancies some twenty years higher than those at the bottom of the hierarchy, as well as being happier. Since few societies have found a way to distribute status more equally, this may be a major barrier in the way of increasing well-being.

The researchers on happiness have found many strong correlations, though there is less agreement on directions of causation (or on the impact of genetic dispositions).[52] High levels of happiness correlate with economic affluence, political freedom, the rule of law, state welfare, income equality, and tolerance, in that order. Together these explain some 70–80 per cent of the differences between countries. Much else is now known about patterns of happiness: how it tends to be higher amongst women, people in stable relationships, with good health and with higher income, and how it tends to be lower amongst the unemployed and the recently separated. Involvement in social activities and the community is associated with high levels of happiness. Across the age range it has a 'U' shape, reaching its lowest point when people are in the mid-forties, and then rising again, perhaps as people's expectations come into line with their real prospects.[53] Most people seem to bounce around a consistent level of happiness, and return rapidly from traumas like becoming disabled, or windfalls like lottery wins. We also know that positive happiness and negative misery are partly independent, and vary in distinct ways. There is even suggestive evidence that blood pressures correlate inversely with national levels of happiness.

What implications does this have for public policy? There is no inherent reason why any nation should make happiness its overriding goal. During times of threat security may become an overriding concern. There are other legitimate goals for governments to pursue too, such as the pursuit of virtue, or leaving a better legacy for future generations. Amartya Sen has argued that 'capabilities' are a better target for policy than happiness—giving people the means to choose for themselves what lives to lead.[54] Others make the case for promoting practical wisdom as more fundamental than happiness or the good life (since a good society depends on its people having the discipline to resist temptations, the prudence to relate means to ends, and the empathy to see the world through others' eyes). One justification for this view is that very similar virtues show up in many traditions (one major recent survey summarized these as: wisdom and knowledge; courage; love and humanity; justice; temperance; and spirituality and transcendence). In the long run governments may focus their efforts on the conditions for human flourishing which, as Martha Nussbaum has argued persuasively, go well beyond happiness (not least because people can too easily accept constrained lives and mislead themselves about their potential). But these are less arguments for ignoring well-being than for seeing it in context as an important transitional goal. The central idea of positive psychology—that good character can be cultivated—is an ancient one and has survived for good reasons.[55] Yet state actions to actively promote happiness appear at this stage less convincing than state actions to alleviate the worst unnecessary suffering, whether that comes from illness, loneliness, or lack of power.

How then should well-being be judged? Today's GDP measures took shape in the 1930s and 1940s and then became standard across the world. They sit alongside a range of alternatives: adjusted GDP measures which try to take account of some of the costs of growth, like less free time, or higher insurance to counter the risks of crime. Some of these measures have shown a similarly flat picture to the data on happiness. Others have tried to integrate economic and social measures—most notably the UN's

Human Development Index which includes such things as child mortality and literacy rates, as well as more obscure alternatives like Fordham University's Index of Social Health. Some governments have begun the systematic measurement of well-being, including its key domains such as happiness with family life, with work, or with the places people live. Many countries have developed more local variants. Seoul in South Korea has a happiness index combining objective and subjective measures in eight indicators and thirty domains. Japan's 'opinion survey on the national lifestyle' has been going for fifty years under the Cabinet Office and has included questions on happiness.

It's possible that none of these will become a standard measure. There are good reasons for doubting whether happiness can be a single thing; it may be so inherently plural and fuzzy that it will resist the intense pressure to find common metrics.[56] But even if no single measure comes to replace GDP, sharper thinking about well-being could recast many areas of public policy and action (even if happiness is a field where individuals and institutions are notoriously poor at following reliable strategies to make themselves happier).[57] Take economic policy, for example. Since losing a job has such devastating impacts on happiness, future governments may set any trade-offs between unemployment and growth or inflation in a different way to contemporary governments. In health there are already signs of a move away from the emphasis on keeping people alive to an emphasis on the quality of life. This may include greater tolerance for patients to control the manner and timing of their own death; a greater status for the care aspects of health; and more power in the hands of expert patients' relative to doctors. Mental health has always had a relatively low priority compared to public health and the provision of cures. But mental illnesses have such dramatic impacts on well-being, both for the individuals directly affected and for all those around them, that this is likely to change.

Greater understanding of social capital, relationships, and trust is also having an impact on public policy. The data on happiness strongly reinforces the importance of strong friendships and relationships, and has encouraged governments to do much more to measure patterns of social capital, and to support institutions and programmes that strengthen relationships: for example parenting advice; mediation services; and support for local institutions—like post offices or clubs—that may appear uneconomic. The success of places like Portland in the USA (which bucked national trends of falling social capital), or of the north European countries (which bucked global trends) have been watched eagerly. This shift of view has also opened up new perspectives: for example, for the elderly, policies that reduce isolation could become as visible as the more familiar policies around pensions. It has also opened up new issues—for example sleep levels appear to correlate with happiness, raising the question of what an urban strategy to help people sleep longer might look like. Other examples would include strategies to cut commuting times (strong evidence from the USA suggests that many people are commuting further than is best for their well-being), or to influence the cultural environment for children (reducing advertising-induced anxiety). Another direction of change may be towards restricting or sharing positional goods (such as stately homes, rare art, luxury tourism, or high-status roles). When positional goods become more prominent in a society, this has a particularly strong impact on happiness as people struggle ever harder to stay ahead of the crowd, and past policies have reduced this effect by opening positional goods up—for example providing rights of way for walkers to enjoy the land around stately homes, or encouraging cheap air travel to foreign countries.[58]

The competing pressures on governments make it unwise to predict which issues will be centre stage. A long economic slowdown, or a long period of insecurity prompted by terrorist attacks, would push these far down policy agendas. If climate change wreaks as much damage as it might—precipitating large flows of refugees, disrupting food supplies, and rendering some areas of high population unsustainable, survival imperatives could overshadow many of the issues described above. But the new knowledge about happiness will become harder for governments to ignore, and it is no longer credible to claim that happiness is an automatic consequence of faster economic growth.

The Balance between Demand and Supply

By the turn of the century a picture had emerged in which some parts of the state were clearly working well, effectively grounded in experience and knowledge, and a reasonable understanding of what mattered to the public. These included macroeconomic policy (albeit severely tested by the crisis of the late 2000s); public health and the main public services, where most countries in the developed world greatly improved their competence and capacity. They also included some classic administrative tasks: like how to shift from driving on one side of the road to the other (which Sweden did in 1967), unifying a previously divided country into a single legal, administrative, and economic structure (as Germany did in the early 1990s), or the introduction of the Euro in 2000. Governments in developed countries are highly competent at these sorts of tasks, albeit with occasional very visible lapses (such as the failure to adequately regulate credit in the 2000s).

There were other areas where performance was patchier—dealing with social exclusion, family policy, mental illness—and where there were wide variations in performance between countries, partly reflecting different histories. In some fields nation states no longer look like the right scale for effective action. Examples include carbon emissions, migration, organized crime and drugs, and water management. But the design of new institutions and powers suitable for dealing with these problems has been slow and fitful.

The net result of these complex shifts is that the upwards and downwards pressures on government remain roughly in balance (see Box 3.3). Even in those countries where the most vigorous attempts were made to roll back the state, a declining role in the economy was more than made up for by widening roles in roles in care, education, and health.[59] The upward pressures on public spending and demand include the positive elasticities of demand for key services (when incomes rise people want to spend a higher proportion of their income on health or education) and the effects of ageing (which generally means a larger proportion of the population who are dependent on collective provision of care). The downwards pressures include competition and individualistic cultures. But what has held them in rough equilibrium is the entrepreneurial activity of politicians seeking new roles for the state, and new deals that balance taxes and spending, freedoms and security, all in pursuit of the ultimate goal for any state: legitimacy.

Box 3.3 Upward and downward pressures on the scale of government

Upward
Positive elasticities of demand for health and education
Ageing and growing needs for care
Insecurity
Risk aversion
More skilled tax collection
Adaptation to climate change

Downward
Individualization and consumerism
Globalization and competition
Inequality and growing opt-out from public services and welfare
Peace
The Internet undermining tax collection

That activity can be remarkably creative. Nations and cities have found many very different strategies for surviving and thriving. The idea that there is only one viable form of capitalism or democracy is a dangerous myth. In recent years, for example, nations have succeeded in building up high technology industries with radically different strategies:

- very heavy public subsidy and national champions combined with strong venture capital and incentives for universities (the USA);
- support for a few dominant conglomerates working in close tandem with government and focused on export markets (Japan);
- strong state support plus national champions (France);
- low taxes for foreign direct investment (Ireland);
- state funding for new ventures, many galvanized by the success of a single dynamic company (Finland); and
- state-led creation of capacity in microprocessors that left the country dominating global markets (Taiwan).

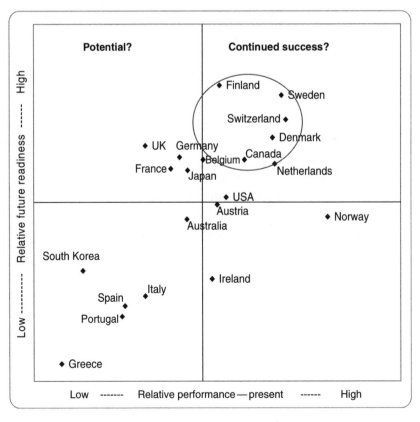

Figure 3.3. Current performance and future-readiness

What works in one country won't in another. But the many league tables and measures provided by the OECD, IMF, World Economic Forum, World Bank, and others, show that the successful nations in the twenty-first century do seem to share some common features. These do not include the size of armies, or the quantity of natural resources, or the presence of charismatic leaders—the things that in previous eras appeared to be the guarantees of national strength. Indeed these can be barriers to success rather than helpers. North Korea has one of the world's largest armies but can barely feed its population. Parts of West Africa have been brought close to destitution by their wealth of minerals. Fig. 3.3 (originally prepared for the UK Cabinet) summarizes two clusters of indicators at the beginning of the 2000s—one on the bottom axis capturing current performance (GDP per capita, happiness, trust, employment, etc.) and the other on the left hand axis including indicators of future performance (such as fiscal sustainability, patents, maths in school, CO_2 reductions).[60]

The most successful societies in the top right-hand corner turn out to be relatively open: able to import good ideas and energetic people, and promote performance and innovation. Institutions and laws underpin this—guaranteeing freedoms and stopping monopolies, whether economic or political. Competitive democratic systems and competitive market economies are quicker to solve problems and more agile in adapting to change. Closed societies, not surprisingly, are slow to benefit from new knowledge and ideas. The most successful societies also have high levels of capacity. They are able to do many things well. That rests in part of what economists call human capital—their levels of qualifications and skill. But it also rests on social capital—the ability to do things together—and on organizational capital, the accumulated capacities of firms and agencies, professions and NGOs. These two qualities are also the two sides of strategy—the combination of sensitivity to the external environment, and intelligence about how it can be shaped or responded to.

A Framework for Adaptive Strategy

WE are now ready to introduce the framework for strategy in public organizations.

The central task is to find ways to achieve profound purposes within the constraints of an external and internal environment. That requires any serious exercise of strategy to address:

- **Why** actions are taken: the purposes, needs, values, aspirations, and fears that most matter to a society, and which cannot be provided without the help of the state. These are shaped and fought over through politics and through the slow movement of culture.
- **What** the context is in which these purposes can be achieved—the possible opportunities and threats; the state of knowledge; and the capacities of institutions.
- **Where to go**: from the interaction of these, definition of a small number of broad strategic directions which can sometimes be translated into more precise goals.
- **How to get there**: policies and actions which take account of the capabilities of the various agencies involved, and can be cascaded down through public agencies, or provide the basis for negotiations between different tiers of governance. These can be linear deductions from analysis or creative jumps that see problems and solutions in new ways.
- **Which**: feedback loops—from users, public opinion, data and pilots—providing information about which things worked and which didn't, leading in turn to further improvements and adaptations.

Fig. 4.1 summarizes the steps. It emphasizes the links between each stage of the process; the importance of learning and feedback (to use the language of

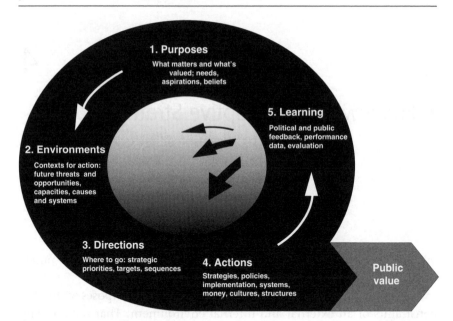

Figure 4.1.   Choices for effective strategy-building

the military, no plans survive their first contact with the enemy); and outcomes. It also emphasizes the importance of focus and priorities: strategies are decisions to do some things and not others (governments run the risk identified by Samuel Johnson, that 'a man may be so much of everything that he is nothing of anything'). In the next sections I explain each of these stages of the strategy process and the issues that they often throw up.

Why?—Understanding Purposes and Priorities

The first preparatory step in devising a strategy is knowing what it's for. Any government, nation, or city faces a near infinite number of things that need to be done. But at any one moment only a few can be done and even fewer can be the subjects of serious attention. So why do some things matter more than others?

The ultimate goals that societies set themselves come from deep within them. They reflect their needs, their values, their aspirations for children or health or well-being, fears of collapse, disorder, or attack. They become energizing when there is an evident gap between aspirations and existing realities: this gap, and the sense of hope and possibility that it can be bridged, provides the drive for strategies. These gaps are sometimes straightforward—like the wish for greater prosperity or better education.

But they can be inchoate, lurking between the lines of political rhetoric, and not always voiced honestly to pollsters.

For a government these values and ethos can be all-important in providing a sense of direction and purpose. They function rather as emotions do in individual decision-making. Recent research in psychology has confirmed the vital role of what Antonio Damasio has called 'emotional rudders' that help people to make decisions in conditions of uncertainty. Without them we're prone to flail around or are incapacitated. Indeed, to think well we also need to feel: 'the high level cognitive skills taught in schools, including reasoning, decision making and processes related to language, reading and mathematics, do not function as rational, disembodied systems, somehow influenced by, but detached from, emotion and the body. Instead, these crowning evolutionary achievements are grounded in a long history of emotional functions, themselves deeply grounded in humble homeostatic beginnings.'[1]

The same must be true of the organizations within which people make decisions. They too have their own memories, feelings, and desires, and work well when these help them to make sense of the world around them and to act. In some cases the values of a government are so clear that it is easy for a junior official to deduce how they should respond to a new situation (for example in a Thatcherite government every new problem prompted the question of whether there was a possible market-based solution). Such clarity saves a lot of transaction costs—but carries risks of dogma and myopia. The general point is that it can often be healthy for governments to reflect on their underying values, the boundary lines that give them definition, and the hopes that give them motivating power. Strategies which are blind to this emotional foundation are unlikely to take hold.

In government the goals which ultimately come from deep within society manifest themselves through many routes. The most important bubble up from political processes—from the manifestos which parties publish in advance of elections and from the great arguments which determine which ways societies move. Over longer periods of time they also come from other sources—the pressures of social movements demanding new rights, or from external pressures such as competition with other nations, or from the requirements of global or transnational bodies. They come from the underlying structure of interests, from aspirations and values, fears and threats. Some societies have experimented with much more open ways of engaging the public in setting goals, and framing the 'why' of public action. The Oregon Benchmarks programme, initiated in the late 1980s, is one of the best known—and survived through several changes of political leadership.

Values and aspirations can be rooted in ideological outlooks. The best account of these underlying world views was provided in 1991 by the American social theorist Albert Hirschman in a brilliant book, *The Rhetoric of Reaction*. He concluded that only three types of argument lay behind the thousands of speeches, pamphlets, and books that had fuelled the Thatcherite and Reaganite revolutions, and that these had been largely constant since the left/right division first took shape at the time of the French Revolution. The rhetoric of futility claimed that any government actions to ameliorate society wouldn't work. So efforts to raise social mobility were doomed because some people are clever and others are stupid. The rhetoric of jeopardy claimed that government action would jeopardize valuable things, like the family. The rhetoric of perversity argued that if government action did have any effects these would not be the ones intended. So wars on poverty would end up with more welfare dependants. A good society, it followed, was one where governments attempted relatively little, and left people to get on with their lives.

Hirschman didn't do a similarly detailed analysis of progressive arguments but they turn out to be equally consistent. First come the rhetorics of justice—the arguments for righting wrongs and meeting needs, whether these are for pensions or affordable housing. All centre left parties draw their energy from this basic moral sense of fairness. Next come the rhetorics of progress, the idea that change is cumulative and dynamic: new reforms are needed to reinforce old ones, or to prevent backsliding. So, for example, new rights to maternity leave are essential to make a reality of past laws outlawing gender discrimination. Then, in a mirror to the rhetorics of reaction, come the rhetorics of tractability: the claims that government action works, and that whether the problem is unemployment or climate change, the right mix of actions will do the trick.

These ideas lie beneath the surface of many governments' programmes and promises, though even the most committed 'reactionaries' can opt for 'progressive' rhetorics on some of the issues they care about: like transforming family values. In different political cultures the polarities will vary, with other issues like identity or religion providing the crucial axes, and the crucial inspiring arguments.

What's There?—Understanding Environments, Contexts, and Capacities

The next question is whether goals can be achieved. It is good to imagine better or worse futures. But imagination has to engage with reality. The language of government can encourage a misleading certainty about the impact that policies will have. Politicians and officials talk of 'pulling levers', 'governmental machinery', 'driving through change', and 'rolling out policies' as if they were lumps of dough. But the people involved in executing policy have views and interests of their own, and the idea of a transmission belt connecting the will of leaders and results on the ground is a long way from reality.

The best strategies achieve a fit with their environment, and go with the grain of its possibilities, for example, building up competences in growing industries. They are also realistic about what's possible, and realistic that changes to the external environment may directly threaten cherished purposes. Anyone involved in strategy—whether to secure agreement to a new road or to overhaul a health system—needs to choose between a variety of mental models for thinking about strategy which have radically different implications for action. Often these models lie unexamined, implicit rather than explicit. Bringing these assumptions to the surface can open out avenues for action which otherwise are missed, and it can illuminate the limits of otherwise impressively comprehensive plans. Any mental model is a choice about what to look at and what to ignore, for example how much to focus on structures (organograms, formal powers), flows (money, messages, people, infrastructures), meanings and cultures (identities, recognition, valuations) or histories (and the path dependence of any particular government).[2]

Our images and practices of strategy depend on what kind of situation we find ourselves in, what kind of field we are seeking to influence. These range from the steady, predictable, and mundane to the fluid and unstable. For an army the strategic imperative of ensuring good catering supplies will require very different responses to the strategic imperatives of a fast-changing battlefield. So, too, in other areas of public life, a vital starting point is clarity about what kind of field being dealt with, and how knowable it is. These can be roughly mapped into four types:

- Fields of **direct causation**, where changes in one variable lead to changes in another in predictable ways. Much of day to day administration is of this kind, as are macroeconomics, a good deal of healthcare, and criminal law. In these areas, a policy move to change interest rates, or perhaps to introduce a new vaccination, has broadly predictable results.
- Fields with **multiple variables** are more challenging, and cannot so easily be modelled. Typically some of the interactions between variables will be reasonably well understood, others much less so. More sophisticated tools such as scenarios and simulations are needed to

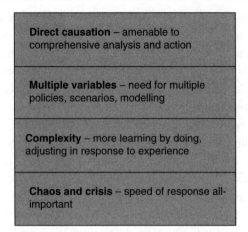

Figure 4.2. Understanding environments for strategy

understand them, and more varied policies to influence them. The evolution of industries; energy policy; or planning are examples.

- **Complex** fields—often involving less well understood phenomena, including human psychology. Crime is a good example. Governments and agencies learn by doing—trying different policies and observing which work—as much as through deductive logic or relying on a settled evidence base (there *is* plenty of evidence: but it is not enough definitively to guide action).
- Finally there are fields of **chaos**: during periods of crisis and transition many of the old rules and relations break down. In these circumstances speed of action and response is all-important; actions cannot afford to be too complex.

Which kind of field is being dealt with affects what kinds of strategy are viable and in particularly how tightly coupled the strategy can be (which is appropriate in relatively predictable circumstances) or whether it needs to be looser and more adaptive (see Fig. 4.2).

What Power and Knowledge can be Brought to Bear?

The next step is to understand how much power and knowledge government can bring to an issue or a task. One of the more bizarre experiences I had in government was seeing a detailed presentation of plans to eradicate opium production in Afghanistan, complete with McKinsey-style targets, trajectories, and milestones. The Prime Minister and his ministers took it very seriously, and the officials who had prepared it, seconded in from consultancies, were clearly proud that they had brought clarity and order to a difficult topic. Yet to anyone who had ever travelled in the region, read any history, or had any knowledge of the current situation, the presentation was absurd. It was divorced from reality, and founded on numerous questionable assumptions. Yet it met a need, and ministers committed significant resources to backing it. Not surprisingly, the target for reducing opium production wasn't met. What I hadn't predicted at the time was that during the period the plan was in theory being implemented opium production rose sharply (as prices rose in a predictable response to the earlier ban imposed by the Taliban).

Some of the weaknesses of the presentation came from the nature of the context—complex, and verging on chaos. But the other problem was that the audience for the presentation, a government based in Europe, was so clearly deficient in either the requisite power or knowledge to act. An all-powerful government can think and act in very different ways to one with little money, staff, or trust.

The many different ways of thinking about strategy can be fitted into four classic frames which reflect how much power and knowledge the strategizing organisation has (see Fig. 4.3). These have been synthesized from the many theories of management and policy in action and they can be simply mapped on two dimensions—one reflecting how powerful the organisation is, the other how much knowledge it has about its tasks and the environment it is seeking to influence.[3] The classic models of strategy are those based on high levels of power and knowledge. Command and control strategies assume that the world is knowable; that the tools for action lie in the hands of the state; and that the primary means of action is

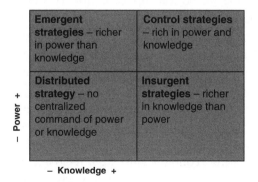

Figure 4.3. Models of strategy

command (law, directive, etc.). In these models what matters most is how those at the top of the pyramid map and respond to the environment—their ability to marshal information, to maintain control, and to monitor results. A strong state responding to a coming water shortage would be a good example.

The category of emergent strategy assumes that the state is powerful but that it lacks sufficient knowledge to act wisely. It therefore needs to learn quickly as events unfold in unexpected directions; action therefore requires persuasion, influence, and alignment of the actions of others, and learning is vital. In some areas the logical consequence is that strategy should focus on creating the conditions for systems to organise themselves: providing laws and regulations underpinning competitive markets, for example. For those at the top the priority is to be ad hoc, opportunistic; and not to become trapped by formal plans. What may matter most is how those on the periphery or at the bottom respond to outside pressures—for example, teachers' collective behaviour (and the behaviour of parents) matters more than education ministries in shaping curriculums over time.

A third category is for those without power who believe that they do have knowledge and know what needs to be done. These are insurgent strategies. States are rarely in this position, though small states may often have to act like insurgents in relation to bigger ones, as may weak departments and agencies. Businesses entering new markets, and NGOs campaigning for change, will often use these strategies, which involve greater use of guile and feints, or operating behind enemy lines, or turning weaknesses into strengths.

A fourth model of evolutionary strategy assumes low levels of power and little concentrated knowledge (power and knowledge are both diffused). It describes both Darwinian evolution, and the evolution of many real world communities. Some see bottom–up, evolutionary and organic change as inherently better than any other kind. What matters is to assist it through communication, encouraging cooperation and trust and growing mutually reinforcing behaviours and actions (for example in international relations the work of arms reduction, confidence-building, mutual transparency).

The appropriate framework will vary according to the issue and the organisation. Some tasks have to be conceived through the lens of command: for example preparing for an Olympics or responding to an imminent threat. Others are largely resistant to command: changing behaviours or cultures or creating economic clusters. A relatively weak nation trying to influence international affairs will certainly have to think more in terms of the third and fourth model.

What Possible Futures?

Understanding environments also involves making sense of the future. The American economist Kenneth Arrow used to tell of his first job during the Second World War, when he was assigned to a weather-forecasting unit in the Pacific. Within a few weeks he realized that their long-term forecasts were no better than simple extrapolations from month to month. He asked his superiors to give him a different and more useful task but received the response that, however flawed the methodology, the data was still needed for planning purposes.

Their reaction is not quite as mad as it seems. It is impossible to think strategically without some understanding of the likely context for change including external forces, trends, and possibilities. Often what is most important is an accurate understanding of the present (one of the most famous comments of recent futurology is William Gibson's claim that the future is already here, it's just unevenly distributed).[4] A range of tools can help to map out a picture of the future more accurately, and the likely pattern of threats and opportunities that a nation or agency faces. Many of these were pioneered by the US military after the Second World War as they tried to think more rigorously about possible disruptive threats through exercises asking 'what if?' These methods now include.

- **Forecasts**—the familiar forward projections of current trends, some reasonably reliable (like demographics) others less so (like economic growth rates), with models of varying degrees of sophistication to take account of multiple factors (such as the various economic models used in the world's central banks). Forecasting is attractive but also always dangerous because it gives a spurious sense of reliability. No one in Germany in 1918 could have easily forecast inflation rates for the next decade, just as no one in the USA in 2000 could have forecast the impact of terrorism. Good forecasters add an error rate to every forecast—which serves as a useful protection against decision makers taking them too seriously.
- **Scenarios**—structured exercises to clarify 3–4 broad possible futures so as to help decision makers ensure that their decisions are robust in as many possible futures as possible. Scenarios can also help warring factions to find room for agreement: a classic example was the 'Mont Fleur' scenarios which in the final years of apartheid helped persuade the top echelons of South Africa's National Party and the African National Congress to reach agreement.

- **Simulations**—role plays which game possible events. A good example was an exercise used to test out the implications of an internal market for the British National Health Service. Titled 'Rubber Windmill', it involved a large number of policy makers and managers playing out how a market would work in practice. The simulation showed that if purchasers competed for limited health services in a market where volume and budgets were relatively fixed, quality would be likely to fall; it also showed that the system would be particularly vulnerable to any financial instability or cuts in funding.
- **Foresight methods**—consultation and discussion to distil the perceptions of networks of experts and practitioners to paint a picture of likely trends, particularly in fields of science and technology, for example cybercrime or the threat of flooding associated with climate change. These can be particularly useful where there is a deficit of political or intellectual imagination.
- A much newer method is the deliberate creation of markets for future knowledge. In the mid-2000s, for example, the Global Risk Network with Newsfutures connected more than 500 traders to virtually trade their predictions about such things as avian flu, global recession, extreme weather events, and oil price spikes and claim to have achieved better predictions than competing alternatives.

None of these methods is reliable. Unexpected events are likely; there will be inherent blind spots; and often the key is to adapt quickly when these become apparent. All of our knowledge comes from the past yet all of our decisions are about the future. Futures tools are often used to encourage a flexible frame of mind rather than prediction. But they can raise awareness of changes which are only dimly visible during the day to day work of government: for example the changing geopolitics brought about by the rise of China and India, Europe's demographic problems, or the long-term impact of carbon reduction. They can also crystallize a vision of a desirable future. Examples of governments that have used these methods include Singapore, the Netherlands, Korea, China, Finland, and Alberta. Handled well, these methods bring to the surface 'predictable surprises' that are familiar to at least some people in the organisation but need to become part of the shared conventional wisdom.[5] They can also be used to consciously challenge the predictable ways in which we misread the future: excessive optimism; excessive attention to easily imagined events or risks; greater fear of loss than hope of gain; and so on.

Hypothetical stories about the future are less challenging to managers and make it easier to talk about difficult issues and options. Shell, which pioneered scenarios in the private sector, used them to acclimatize managers to apparently improbable possibilities—like very sharp fluctuations in oil prices (which then often did occur). Within governments futures work has both direct and indirect benefits. The Singapore Government's Scenario Planning Office describes scenario planning as

> a set of tools for generating a strategic conversation about what we can do today to prepare for an uncertain future...Scenario planning helps to free our minds to expect discontinuities in our environment. It approximates a strategic fire drill— we learn to be forward-looking by 'living in the future', whilst positioning ourselves to react to change quickly and nimbly.

This sort of work is best facilitated by groups that are detached from day to day politics and administration. The Netherlands National Environmental Policy Plan (NEPP) is a good example, drawing on a semi-independent Environmental Planning Agency which generates the issues which the plan is based around and then monitors whether the targets have been achieved. The Social and Cultural Planning Office which advises the Cabinet has a similar status—simultaneously outside government and able to think independently, but also with a formalized status within.[6]

What Causes What: Mapping the System

The next important preparatory step is to map the system: to be explicit about what causes what. Various methods can be used to map links between system elements, including feedback loops and lines of causation. There are some standard methods for surveying the key variables such as TOWS, STEEP, PEST, PESTLE, and others drawn from business and the military. The best tackle head-on the challenges of 'zooming' and 'granularity'—how to move between levels of analysis from the large to the small and back again. Often these will identify gaps in knowledge, gaps in data, or issues on which there are competing accounts and theories. These overall systems maps can be built up from any source which provides insights into what causes what:

- evidence and literature reviews (of the state of knowledge globally, drawing on all relevant disciplines and assessing their levels of certainty);
- modelling (to show the interactions of key variables);

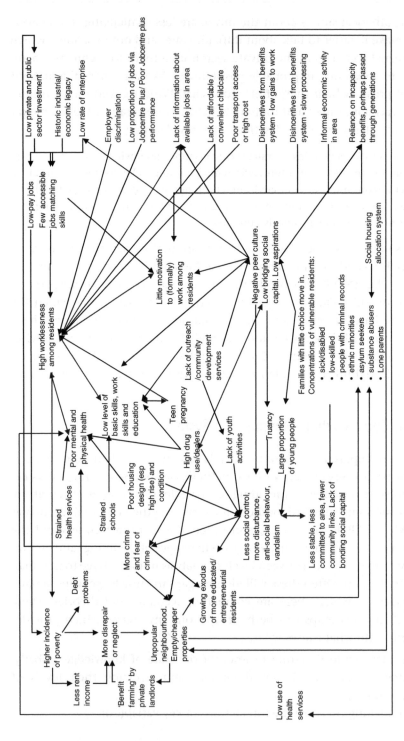

Figure 4.4. Mapping the system: urban regeneration as an example. *Source:* UK Cabinet Office.

- historical reasoning by analogy (looking at how decision makers succeeded or failed in comparable situations);
- benchmarking (finding the best available alternatives worldwide and learning lessons from them); and
- logic trees (the formal dissection of an issue into its component parts).

Fig. 4.4 is an example of a systems map of the influences on regeneration in low-income neighbourhoods, showing some of the complex feedback loops and pointing to the best points of leverage for policy intervention. Fig. 4.5 maps some of the influences on obesity, and some of the issues which arose from an analysis of the issues. It is a particularly good recent use of systems maps and a prompt for further research and discussion, offering an open view of the problem.

To shape these systems maps formal analysis needs to be complemented by informal tools. One that's often missed out is careful listening to people involved in the system at every level (including frontline practitioners, or users) since their perspectives, insights, and ideas may challenge the picture derived from quantitative data. It's notorious that tacit knowledge is often the most valuable—particularly about imminent disasters, or problems that are unpalatable for leaders. Issue trees can help to disaggregate

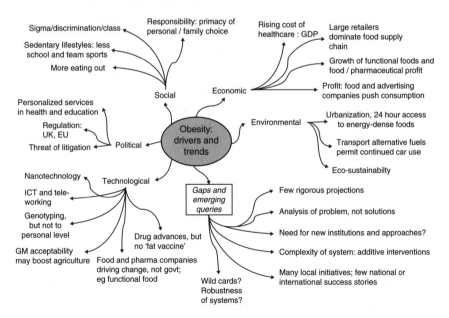

Figure 4.5. Mapping the system: pinpointing research needs.

Source: Foresight, *Trends and Drivers of Obesity,* a literature review for the Foresight project on obesity, 2007.

the key problems, showing whether they are the sum of several different phenomena, what's known about different causess and what's known about possible solutions.

Good analysis shows the connections between things and the non-obvious facts that lie beneath the surface. Good strategy is often analytic-ally rich, though there is always a trade-off between time and resources. 'Boiling the ocean' to achieve the most comprehensive possible under-standing of the facts is pointless when time is short. But the quality and depth of analysis is often the critical factor behind good strategy because all bureaucracies build up systematically distorted views of the world around them. Analysis helps to peel away false assumptions.

Analysis particularly comes into its own in relation to apparent regular-ities—correlations between a cause and an effect. Implicitly—and some-times explicitly—governing involves judgements about the links between correlation and causation. Leaders provide diagnoses—of why crime is up or unemployment down—and they provide prescriptions which claim that action X will lead to result Y. At one extreme decision makers can rely on hunch and improvisation to guide their claims. At the other there are the full rigours of randomized control trials (RCTs), widely used for medical experiments but not easy in most areas of public policy (though they were first used in agricultural policy in the 1920s). In between decision makers have to make do with data and the patterns that can be found in them. This is where common sense most often comes unstuck. In many areas of great interest to the public judgements have often been wrong. Apparent correlations which appear to be common sense, or to be backed up by science, have dissolved in the face of new evidence. So the good decision makers have learned how to rigorously question and investigate patterns, however appealing they may seem.

For example, it's widely assumed that inequality causes high levels of crime, and there are indeed many examples of correlations. Yet the UK is not alone in having experienced steadily rising crime during the decades after 1950 when inequality fell, as well as falling crime during the 1990s and 2000s while inequality rose. Here are a few of the issues that arise in relation to any apparent correlation, of the kind that appear every day in the media and in parliaments (usually taking the form 'research shows that x causes y'):

First, any correlation may simply be using the wrong categories. A good example is the long-standing belief that children from broken homes are more likely to commit anti-social behaviour, which appeared to be backed up by mountains of evidence. But more detailed studies later showed that the key variable was not family break-up, but rather family discord (implying that sometimes it would be in the child's interests for the family to break up).

Second, care needs to be taken to ensure that there isn't another missing factor which explains patterns. For example, the much higher rate of homicide in the USA can be attributed to features of US culture (Oscar Wilde blamed it on the bad wallpaper; others have suggested violent TV). But more detailed analysis shows that the differences in murder rates between the USA and other countries are mainly attributed to homicides using guns, not to homicide as such. In other words the risk of homicide is related to the much greater availability of guns, and to attitudes towards personal use (which helps to explain why Switzerland, a country where every male householder eligible for national service can have a gun, avoids high homicide rates).

Third, causal patterns need to be disentangled. It used to be thought that early drinking was likely to lead to alcoholism in later life. But more detailed genetic studies suggested that both had the same cause, a genetically shaped tendency to substance misuse.

Fourth, causes may work in surprising directions. For many years it was assumed that children who had been smacked by their parents risked psychological harm. But then psychologists suggested that the lines of causation might work in the opposite direction: children with behavioural disorders might elicit more violent behaviour from their parents. The current thinking on this issue isn't settled—some research appears to show that it is how parents smack that matters most (whether it is straightforwardly disciplinary or verges on abuse). But there are many other examples where causal directions are the opposite to what they appear.

Fifth, the right interpretations may challenge assumptions. A good example is the higher rate of schizophrenia amongst black people, particularly men in the UK and the Netherlands. This could be genetically caused, or reflect a greater tendency amongst white doctors to diagnose black men as schizoid. But detailed studies show that the illness is associated with the problems of migration—not with genetics or the biases of the medical profession.

Sixth, causes may lie in surprising places. Steve Levitt's research on crime in the USA debunked the proud claims of many police officers that they had personally overseen an unprecedented drop in crime. His research showed that the key factor was the change to abortion law which led to fewer boys being born to poor women in the 1970s. A decade and a half later this showed up in the crime figures. Although serious errors were found in his analysis, the basic finding has remained solid.

Seventh, actions may have non-obvious effects. More intensive action to arrest drug dealers can simply push up the price of drugs and attract more people into crime. In the classic example paying teenagers to collect rats during an epidemic encouraged more teenagers to become rat breeders and drove up the rat population rather than cutting it.

That one factor correlates with another, or that one risk factor correlates with a particular outcome, never constitutes proof of causation. To become more solid, a correlation has to be replicated in both halves of a large data set; found in other data sets; confirmed by a meta-analysis of many similar studies; and investigated for sampling biases or 'confounding' factors. This is rarely going to be possible amidst the pressures of making policy and enacting change. But devoting even modest resources to investigating the complex patterns of cause and effect that lie beneath the surface of every government pronouncement or ministerial speech is usually money worth spending.

This knowledge can then feed into the maps of how systems work that were mentioned above. This is where analysis matters most. Around any public policy goal there will be many pieces of potentially relevant knowledge, but these are unlikely to have been synthesized into a comprehensive view of the dynamics of change. Take, for example, the issue of school retention for teenagers from poor backgrounds. There are many different theoretical models for making sense of why some may drop out:

- Through an economic lens the most important issue may be incentives—can they earn more in the labour market than staying on at school?
- For educationalists the decisive factor may be how engaged they are in their early years at secondary school, from 11 to 13.
- For sociologists the decisive factors may be the influence of family or peers.
- For psychologists the critical issue will be their own cognitive abilities, for example their willingness to delay gratifications.
- For authoritarians the problem may be a symptom of insufficient punishments for non-attendance.
- For youth workers the problem may be the absence of case workers who understand their needs and can guide them through difficult transitions.

All of these viewpoints contain some truth. But policy makers need to be forensic in working out which explanations apply to which teenagers, and to pull together a clear map of what is and isn't known, setting out the various feedback loops and interdependencies. This is not easy to do—it involves capturing and interrogating the knowledge from many different sources, some academic, some in the minds of practitioners or the public, to create an ever more sophisticated and comprehensive description of the system or ecology that surrounds an issue. Often this involves forcing implicit assumptions to be made explicit.

Take heroin use. Everyone involved in the drugs field will have some implicit and explicit assumptions about what explains changing patterns of addiction. Some will see the issue primarily through a policing lens—if only the penalties could be high enough or enforcement sufficiently robust to cut off supply routes, the problem would go away. Others prefer a social lens and emphasize the blocked opportunities and the peer encouragement that leads people to addiction. Others see things in terms of personal stories and tragedies—including the impact of child abuse or family breakdown or bereavement. Again, all of these will have some grains of truth, but what matters is their relative importance and how different factors interrelate. Sharply reducing heroin use will generally require a combination of coercion (for example harassing local dealers rather than only focusing on the much less visible big dealers), treatment, social action, and changing peer cultures.

Good systems maps can directly shape strategy and policy—helping to guide where the most useful interventions can be made.[7] Alternatively, they may clarify where the most promising experiments and pilots can be set up to test and compare different approaches, for example comparing school retention strategies which use financial incentives against others which use the same money to improve school experiences or provide personal advisers.

What do all of these amount to? The key test is whether there is a plausible and credible account to be given of how the system works—how it responds to changes in key variables, ranging from the level of economic growth to shifts in public attitudes—well before possible solutions are looked at.

Where: Setting Directions and Strategic Goals

These preparatory steps—defining goals and why one task matters more than others; understanding the field, recognizing the scope of power and knowledge, situating action in possible futures and mapping systems—provide the foundations for more effective strategy. In a rough and ready form they are good disciplines for any organisation to review itself with at regular intervals. Is it focused on the things that matter? Is it realistic about the nature of the field it is acting in? Is it deluding itself about its power and knowledge to act? Are its policies and strategies robust in the light of possible futures? Are actions grounded in a plausible account of how the system works?

But these are of course only starting points. The hard graft of strategy then involves using the dialogue between purposes and environments to define the direction a society or a nation is to take.

There are many things that governments and societies would like to achieve but cannot. This is particularly true in foreign affairs where the political leaders of powerful nations have considerable capacity to imagine solutions to other people's problems—conflict in the Middle East is perhaps the classic contemporary example—but which rarely work. There are many aspects of human nature that irk political leaders. But there are tight limits to what any government, especially a democratic one, can do to influence them. Indeed the ability to distinguish achievable goals from unachievable ones is a mark of good leadership. Vigorous internal debate—which may have to be very secret—helps to clarify the doable and the undoable, and then with a wider strategy-making process helps decision makers to decide what really matters, which goals to focus on and how to sequence different priorities.

This can be very high-level. Table 4.1 sets out some of the vital statistics of two very different models of development, the USA and Norway, which have almost identical levels of GDP per capita. These very broad directions—whether to create or retain a strong welfare state, or a highly individualistic and competitive society, or a strong emphasis on security—are at the heart of democratic politics and the arguments societies need over their overall direction and priorities. They are not options that societies can simply choose from a menu: they are path-dependent, and they involve 'elective affinities' (to use the phrase Weber adapted from Goethe), that make systems more or less coherent. But societies can choose to shift direction—as the UK did after the Thatcher years when it

Table 4.1. *Models of development, USA and Norway*

	USA	Norway
Income per capita	$37,624	$37,108
Taxes as % share of GDP	26	43
Gini coefficient (income inequality)	0.41	0.26
Spending on the military as % of GDP	4.1	1.9
Spending on health as % of GDP	15	10
Life expectancy	77.2	79.5
Under-5 mortality per 1,000	20	4
Annual working hours	1,824	1,363
Private cars per 1,000 people	765	494
Prison population per 1,000	715	64

sharply raised public capital investment and spending, or as Germany did a few years later when it started to deregulate labour markets.

These shifts can be distilled into more precise objective and strategic directions, and then translated into instructions that can be made sense of by large systems and bureaucracies. In some cases they may be quantitative—for example improving children's literacy levels, cutting mortality rates, bringing down unemployment by a million, or building 300,000 new homes. Britain's government set several hundred goals in the 1990s and 2000s, ranging from improvements in exam results to declining cancer mortality. In the 2000s South Australia set ninety-eight targets ranging from opportunities for aboriginal people to cutting water use. Texas embedded its quantitative goals in law. In other cases goals may be equally precise but less numerical: securing entry to the European Union, avoiding a war with a neighbour, achieving a major devolution of power. Vague goals—and rhetoric—can let people down. Clarity and accountability are linked, though as we'll see all numerical targets can lead to distortions and 'gaming'.

In some circumstances the best directions are very precise but leave plenty of room for intelligent adaptation. In the US and UK military the 'commander's intent' is put at the top of any order, specifying the desired end-goal. The aim is that this should never be so detailed that it cannot survive unpredictable events, but that it should be clear enough to guide decisions. This is what governments often need too if they are to galvanize bureaucracies—for example, the goal of ending child poverty, or putting a man on the moon, or becoming ready to join the European Union.

For strategic directions to work, and for these 'intents' to be meaningful on the ground, there needs to be a clear sense of what can change and how fast. Governments generally overestimate how much can be changed quickly—and jump to announcements and laws which have little chance of succeeding. Ministers who can expect to be in office only briefly find it hard to be patient. But governments' other vice is to underestimate how much can change longer term. Being too firmly located within a system makes it harder to spot where cumulative change can over a period years transform a situation. The stage of turning the high-level goals into strategic directions can be greatly helped by strategic analysis. This is the point at which a team within the bureaucracy can advise about what is achievable; about which goals make most sense; about how different goals support each other or are in conflict.

Setting directions also involves clarity about sequencing as well as timescales—what steps are the preconditions for other steps? So, for example, if a society wants to take radical steps to cut carbon emissions, what steps may be needed before full-scale carbon taxes are introduced or comprehensive road charging? What will help prepare businesses and households for fundamental changes to their daily lives?

Finally, setting directions also involves reflection on government's appetite for change and the extent of the change margin (which is described later in this chapter). This margin can be understood in financial terms—what proportion of today's spending can be redirected to future priorities? But it goes much deeper. A North American state that chose quickly to move away from a highly dispersed, car-dependent model of living towards a west European one of dense cities and highly developed public transport systems (Europeans currently use half as much energy and produce half as much CO_2 as North Americans) would require great will power and commitment. One that wished to go even further towards mandating hybrid or electric vehicles, combined heat and power and other systemic alternatives to the high carbon status quo, would need even more. Many societies in the past have shown themselves to have just such radical appetites for change. But generally these depend on exceptional qualities of leadership as well as a widely shared sense that the status quo is no longer an option.

How? Policies and Actions

Strategic directions then need to be turned into policies, plans, and actions. One of the common vices in government is to publish strategies which simply sit on shelves. Another is to create many stand-alone policies that reflect the personal enthusiasms of ministers or officials. The fact that ministers' tenure in their jobs is usually short—1–2 years in many countries—gives them strong incentives to emphasize initiative over outcomes, and to use public relations as a substitute for achievement. The best of these may turn out to be invaluable reforms. But often these create a clutter that diverts attention from more important priorities.

So strategies, policies, and plans should be coherent, and should follow from the directions that have been chosen, and from what's known about causation. All public agencies have at their disposal a wide toolkit—much larger than was available a generation or two ago. The most recent attempts at a comprehensive map of policy tools were provided by Lester Salamon's *The Tools of Government: A Guide to New Governance*, which is particularly strong on economic tools, and Christopher Hood and Helen Margett's *The Tools of Government in a Digital Age*, which takes a rather broader view.[8] The tools available to governments include:

- Laws, directives, commands. These are the traditional tools of governments, but they are often blunt, inflexible, and hard to enforce. Many legislatures, perhaps inevitably, see legislation as the best solution to problems—to anyone with a hammer most problems look like nails.
- Finance, in the form of subsidies, tax incentives, or penalties and funding for programmes. This is the other main means of encouraging change, though experience of public sector reform shows that in practice finance plays a more limited role than is often expected.
- Allocation and development of people, from managers to frontline staff.
- Changed structures that create agencies or teams with new tasks. There will always be trade-offs between the costs of structural change and the benefits, and between the higher transaction costs of more collaboration and higher likelihood of doing what matters.
- Knowledge: ensuring that information or knowledge is used in new ways, for example through public information campaigns, retraining for professionals or more sophisticated tools of knowledge management (which is usually essential for implementation, though difficult if there are weak incentives or cultural encouragement for knowledge sharing).
- Use of third parties (where there is a long history of what works and what doesn't in using agents and agencies).
- Contracting out of tasks.
- Partnerships, and the many organizational devices through which public, private, and non-profit organizations can share risks and opportunities, for example to build roads or run hospitals.
- Regulation and rules for empowered bodies to enforce them.

There are also a host of other types of tool, some very ancient, for licensing activities, requisitioning information or goods, providing warnings or instructions, rewarding compliance, or distributing punishments. Table 4.2 sets out the mix of tools in more detail.

Some of the most important new tools are evolving to change behaviour, through combinations of incentives, persuasion, and peer pressure, drawing on lessons from psychology (discussed in more detail in Chapter 11). The use of web-enabled and other IT tools as ways of organizing public information, transactions, and feedback is also becoming increasingly important, after a slow start.[9]

Fashions change in relation to these tools. The most commercially successful book on government over the last two decades—David Osborne

Table 4.2. *Tools of government*

Information, education, and advice	Command and coercion	Economic instruments	Regulation
Provision of information *League tables; online information; statistical data*	**Taxes designed solely to raise money** *Income tax, sales tax*	**Taxes designed to change behaviour** *Tobacco duty; fuel duty, carbon taxes*	**Price & market structure regulation** *Pensions; privatized utilities; competition laws;*
Public education campaigns *Teenage pregnancy; AIDS campaigns; diet*	**Laws** *Compulsory education up to 18; prohibitions on drugs*	**Charges** *Congestion charges; road pricing*	*Price regulation*
Reporting & disclosure requirements *Financial services, public agencies, audit functions and inspectors advising public agencies on best practice and performance*	**Penalties** *Anti-social behaviour orders* **Policing** *Bans or restrictions on demonstrations*	**Subsidies, tax credits, & vouchers** *R&D tax credits; child tax credit; pre-school education vouchers*	**Production & consumption regulation** *Planning rules; Public service obligations on privatised utilities; Compulsory motor insurance; Renewable energy obligations; Licensing*
Labelling *Food ingredients, energy efficiency, carbon footprints*		**Benefits & grants** *Disability benefits; subsidized trust funds for children; personal budgets for welfare beneficiaries*	**Standards setting regulation** *Accreditation of vocational qualifications and exams; Trading standards; Health and safety*
Advisory services: *for teenagers, small businesses*			
Representation services *Ombudsmen*		**Tradable permits & quotas** *Carbon emissions trading schemes*	**Prescription & prohibition legislation** *Criminal justice; Banning tobacco advertising or smoking in public places; penalties for drunk driving*

	Award & auctioning of franchises and licences	Rights & representation legislation or regulation *Human Rights; rights of redress*
	Mobile phones and spectrum; airport landing slots	
	Government loans, loan guarantees, and insurance	
	Student loans; export credit guarantee	

Direct intervention	International	Self-regulation
Direct provision of services (including co-production) *Police; armed forces; hospitals; schools* New kinds of agency: *executive agencies, government-owned charities or private companies; joint ventures*	**Open co-ordination** *EU budget and social policy*	**Voluntary agreements** *Advertising standards; Corporate Social Responsibility initiatives*
Commissioning of services (from public, private and/or voluntary sectors) *Private prisons; welfare to work; subsidized social care*	**Special vehicles:** e.g. HIV/AIDS, IFF	**Codes of practice** *Banking Code*
	Global justice: e.g. International Criminal Court	**Co-regulation and arbitration at work**
	Global public goods: CDMs and carbon trading	

and Ted Gaebler's *Reinventing Government*, which popularized the new public management—advocated that the state should concentrate on 'steering' rather than 'rowing', using more arm's length tools and acting wherever possible as purchaser, commissioner, or regulator rather than as a provider. But the combination of new security threats and experience of the problems associated with arm's length steering has encouraged a partial swing back of the pendulum towards more direct control.

The choice of tools depends on many factors: evidence about effectiveness; the political authority for using more or less coercive means; the degree to which the public—or business—want to change behaviour; and the degree to which the key tasks are measurable, repetitive, and high-volume (and therefore easier to delegate top–down).[10] Other issues include:

- **Substitution**—where there are direct alternatives or trade-offs, for example between financial incentives and legal requirements. Departments and agencies tend to become habituated to particular tools—without considering the alternatives (for example, making too much use of legislation like Britain's Home Office which passed fifty-five criminal justice bills in a ten-year period, or tax incentives which are the favoured tool for Treasuries).

- **Complementarity**—will doing more of one thing make it easier to do more of other things? For example, policies to charge motorists for driving into cities will tend to increase public demand for cycling facilities; increasing performance amongst schoolchildren at 11 will tend, five years later, to improve performance at 16, and seven years later to increase demand for higher education.

- **Sustainability**—some policy tools prompt people to adjust their behaviour in ways which make the tools less effective. 'Goodhart's' law refers to this in monetary policy: any definition of money that is used as a policy instrument in time becomes less effective as economic agents find ways to bypass it. Similar phenomena have been observed with many other kinds of target. Sustainability also matters in other ways too. For example, programmes like Headstart in the USA and Surestart in the UK which are aimed at helping children of low-income families, can have a significant initial impact—but this is sustained through to adulthood only if the interventions are kept up.

- **Dosage**—some tools will work only if the intensity of the intervention is sufficient. This will apply to incentives and penalties, as well as to providing new services. Dosage may involve levels of treatment (for something that's gone wrong), provision, as well as enforcement.

So, for example, a minimum wage will only 'work' if there is sufficient policing of employers so that the cost of being caught is greater than the cost of paying higher wages. Dosages also reflect the scale of underlying problems. In the UK, for example, cash benefits now take off 15 per cent of the Gini coefficient (the standard measure of income inequality), compared to 8 per cent in the late 1960s and 5 per cent in the late 1940s: in other words the welfare state is having to work much harder to balance increasingly unequal market rewards.

- **Capability**—some policy tools work much better on paper than in practice, because they depend on a high degree of judgement in their implementation. For example, welfare to work policies offering more personalized deals to the long-term unemployed depend on frontline staff being able to make assessments of whether the claimant has a drug, alcohol, or mental health problem.
- **Dynamics**—some policies have much greater indirect dynamic impact than their immediate effects. For example, welfare programmes that directed money to women rather than men (like Brazil's Bolso Familial) set in motion far-reaching changes within families as well as having the direct effect of rewarding families for sending their children to school. In other cases the effect runs out. Using energy efficiency programmes to cut carbon emissions in the long run turns out to be self-defeating: the savings achieved simply drive up spending on other (high carbon) goods and services. Lasting success depends instead on decarbonizing the economy.
- **Cost structure**—many policies work well if they can be tailored to individual needs, but this generally drives up costs. So there is little purpose in proposing detailed assessments of individual readiness for rehabilitation in a prisons system if there isn't the finance to support it. The general point is that there is no point piloting models which are clearly too expensive to be scaled up. Equally some policies may start off expensive but become cheaper over time because of 'learning curve' effects and other economies of scale.

Shaping policies is the point at which governments most need creativity. Sometimes the best solutions will be very lateral in nature: taking an idea from one field and applying it in another (for example applying the zero waste ideas of lean manufacturing to the environment or social policy); sometimes they will be hybrids, like call centres providing diagnosis for health problems; and sometimes they will turn weaknesses into strengths. Just as any disability also heightens other abilities (for example, the acute hearing of the blind or the oral communication of the dyslexic), so can every apparent problem be seen in a different light as a creative possibility. The huge costs involved in avoiding climate change can also be seen as an opportunity to speed up advances in economic efficiency; ageing can be seen as a looming cost or as providing a new source of labour and social capital.

The converse of this is that apparently sound solutions may disappoint. A good example is seatbelt legislation which appears at first glance a very straightforward example of effective government policy. Wearing a seatbelt was made compulsory in over eighty countries during the 1970s–1990s following the lead taken by Australia. In each case evidence was cited showing that wearing a seatbelt reduces the risk of injury and death. Yet the evidence comparing countries which introduced compulsion against those that didn't shows that in the latter cases the rate of decline of deaths was higher. The reason is simple and is sometimes described as the 'risk compensation hypothesis': people adapt their behaviour to balance their propensity to take risks (which is shaped by the apparent rewards) with the costs of taking risks. If new safety laws reduce the risk of a behaviour that people enjoy, they are likely to do more of it.[11]

Another example is the sometimes counterintuitive impact of equality laws. Many countries ban discrimination on grounds of race in order to become more integrated, and prohibit numerical targets or quotas which have the effect of discriminating for or against particular individuals. Yet the effect of this well-intentioned policy in some places has been to make institutions like schools and football clubs more, not less, mono-racial. As Mark Bovens and Margo Trappenburg have shown in their work on 'segregation through anti-discrimination', the absence of quotas or targets for racial groups encourages people to choose to stick with others like them. Housing policies have tended to encourage greater choice and to give migrants rights to social housing. Attempts to direct the location of migrants more actively have tended to falter. People in wealthier areas have been quite happy to see the poor newcomers locating in enclaves in poor cities, even though this has often stirred up tensions.

The same dynamics apply in schools. Where choice has been allowed, schools have ended up highly segregated. Yet, when asked, parents say that on balance they would prefer schools to be more mixed, and with good reason, since segregation isn't good for the pupils. Even though the Netherlands pays 1.9 times as much to schools for each ethnic minority pupil, white parents generally choose to avoid schools with large proportions from ethnic minorities. Thomas Schelling's famous work on the dynamics of choices (the 'Schelling Segregation Model') is relevant here. His model used a notional chess or draughts board and placed counters of two colours on them, which could represent people from different races. He then specified decision rules for how a counter on a particular square would respond to the patterns around them (the eight neighbouring squares in the case of the interior, three or five squares for those on the outside). For example, a rule in which any counter would switch colour if more than three of its neighbours were of a different colour set in motion a very quick dynamic which would turn a very mixed picture into a wholly segregated one. Even very mild preferences could have the same effect. Ironically, those places that have tried to enforce more mixed communities have been blocked from doing so. Rotterdam's policy to do this was declared illegal as far back as 1974. In the municipality of Tiel a rule was introduced that whenever a school reached the same proportion of black pupils as the overall proportion in the area, black parents seeking a place would be directed to other schools. This policy had succeeded in ending school segregation and white flight. But in 2005 the Equal Treatment Commission ruled that it was discriminatory. As a result policies that were designed to achieve equality and integration ended up achieving the precise opposite—and have left the Netherlands as a rather anti-immigrant country.

Sequencing

The hardest design task is to get the right rhythms and sequencing for strategy. Many new policies and strategies need new capacities and institutions to be in place before they can work. Britain tried to create a brand new service (called 'Connexions') to provide advice for socially excluded teenagers to help them navigate away from truancy, crime, drugs, and towards qualifications and jobs. The policy suffered early on from distortion (it had been intended to be a highly targeted service but was redefined as a universal one) and was then implemented too quickly with the aim of reaching complete coverage within three to five years rather than the decade or more it takes to create a new profession with distinct skills and norms. Not surprisingly the results were very uneven (although they were positively endorsed by evaluations and audits). Timescales matter greatly too for any strategies that depend on community engagement (which takes time to coalesce) as well as for physical infrastructures.

In other cases the sequencing involves high politics and public opinion. Many governments have tried with great difficulty to reform their pensions systems. During a time of rapid ageing this is bound to be hard because almost everyone appears to be a loser: the only viable options involve people working longer, saving more, or being taxed more. Individually sensible policies risk being knocked back by angry prospective losers. So this is a field where there has to be widespread public understanding of the problem, and widespread recognition that current policies are not sustainable, before any specific solutions can be suggested. In the UK in the early 2000s ministers had fudged the problems but Tony Blair felt impelled to grapple with them. An independent review was set up to examine the nature of the problem and spark off a national debate. Only after that had run its course were specific options floated, and then turned into policy (including raising the retirement age, clearer obligations for employers, as well as a higher contribution from taxes), and these were then spread over several decades. Other big policy issues, from charging for road use to climate change, also depend on a widespread consensus before rational policies can be floated, and similarly long timescales for implementation.

There is a large literature on how to organise change in big organizations and systems.[12] A common theme is that moving quickly into action, even on a small scale, can create positive feedback loops. It means that some people now have a stake in change; it provides learning about what will work; it signals that change is real; and it builds up the confidence of those who have initiated the change. In one of the best recent empirical studies of change in the public sector (looking at procurement in the federal government in the USA), Steven Kelman identified eighteen different feedback mechanisms, from learning curves to growing confidence.[13] In some very different contexts too the first step in a strategy can be superficial or symbolic, so long as it creates a momentum for change. When Edi Rama became mayor of Tirana his first move was to paint the buildings bright colours—a quick and cheap mark of change. Others have painted the lamp-posts or organized public festivals. An artist in residence working for the New York waste department sought out all ten thousand employees to thank them, a simple act which symbolized a changed relationship of respect. These are just a few of the steps that can build the confidence that later sustains a strategy through difficult times. Later on there are many other tools which can embed a process of change: installing new people and removing resisters; building new institutions with a stake in making change succeed; and rewarding supporters.

Financing Strategy

Throughout history rulers have worried about money; there's never enough of it. Money gets stuck on old priorities (one political scientist estimated that after Margaret Thatcher's radical administration had been in power for more than a decade over 90 per cent of expenditure was still devoted to programmes established by previous governments).[14] Even presidents and prime ministers have to scrabble around for small amounts of money for their pet projects because of the difficulty of cutting existing programmes which have accumulated their own vested interests. Being strategic means being tough in freeing up resources—and taking on interest groups that have become habituated to public subsidy. But for that very reason it's hard in a political context. David Stockman, who was Ronald Reagan's budget director, describes his mounting disillusion at budget meetings. Reagan didn't understand the issues and his counsellor Edwin Meese excluded any discussion of difficult issues. Stockman had to set up parallel structures to get to grips with budget options, and then found himself the inevitable target for resentment from Cabinet ministers whose favourite programmes he was trying to cut. The net result was that an administration that was ostensibly in favour of smaller government left the USA with its largest ever public deficits.

Strategy is closely bound up with money—getting the economics wrong generally guarantees that the strategy will fail. Richard Musgrave's classic work on public finance distinguished three areas of government activity relating to money:[15] stabilization (keeping the economy at full employment, and ensuring the background conditions for strategies to be implemented); allocation through taxes, subsidies, and provision of services; and distribution, dealing with equity and entitlements. In the past economic instability has been the biggest threat to strategy. Without reliable revenues and predictable prices it is hard to plan with confidence. Any policies that are likely to affect the relationship between total revenues and total expenditures are particularly risky (for example reorganizing tax-raising services). And any measures that change distributional arrangements bring with them strong political reactions (many apparently well-thought through policies and strategies have simply ignored distributional impacts. Yet the people and interests affected by changes rarely ignore them and all politicians worth their salt look at proposals through a distributional lens). Bureaucratic arrangements for finance can also often impede strategy. Many governments are as concerned to spend money (particularly towards the end of financial years) as to account for it well, and money is bound to be tied up with the micropolitics of bureaucratic battles.

The last twenty-five years have brought many reforms to how governments use money, from planning to performance management. The best of these have tried to put money in the service of strategy, or desirable outcomes. It has become a commonplace that financial discipline is the precondition for almost everything else, and that this requires clear rules including limits on total spending that are set, usually over a three-to-five-year time horizon, before any bids are considered. The credibility of these rules depends on the authority of a strong finance ministry or cabinet committee to hold the line and maintain the overall fiscal position in negotiations with departments. There then has to be monitoring of what is being spent and how it is being spent, so as to trigger intervention if particular budgets are overshooting (for example, demand-led categories of spending such as entitlements). This task of monitoring can be organized within government—or it can be shared. In India recent legislation conferred powers on local tribal communities to confirm that budget allocations were actually spent on the promised roads and hospitals. Greater transparency, including public information about budgets, unit costs, and individual items, reduces the risks of corruption. Equally, greater transparency can bring the public into arguments about relative priorities and relative performance. The more that society can be mobilized to scrutinize performance the better.

There are then more detailed policies that have been widely used to ensure that monetary allocations fall in line with strategic priorities. The most important of these are processes for reallocation from programmes and activities that create less public value to ones that create more: for example, biannual reviews of spending or zero-based budgeting, in which every budget is taken as up for grabs. These require vigorous Treasuries to interrogate and investigate value for money. Strategic government is very hard when Treasuries are too weak and have to treat existing spending levels as given. For the same reasons all governments need regular exercises that question existing commitments—however politically untouchable they may appear. How public finance is designed can also encourage more strategic behaviour. If under-spending is immediately clawed back officials are much less likely to act strategically. Longer budget commitments—over three or four years—give more reasons for departments to think more rigorously about their own commitments. The same is true of rules which allow them to keep a proportion of receipts from capital sales or charges. These principles can also be extended: contracting with providers over similar periods to incentivize them to create new value, such as lower unemployment or crime.

Budgetary allocations then need to be closely tied to strategic objectives. When stated priorities are not reflected in the allocation of new money, and the reallocation of old money, this is generally a sign that political leaders don't have an adequate grip. Wherever possible budget allocations should be linked to outputs and outcomes, preferably with broad targets for departments or units to achieve, and mechanisms to compare results against these. Within departments, or governments as a whole, benchmarks can be set using the better performers as the baseline. Poorer performers can be replaced or taken over. Scandinavian countries such as Finland and Sweden pioneered 'results-oriented budgeting' in the 1970s and 1980s and this has become a worldwide movement away from controls focused solely on inputs to controls much more closely tied to results and outcomes, and, in some countries, to budgeting on an accruals basis rather than cash.

The next stages—which are still out of the reach of most public agencies—involve more precise costings of different activities, outcomes, and outputs so that decision makers can compare the unit costs and marginal costs of alternative policies or providers. Money can then be used more strategically to drive change and improvements, for example through purchasing outcomes in competitive markets, or overtly linking funding allocations to milestones of achievement. More radically, the public sector can be opened up to alternative providers, or to communities which wish to provide for themselves.

Appetites for Change: The Change Margin

Effective strategy requires that money is liberated from the past for the needs of the future. As we look forward from today the future presents itself as a funnel extending into the future, from a certain now to an uncertain future. Within any organisation there will be a varying appetite for what can be called the 'change margin' (see Fig. 4.6). This is the proportion of that funnel which is open to change. This margin partly reflects the flexibility of organizations and procedures and it is partly a matter of budgets—whether they are designed in such a way that new programmes have a good chance of being funded. In most governments this margin is pretty narrow: past commitments soak up all available resources, and any growth in revenues is taken up by pay increments or inflation. Few can free up more than 1 or 2 per cent of spending within a year.

Much of the machinery of government tends towards rigid allocations where the criteria for anything new are far more demanding than for what exists. External shocks and political catharsis can unlock resources. But the best governments also cultivate their own change margin, setting aside resources for new initiatives and programmes, promoting newcomers, and

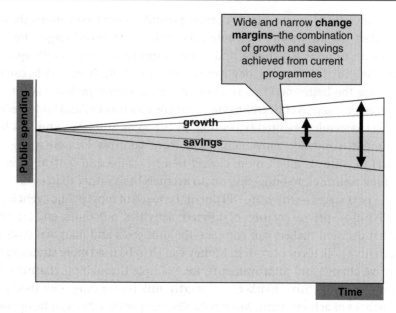

Figure 4.6.   Change margins

opening up services to competitive pressures. These are the ones that have mastered how to refuel while in mid-air.

Structures and Strategy

Most strategies follow structures rather than the other way around. But at some point any strategy needs to consider whether structures are fit for purpose. Restructuring can be a costly diversion of time and energy, and it is striking that the nation with the highest life expectancy, Japan, is also unusual in having avoided any major restructuring of its health system over fifty years. All too often fiddling with departments and agencies gets in the way of achieving results. Yet there are undoubtedly better and worse structures, and in some circumstances changing structures can unleash great energies. NASA, for example, was restructured five times in its first eight years (and was led by a triumvirate with very different skills and experience, who all had to agree any major decision—a formula that helped to combine decisiveness with flexibility).[16]

In the classic works of twentieth century business strategy—in particular the writings of Alfred Chandler—it was argued that structure should follow strategy. For any possible strategy there would be an optimum structure, aligning powers and accountabilities in the best possible way.[17] In the public sector this should align the incentives of politicians, key bureaucrats, and the public. Most would agree that strategy and structure need to be aligned and that any strategy has to fit with aspects of the organisation. John Roberts, for example, describes in his book *The Modern Firm* the four key elements that need to be aligned with strategy in business:[18]

- the people—skills, motivations;
- architecture of organizations—structures, governance, how tasks are divided;
- routines—processes and procedures; and
- culture—shared beliefs.

In other words the job of leaders and managers is to align both the hardware—the formal organograms—and the software of processes and cultures. But the structural choices that follow from this are not straightforward. So for example if the priority is crime reduction how far should a single organisation control the various activities of government which might contribute to it, which range from supporting problematic families to truancy, urban design to surveillance technologies? Or how far should a government concerned to cut carbon emissions bring together the many sources of emissions, such as transport policy, energy policy, and housebuilding regulations?

The US Commission on public services led by Paul Volcker in the early 2000s had as its first recommendation that 'the federal government should be reorganized into a limited number of mission related executive departments'. This view reflects current conventional wisdom, and appears sensible. But it is not as helpful as it appears. It implies that government's missions are distinct and that government should be constantly reorganized as missions change. Yet while some missions are sharply delineated others are necessarily fuzzy. As B. Guy Peters put it in a major survey of public reforms 'organisation theory in the public sector is not yet sufficiently advanced to provide adequate guidance for would-be reformers . . . there is not sufficient evidence to make good predictive statements.'[19]

The classic departmental and agency structures were primarily shaped around knowledge—how best to tap pools of expertise. In other governments structures were designed to prevent concentrations of power. Hitler promoted intense competition between his agencies to maximize his power and room for manoeuvre. Fashions swing between specialization and consolidation, bundling and unbundling, without much evidence to back them up. The UK, for example, created well over 100 specialist executive agencies in the late 1980s in a burst of specialization that was then paralleled in many other countries (for example, Canada's Special Operating Agencies and France's 'Centres de responsabilité'). This worked well in fields where the tasks were easily specified and measured and, where the issues were not politically controversial, but badly elsewhere. Predictably too it led to many failures of coordination and handling of cross-cutting issues.

In principle structures work best where they have a reasonable fit with the most important tasks, and ensure some clear lines of accountability. They should:

- reflect the manageable span for a top leadership;
- minimize the proportion of transactions that cross departmental boundaries relative to remaining within them;
- be suitable for coping with the pressures likely during periods of crisis;
- gather the right cluster of related issues; and
- ensure clear lines of accountability for outcomes.

In many fields there is at least a logical virtue in structures that ensure some authority to oversee and respond to coherent whole systems, viewed either in terms of fields (e.g. crime) or groups of people (e.g. the elderly), but this is itself a principle that can only be adopted in part because such systems are never self-contained. So there is a logic to bringing all the functions around welfare for people of working age into a single department, or all the functions relating to the development of the countryside. But the health services needed by old people overlap so much with the health services needed by younger people that departmental separation would probably be counterproductive.

No government can function without some boundaries and separations. A government solely made up of horizontal functions would face just as many coordination problems as one made up solely of vertical functions, as would a government made up solely of project teams. The key is to minimize the number of critical boundaries rather than to eliminate them.

But there are no ideal structures—only structures which are more or less obstructive to the ends which are desired. There are many types of structure that are bound to impede strategies—particularly if they embed conflicts between the interests of bureaucrats, politicians, and the public. So, for example, if an important task straddles two agencies with divergent missions—for example a transport department committed to maximizing mobility and an environment department committed to reducing carbon emissions—then structures may have to change as a precondition for success. Equally if an agency or department was designed for a role in provision but has become a regulator this is bound to require new structures, skills, and cultures. But it's common to devote too much attention to formal structures, which, though important, are not all-important. Restructuring can be a displacement activity for ministers. It provides them with something to announce and gives the appearance of being in charge. But the majority of restructurings that I've observed achieved less than they promised, and diverted scarce energies. One reason is that organograms can be very misleading and give a spurious appearance of logic and clarity to systems that are much messier, and more dependent on personal relationships or networks. The growing range of methods that are used to analyse these networks—showing who is helpful to whom; who provides information, collaborates, or supports others—are a marvellous corrective to the decision makers who take organograms at face value. They always show patterns that are at odds with the formal structures, often with relatively junior individuals playing critical roles in joining public agencies together.

It's likely that future public strategists will think about structures in very different ways. Already in many fields more organic or biological metaphors are being used to think about organizational forms: how to spread models more like spores; how to design organizational algorithms that can then evolve; how to consciously manage networks that cut across organizational boundaries; how to encourage cycles of growth and shedding rather than creating structures as if they have to be permanent. These ways of thinking are in their infancy but could in time liberate public sectors from block-like organograms.

Implementation

Strategies become real when they move from paper and discussion to become part of everyday jobs: routinized, planned for, monitored, overseen, and funded. Getting strategies—or indeed any reforms—off the ground usually requires:

- champions, the more powerful the better;
- money to reward changers;
- early wins as well as the slower slog of fundamental change;
- effective communication not only of the content of change but also of its inevitability, or irreversibility;
- wide political support—so that it isn't reversed if there is a change of party or faction in power; and
- pull from public opinion or a social movement.

As I show in Chapter 7, there are many ways to integrate strategy and implementation: ensuring that the same people work on both; providing constant feedback on progress (as with Tony Blair's stocktakes where ministers and senior officials reported on progress against targets, and where Blair had his own independent sources of data provided by a Delivery Unit). Competent Cabinets shouldn't accept ministerial submissions unless they have fully analysed what it will take for the policy to be implemented—not just in terms of money, but also in terms of skills, organizational capacities, and technology. The UK's Social Exclusion Unit went a step further, inviting people with direct frontline experience to report to ministerial committees on what they believed to be happening on the ground, for example around rough sleeping or teenage pregnancy. All of these approaches introduce a healthy reality check.

The general message is that the lines between strategy and implementation should not be too starkly drawn: managers and implementers should be involved in shaping strategy and vice versa. Take, for example, a strategy to build up neighbourhood policing, influenced by public demands for more localized policing methods, or by evidence showing that certain kinds of community-based policing cut crime and build public confidence. This strategy can be implemented with:

- structural changes to local police forces to create new neighbourhood units;
- formal public rights to consultation or direct election;
- budget allocations—and new dedicated funding streams (either genuinely new or top-sliced); and
- regulation of higher-level police agencies holding them to account for the degree to which they have implemented particular policies.

But these are bound to be incomplete if they do not also include attention to the practical preconditions, such as:

- retraining police officers to prepare them for a different style of day to day work, in which public concerns about antisocial behaviour may matter more than the priorities of police chiefs;
- bringing in new types of people—for example to better reflect the communities being policed, particularly in multi-ethnic cities; and
- setting-up information systems that provide the public with good information about crime levels in their area and what results are being achieved for them.

It is not the job of people designing policies to do this work in detail; but it is essential that they involve people with an understanding of the street-level realities of policy.

Which? Learning about What Worked and Why

All strategies are born flawed and partial. Unexpected results are inevitable. In a few areas there is reliable knowledge about what causes what, and about the likely effects of policies. But in many fields patterns are hard to predict with any confidence. The key to success is rapid adaptation, learning from failures as well as successes. For leaders that means getting their mistakes in early, and remaining sceptical of their own propaganda. Politics provides one very direct feedback mechanism—whether through complaints, media comment, or campaigning. Many of the tools being developed in the field of engagement, from consultations to citizens juries, are designed to provide richer and more direct feedback. For bureaucracies, learning depends on rich and comprehensible performance data becoming available in as close to real time as possible. For all the people involved in a system, learning can be helped by formal means such as collaboratives, peer networks, 'what works units', and the many other means of institutionalizing reflection. All of these can be strengthened by the formal accumulation of evidence through research, and a culture in which leaders are seen to admit to errors and to learn from them. Legislation can play a part—like the US Data Quality Act—that provides a pressure on decision makers to show how they have made use of the best available evidence.[20] Part of the task of strategic design is then to leave systems better able to learn quickly without external interference.

Learning is paradoxically hardest when things are going well. The minority report of a group monitoring how well NASA was making the space shuttle fleet safer after the loss of the Columbia said in 2005 that NASA 'must break [the] cycle of smugness substituting for knowledge'. Complacency is common in all big organizations, and past success makes for smugness. Just because experts are often more right than laypeople it doesn't follow that they always are. Just because past methods worked doesn't mean that they always will. Organizations committed to learning work hard to counter these tendencies. Analysts can be organized in structures that are separate from line management. In the World Bank, the Operations Evaluation Department (OED) reports to the board of directors rather than to the president of the organization. Organizations like the UK's Audit Commission provide a running commentary on issues and effectiveness. Other methods include communities of practice which provide a safe space for dissenting opinions; peer reviews which use outsiders to comment on strategies and implementation; 'pre-mortems'—reviewing a prospective programme with the assumption that it has failed;[21] and role plays which bring out the dynamics of situations that otherwise get buried in analysis.[22] None of these can be guaranteed to work against the pull of hierarchical smugness. But without constant effort to learn and question, all organizations default back to the assumptions they feel comfortable with rather than the ones which are actually true.

Alignment

We started this chapter with missions and purposes, and went from there to the practicalities of implementation. What makes a strategy truly powerful has to do with the coherence or alignment of each of these elements. Figure 4.7 provides a framework for thinking about any public organisation. At the heart are the defining missions and values of the organisation: the purposes that most motivate it and which define its moral boundaries. Next out come the architectures and structures through which it operates, the agencies, departments, and units. Then, there are the tools and delivery mechanisms through which it interacts with the public—the schools and tax offices, police stations and websites. And finally there are the people being served, with their own needs and concerns.

In the best organizations these layers are aligned. The structures are well suited to what they are trying to achieve. The behaviour of frontline workers reflects the underlying values of the organisation, and how they

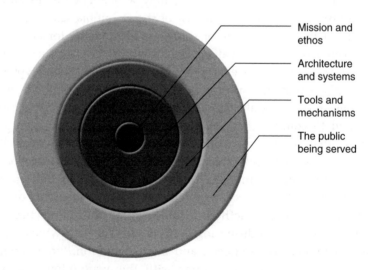

Mission and
ethos

Architecture
and systems

Tools and
mechanisms

The public
being served

Figure 4.7.   Alignment in organizations

explain themselves corresponds with what the organisation says at its highest levels. When this happens organizations buzz; the messages from the top and the bottom resonate—they make sense, and this helps people to align their own personal motives with the needs of the organisation, and of the people they are there to serve. In most organizations, however, there are dissonances. The architectures and structures may reflect historical accidents and powerful interests rather than being fitted to the mission and purpose. The day to day behaviour of the organisation may be at odds with its stated values—for example, people getting promoted according to personal networks rather than merit; or formal missions existing only to be paid lip service. These dissonances are likely to be very visible to the public and to the people within the organization—and they leave people cynical and sceptical, and less willing to commit their all. The more missionary the organisation, the more this is likely to matter: so reducing cognitive dissonance is critical to all-encompassing organizations like the Catholic Church or the Chinese Communist Party, or to companies like Google that make a moral claim for their work ('do no evil') but less important for organizations whose missions are more mundane (fixing the traffic lights or manufacturing baked beans).

Good leaders try to get this alignment by revitalizing the sense of core mission—which can be helped by talking to people at all levels around the organisation to clarify exactly what they care about most, and what missions galvanize them. Having done this the structures can then be adjusted (which usually involves simplification), as can the tools. A good example was the overhaul of public agencies involved in unemployment—such as the Employment Service/JobCentre Plus in the UK. In many nations these had become policers of welfare benefits. Their cultures had come to see the public as the problem—their laziness, or venality, had to be sharply curtailed, and customers were viewed with distrust. The work was generally de-motivating, poorly paid, and divorced from any higher ethical goal. Then, in successive countries, the emphasis was shifted to raising employment rates. Labour market agencies were merged with the agencies responsible for benefits (to varying degrees in countries including Australia, the Netherlands and the UK). Frontline staff were retrained as personal advisers (there are now 9,000 in the UK), charged with doing whatever it took to help people find and keep jobs. This work was inherently more motivating. The roles still involved tough judgements about individuals who claimed not to be able to find work, as well as sympathy (and some frontline staff became much too emotionally involved with particular clients, telephoning or visiting them each morning to encourage them to turn up at work on time). But over time people at every level of the organisation were able to give a much more consistent account of what they were trying to do and why, with a clear line of sight between their daily actions and the organization's mission.[23]

A very different example is nuclear proliferation, an issue that is likely to soak up a great deal of government leaders' time in the twenty-first century. In the years after the invention of the atom bomb governments struggled to find the appropriate moral frame for thinking about their uses. John Foster Dulles, the US Secretary of State in the 1950s, reported President Eisenhower as saying that nuclear weapons needed to be treated as essentially no different from conventional ones. Yet over time the military and civil elites responsible for nuclear war concluded that nuclear weapons had to be treated as *sui generis*: so appalling that their use could scarcely be contemplated. Operational assumptions that treated them as similar to conventional weapons were out of alignment with the higher mission. Weapons which appeared to make nuclear war more feasible, like neutron bombs (which destroyed people but left buildings and tanks intact), had to be abjured. During the Yom Kippur War Golda Meir is said to have forbidden any contemplation of use of Israel's nuclear weapons, perhaps, too, out of a sense that if Israel broke the nuclear taboo it would ultimately become the victim.

The ultimate mission of a nuclear peace therefore required very different moral principles; different architectures (including in the end mutual transparency); and different tools (including much stricter controls on usage than were needed for conventional weapons). Any misalignment of these levels could spell disaster. This moral sense, and its accompanying structure, appears to have been widely shared by the many people involved in planning and overseeing the huge stockpiles of warheads that the USA, USSR, and China accumulated. Whether it is shared by the new nations acquiring nuclear weapons is less clear.

PART II

PART II

Locating Strategy: Structures, Processes, and Cultures

STRATEGY can be run from prime ministers' offices, from Cabinet Offices, or distributed across departments. It can be delegated to arm's length bodies charged with thinking about the long term or controlled by tight, but informal, circles around a strong leader. There is no one right place to run strategy in a government: much depends on the balance of roles between politicians and officials, and the balance of power between different politicians. But there are some demonstrably wrong ways to organise it. If strategy is given no time or no resources, it's unlikely to flower. Subordinating it too much to political management or media management virtually guarantees that a government won't be strategic in any serious sense. Equally, if it becomes too detached from politics it risks irrelevance, however brilliant its analyses.

Many strategy teams erred in each of these directions. Some famous political strategists—such as George Bush's adviser Karl Rove—turned out to be poor at galvanizing change through government. Their very brilliance at managing messages and poll results left them ill-equipped to understand complex systems. If your currency is the announcement, the speech, and the election campaign, it's psychologically difficult to adjust to the slower rhythms of change in healthcare systems or energy infrastructures. The mirror weakness of strategy teams has been to take refuge in formal analysis—for example in think tanks like RAND—and to lose either a political or a moral compass, or any sense of the public mood. If you can't translate a long-term strategy into short-term actions, and, ideally, actions that build confidence, your recommendations are unlikely to find favour.

To work well the centre of any government needs a number of people who can move between the different horizons, linking the long-term to the immediate, while also synthesizing the political and administrative aspects of policy. This group needs to be small enough, and committed enough, to cope with fierce arguments. They have to be able to trust each other enough to risk airing radical possibilities without the fear of leaks. Around them there then needs to be a wide range of more specialist functions which I describe below.

The relationship between the inner circle and the next circle out is likely to be fluid. Many political leaders have recruited consultants to provide them with a streamlined and rational way to organise their staff. Typically they come back with neat organograms, and straightforward lines of authority. Mayors and governors from business backgrounds tend to be particularly attracted to the crisp neatness of simple structures. But effective leaders intuitively surround themselves with more variety than this. They know that what works in one period won't in another, and so they ensure that they have access to competing sources of advice which provide them with the resources to change direction if necessary. That applies to political tactics and strategy as much as it does to governmental strategy, and it's one of the reasons why the very best political leaders often played their staff against each other and acted deceptively.[1]

Hence the often strange architectures of strategic advice. China has an Academy of Social Science (CASS) with several thousand members which shaped some of the most radical shifts of direction in the 1980s and 1990s, a National Development Reform Commission in the State Council, as well as numerous smaller groupings in and around the party. France has had Presidential aides, task forces, planners, and commissions as well as formal bodies like the Commissariat de Plan. Denmark's Prime Minister, relied not just on a small group of political advisers, and a strong civil service, but also created a Globalization Committee in 2005 to advise on how the country could become a world-class player in fields like education and innovation—which resulted in some 350 recommendations.

It helps if the culture is open to learning and adaptation. In recent years smaller countries have proven more adept at building strategy into their DNA. Finland, Switzerland, Denmark, and the Netherlands have all shown greater realism about the external environment they are operating in and have arguably responded to external events better than bigger countries. Singapore has cultivated a strategic outlook amongst its senior officials, and an energetic interest in possible threats and opportunities, from having its water supplies cut off to revolutions in neighbouring countries. Finland has been adept at organizing discussions to engage its elites—including politicians as well as officials—so as to forge consensus on changes of direction. Iceland under its president Ólafur Ragnar Grímsson has deliberately presented itself as a laboratory for the world, using its relatively small scale to pioneer innovations around genetics and hydrogen-based energy.

By contrast, large countries more often get stuck. France's Commissariat de Plan, which prospered during the boom years, failed to adapt in the 1990s and 2000s and ministers became increasingly dissatisfied with its high-level machineries. In the USA, political strategy continues to squeeze out governmental strategy, one of many reasons why in fields from healthcare to the environment this remarkably innovative country has had such backward government. Germany has occasionally tried to insert new strategic mechanisms into its decision-making machinery—and between 1999 and 2002 had a department of political analysis and strategy. But these have generally fallen foul of the dispersed character of power in the German system, and ingrained distrust of over-centralization.

Where Should Strategy be Done?

So how, and where, should governments organize strategy? The narrowly defined function of strategy sits best alongside a strategic centre of government able to handle the three horizons described in Chapter 2, from the all-consuming crisis to slow steady actions. Many centres of governments have accumulated functions over time without much logic. Some simply mirror departmental structures. But it's better to combine at the centre the functions which are essential to the overall effectiveness of government and cannot be devolved or delegated. This results in a fairly short list:

- setting the overall direction and priorities, with a strategy function to do this at a high level, and to address cross-cutting issues;
- ensuring that the key resources are allocated in line with the strategy, including finance (the job of ministries of finance and treasuries), legislation and people;
- allocating jobs and managing ministerial and official performance;
- tracking the implementation of the most important strategies and policies—and intervening if they are going off track (for example, through delivery units);

- overseeing committees of Cabinet and ensuring good processes for reaching decisions;
- managing politics—including coalitions and relations with representatives of the ruling party;
- communication—including coordination of departmental communication;
- listening—remaining in touch with public mood and experience;
- oversight of the civil service to ensure it has the right skills, structures, and methods;
- geographical coordination—ensuring that the different arms of government are aligned in their work in cities, towns and rural areas; and
- external affairs (including traditional diplomacy but also the many issues that cut across international and domestic policy).

Not all of these need to be run from a single central department. In most governments external affairs are run by a foreign ministry, albeit with close involvement of the President or Prime Minister. The allocation of money is usually given to a finance ministry or an office of the budget. There are then various other functions which may be located in the centre, or passed out to other central departments to manage on behalf of the whole government: coordinating purchasing, coordinating information, and communication technology to ensure interoperability and effectiveness, or the roles of heads of profession (chief scientists, statisticians, economists, etc.).

Centres of government can perform any of these tasks through at least three different registers. They can issue commands and directives, they can coordinate, helping agencies and departments to negotiate with each other, and they can exercise influence through their expertise, for example over technology. Which style is right will change according to the issue and the moment, though since the political capital of leaders is a scarce resource, most will try to do as much as possible through influence and negotiation rather than dictat.

The currency for much of the work of centres of government is the 'live issue': the topic that captures the attention of leaders. Many of the methods described in this book intersect with centres of government when they become useful for dealing with the small list of live issues. These come to the fore either for a short period because of a crisis, or for a longer period because of their political salience, or because they are pushed there by periodic processes like budget reviews or strategic audits.

At these points a critical question for any government is whether it has the right architecture of brokers, capacities, and networks to bring in the requisite knowledge and skills, as well as to make the right links to power. From the perspective of strategy the critical issue is to have brokers who can tie the longer-term work of strategic thinking to decision-making in departments, cabinet committees, and agencies. The brokers need to be powerful enough, canny enough, and bold enough to fight their corner against shorter-term advice and imperatives. They also need to work against the typical vice of governments, which is to make critical decisions without the presence of anyone with deep knowledge of the issue at stake. Part of the job of brokers is to pull in the right knowledge at the right time.

With good brokers in place, strategic capacities can be organized more at arm's length, in specialized teams which can define and assess options with an ethos that's more about finding the best answers rather than the most expedient ones. These work best if they combine experience from within government with experience and methods from outside. A useful rule is to aim at combining half civil servants and half people from academia, business, NGOs, and to combine a stable core staff with a high turnover of secondees, partly to ensure plenty of friends across government, and networks which can provide an additional source of intelligence.

In shaping the units in the UK government we worked hard to build in design features that would keep them relevant and influential. Wherever possible their projects were taken through Cabinet so that they could be announced as statements of government policy, rather than as recommendations to government. Wherever possible we recruited ministers and senior officials to be project sponsors, as well as engaging the Treasury early on to ensure that recommendations had a good chance of securing funding.[2] A lot of effort went into winning over departments that would typically resent any review of their own policy responsibilities, and within a few years achieved a target that 50 per cent of the work should be commissioned by departments, rather than by the centre of government. We also worked hard on encouraging processes that would favour long-termism (such as regular fundamental spending reviews) as well as cultural signals that would influence behaviour (such as visible encouragement from senior officials). Figure 5.1 summarizes the stages of a typical strategy project and some of the tasks and outputs involved.

Strategy teams' most important challenge is securing sufficient time and attention from political leaders. All of government is a struggle for attention in which the immediate and dramatic usually triumph over the

Phases

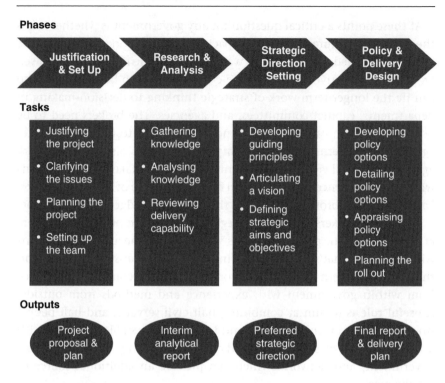

Figure 5.1.   Strategy project phases

long-term and gradual. A high proportion of any leader's time has to be devoted to day to day pressures, and the demands of sustaining relationships, whether with other governments or powerful interest groups. But it's vital that some time is dedicated to long-term decisions within the daily diary, along with regular awaydays and retreats (and their extent is one of the marks of how serious a leader is). Around 20 per cent should be devoted to the long term, preferably in longer chunks (e.g. two-hour sessions during the working week, along with occasional half or whole days) if the leader is to remain fresh and strategic.

Even when that's the case, strategists need to be able to make the most of the conversation in a corridor, in a car, or in an elevator to crisply communicate an issue and possible solutions. My own experience working for Tony Blair warned me against being too impatient for decisions. He made much better decisions when he had sufficient time to immerse himself in an issue—the decisions made on the fly reflected his instincts or recently heard anecdotes and were often worse for that.

Open Strategy

Sometimes work has to be done confidentially with a few trusted advisers—premature leaks can kill radical ideas. But in many fields governments increasingly opt for more open models of strategy in which they deliberately relinquish their monopoly power to think, decide, and act. The ubiquity of Freedom of Information laws is already pointing in this direction, and many governments now publish legislation in draft. In the purer open models being discussed in some countries every step of the process would be opened up, making the fullest use of the web and its successors. Analysis would be opened up to researchers and practitioners to comment and suggest; there would be open deliberation about alternatives and their implications, in which anyone could comment, propose, or petition; and there would be regular opportunities for the community to interrogate itself and ask how people feel about emerging alternatives. Open models of this kind are likely to become familiar as collaborative work tools enter the mainstream, helped by the ubiquity of social networking.[3] New Zealand's use of a wiki for police legislation and the relatively open method used by the Spanish socialist government to draft its (winning) manifesto in 2008 are two examples that are likely to emulated.

The limits of these models match those of open-source methods. The models that produced *Wikipedia* or Linux software work well where there are unambiguous goals, leaders with the authority to intervene in what are otherwise open processes, and few if any competing interests. In most public fields these conditions do not apply. There are divergent interests, obvious risks of capture by particular groups with an axe to grind, and constitutional reasons why some people will ultimately be held to account for decisions and others will not.[4] As a result the more open methods of strategy formulation are better understood as tools that can help leaders make judgements with a much wider circle of collaborators while still being held to account for their decisions.

Between the more open methods, and the closed methods used within governments, there is the potential for parliaments to play a much fuller role, investigating possible futures (as the Finnish Parliament did with an ambitious programme of futures work), scrutinizing strategies, hosting debates with other stakeholders, and using technologies to allow the public to take part more fully.

There are healthy traditions to build on. Britain's nineteenth-century select committees were at times models of serious reflection:

Through session after session, through hundreds of inquiries and the examination of many thousands of witnesses a vast mass of information and statistics was being assembled. . . . all this enabled the administration to act with a confidence, a perspective and a breadth of vision which had never hitherto existed. It had also a profound secular effect on public opinion generally and upon parliamentary public opinion in particular. For the exposure of the actual state of things in particular fields was in the long run probably the most fruitful source of reform.[5]

Perhaps this is how parliaments should reinvigorate themselves—combining their role as legislators with their role as the guardians of a much more inclusive public conversation about what needs to be done.

Knowledge: How Can Governments Know Enough to Govern?

IN the 1990s, Lawrence Sherman was commissioned by the US National Institute of Justice (NIJ) to investigate patterns of domestic violence, which was becoming increasingly prominent as a crime category, having in the past been largely ignored. His findings were surprising: where acts of domestic violence were committed by employed people living in middle-class areas an arrest would have a big impact and would sharply reduce the risk of re-offending. But if the offender was unemployed and living in a poor area arrests made them more likely to re-offend. The recommendation that in such circumstances no arrest should be made was unpalatable, to say the least, and the report was buried.

Any government needs knowledge: about enemies, citizens, and options. How it is collected, organized, managed, and then either used for positional advantage, or shared with citizens, is one of the most important issues facing any state. But, as in the case of Sherman's work, knowledge is rarely neutral. It may lead to morally unacceptable conclusions—like not taking action against a criminal. It may point in the opposite direction to public opinion and values. And it may simply be wrong.

In my experience governments rarely know either what they need to know, or even what they already know. The relevant knowledge may be held low down the hierarchy and isn't called on when critical decisions are made. Alternatively a version of reality, usually rose-tinted, may be confused with knowledge. A good principle is always to 'triangulate' any piece of knowledge that comes from a public agency: if a department claims that something is happening, never fully believe it until a random visit to a school, hospital, or police station has confirmed from below what was claimed from on top. The same principle applies to research: it's very unwise to believe any single research study, whether in medicine or social policy. Only when multiple studies, using different methods, have come to the same conclusion is it safe to believe that it's true.[1]

John Maynard Keynes once commented that 'there is nothing a government hates more than to be well-informed; for it makes the process of arriving at decisions much more complicated and difficult.' But his worldly scepticism is now coming to look somewhat anachronistic. Governments have become ever more ravenous for information and evidence. A few may still rely on gut instincts, astrological charts, or focus groups to guide their decisions, but most recognize that success depends on much more systematic use of knowledge than in the past.[2]

This demand cannot be understood in isolation from the political and international context. The political climate of the early twenty-first century is unusually non-ideological (with some exceptions, such as the Bush administration in the USA), by comparison with the heydays of Christian and social democracy in Europe, communism in the east and, more recently, of neo-liberalism in the English-speaking world. More pragmatic governments place a higher premium on what works, are more willing to copy good ideas from elsewhere, and may be less constrained as to the solutions they adopt. Such pragmatism has been reinforced by greater international transparency. The work of the UN, World Bank, IMF, OECD and EU means that all governments are now continuously assessed according to their performance on a range of indicators. These in turn shape how they are judged, how successful they are at attracting investors, and the perceptions of their own people. We live in a world where people see much more quickly if their trains work worse, their cars cost more, or their streets have more homeless people on them.

Demand has to some extent been met by supply from international organizations, policy analysts, and social scientists working in universities, think tanks, and corporate research, market research and non-governmental organizations. More formal supply has come from institutions designed to synthesize knowledge, like the UK's National Institute for Clinical Excellence (NICE) which assesses the evidence on effectiveness of different treatments, and the worldwide Cochrane and Campbell Collaborations.[3] Access to knowledge is greatly helped by a panoply of web-based tools. These include fairly comprehensive resources like policy.com in the USA; the more strictly quality controlled web-accessible systematic review and primary research database;[4] and ever smarter search engines (such as Google Scholar) which allow policy makers to pull in thousands of research papers and examples of good practice almost instantly. These are still in some senses prototypes—their future counterparts should be able to sift better by quality of evidence, to manage and interpret. They have the weaknesses of the web more generally—many lack sufficiently rigorous means of judging the authority of information. Yet they have already transformed the day to day business of policy-making, even if governments have been very slow to adopt comprehensive knowledge management systems with smart search engines internally.[5]

The Knowledge Used by Government

Past states used many forms of knowledge, ranging from academic evidence (the early nineteenth-century economics of Ricardo or the embryonic medical science on which public health measures were based) to intelligence in all its forms (from conversation and anecdote to hard data). Today the types of knowledge have grown to include:

- statistical knowledge (for example, of population size and migration);
- policy knowledge (for example, on what works in reducing reoffending);
- scientific knowledge (for example, on climate change);
- professional knowledge, often informed by rigorous testing (for example, on the impact of vaccination);
- public opinion (for example, quantitative poll data and qualitative data);
- practitioner views and insights (for example, police experience in handling organized crime);
- political knowledge (for example, the balance of opinion in the ruling party);
- economic knowledge (for example, on which sectors are likely to grow or contract); and
- 'classic' intelligence (for example, on the capabilities and intentions of hostile states or terrorist networks).

A striking feature of this list is that each type of knowledge has its own professionals and interpreters. In some cases they have their own semi-independent profession within government. For example, in the British government, economists, operational researchers, and statisticians each have their own professional structures.

In theory a generalist civil service can provide all of these types of knowledge. But in many governments, the ability of civil servants to be intelligent users and customers of different disciplines has fallen behind. One of the units which I was responsible for setting up in the UK government was a consequence of this. The Strategy Unit was charged with promoting a more analytic approach to policy. It did this partly through its own work on issues as varied as energy policy, childcare, and drugs, which brought together in a single process analysis, policy design, the securing of Cabinet agreement, and the preparation of implementation plans. It also had a role in providing coaching, methods, and support to a network of strategy units across government. With around 100–150 staff, half from within the civil service and half from outside, and a fairly high turnover of people back into other parts of government, the SU tried to spread new practices across government, spawning equivalents in most of the main departments in UK government, with board-level heads of strategy.

Our experience highlighted some of the crucial conditions for the more effective use of knowledge. One was that the formal processes of government needed to demand good analysis. These included regular policy reviews and spending reviews that systematically drew on the state of knowledge, and sent a strong message to ministers that bids for funding would stand a better chance of success if they were founded on evidence of which inputs would achieve which outcomes. It was then vital that knowledge was integrated with action, which required people in senior positions who understood different kinds of knowledge and how to integrate them. We explicitly rejected the division of labour which had shaped the organisation of research functions within government (formalized in the UK in the 'Rothschild principle' that researchers should work on commission to clients), and the 'new public management' principle that policy should be separated from delivery. Instead the experts needed to be embedded in the same teams as the policy makers and the practitioners. Another vital factor was networks that allowed easy access to data, to research, to 'lessons learned' reviews at the end of projects, or directories of individuals with useful experience. Getting the right knowledge to the right decision makers at the right time is rarely straightforward, and most of the experiences of knowledge management in the private sector have been problematic. The difficulties involved in using knowledge are particularly daunting in large bureaucracies where departmental and disciplinary boundaries create disincentives to sharing, and where the corporate memory is often remarkably hard to find.

How is Knowledge Used in Different Types of Field?

Some of the earlier writing on the use of evidence in policy-making assumed a linear path from academic research, through policy design, to implementation. But the ways in which knowledge can be used vary greatly according to the state of knowledge. Three types of field can be identified.

Stable Policy Fields

First, there are the areas where knowledge is reasonably settled. The theoretical foundations are strong, governments broadly know what works, there is a strong evidence base, and most new knowledge is incremental. Research focuses on filling in the gaps, and refining insights. Pilots can be designed relatively easily to isolate the key factors. In these examples—macro and some microeconomics, labour market policy, some curative and preventive health—the field is closer to a normal science. The professional bodies and leading experts can generally be relied on to give good advice, systematic reviews can generate clear-cut conclusions, benchmarking is straightforward, and good innovations spread fairly quickly through formal networks.

Policy Fields in Flux

Second, there are fields in flux. In these fields there is argument about what's known and which categories or theories are relevant. People may agree that policies which once worked are no longer working, but they can't agree on either the diagnosis or the solutions. In these areas—which include a fair amount of education, some environmental policy, crime, and the organisation of public services—there is often a great deal of fertility and experimentation. Evidence is patchy and is more likely to reveal the weaknesses of policy rather than providing convincing evidence about what will work in the future. The professions in these fields may be as much part of the problem as the solution. The most promising innovations are as likely to come from the margins. In these areas new mechanisms are often needed to make use of knowledge: the collaboratives in health used in the UK are one example, bringing together a diagonal slice of practitioners, researchers, and decision makers to consider what works, and valuing direct experience alongside formal research evidence. There will also be a need to support heterodox ideas, pilot promising innovations, and exercise a healthy scepticism about any methods that are over-reliant on peer review or control.

Inherently Novel Policy Fields

Third, there are genuinely new areas whose very newness precludes a strong evidence base: the regulation of biotechnology; e.government; privacy on the net; new forms of governance at the European or global level are all examples. Climate change is another. The IPCC has made forecasts and the UK government's Stern Review has made economic estimates that without action the overall costs and risks of climate change will be equivalent to losing 5–20 per cent of global GDP each year, with an increased risk of catastrophic natural disasters.[6] But no one can be certain how reliable these forecasts are, and no-one can know what will or won't work because these are virgin territories. The pioneers are likely to make the most mistakes, the experts will be only just ahead of the amateurs, and the task of good government is to keep a very close eye on what is and isn't working to reduce the risk of big mistakes. In these fields, again, trad-itional bodies may not be effective ways of organizing knowledge (the IPCC is a good example of a novel approach to knowledge to deal with a novel situation). Systematic investment in innovation is vital, but through fast-learning models rather than the piloting of fixed approaches. As Karl Weick once wrote, in the truly novel situation the only thing 'one can do is act'.[7] In all three types of field evidence has a critical role to play. But it will only be in the first that it is meaningful to talk of policy as based on evidence rather than informed by it.

Evidence and Theory

The differences between these fields underscore the importance of theory. In the second and third categories the questions are changing as well as the answers. In such situations evidence doesn't exist in the abstract, floating free. It exists in relation to theories and concepts which provide the prisms through which the world is seen. These theories are not alternatives to hard facts and evidence: they are the only ways of making sense of them. Indeed, as Kurt Lewin famously put it, there is nothing so practical as a good theory, and when fields are in flux what we often need most is better theory.

The importance of theory, or basic research, should be self-evident. The influence of modern economics would be inconceivable without a strong body of macroeconomic and microeconomic theory that provides frame-works for thinking, testable hypotheses, and directions of policy innov-ation both within economic policy and in neighbouring fields: for example, road pricing, internalization of externalities, vouchers for learn-ing, or insurance for long-term care. The social theories growing up around concepts of social capital also provide a frame for understanding the world, a series of research projects, testable hypotheses and directions for policy-making in everything from housing design to volunteering.[8]

Theories may be part of large and sophisticated systems, or they may be more detached ideas. But it is often the concept, not its application, that is the key unit of policy development and transfer in cases as various as monetarism, quasi-markets for health, public service broadcasting, equal opportunities, renewable energy, regulated utilities, or contract compliance.

The spread of new approaches to the labour market is a good example. Many of the most successful models were designed by labour market economists, drawing on solid microeconomic theory. They were subsequently pioneered in Scandinavia (for example, taking form in legislation like Norway's 1991 Social Services Act which entitled local authorities to impose work requirements on welfare recipients), in Australia, and, for lone parents, in the USA. They were successfully promoted by the OECD, and then reinforced as the academic work became more sophisticated and was able to draw on extensive evaluation.

Theories wax and wane in part because of the power of their ideas and in part because of the evidence. The influence of neo-liberalism grew not just because it fitted the world view of powerful interests but also because of its clarity and simplicity: it offered a clear narrative explanation and diagnosis of many of the problems governments faced, with the added patina of close links to economic science. More recently its influence has waned, in part because of its poor analysis of motivation, culture, public goods, and the collective handling of risk.

Sometimes theory leads practice and shapes the field for research and its application. Yet in matters of public policy concepts don't necessarily come from theories. They can be embodied in applications, with the theory coming later. This was true of one of the most important diffusions of the last 100 years, the spread of Keynesian economics and, in particular, demand management to sustain full employment. During the 1920s and 1930s Keynesianism in different forms was separately 'discovered' in New Zealand, Scandinavia, and Roosevelt's USA before, not after, the theory had been first formalized by Keynes himself. It was then popularized (some said bastardized) to become the conventional wisdom of the post-war era. In this case, as with much science, the story is in part one of parallel invention, of great minds thinking alike.

Learning from Elsewhere

Much of the knowledge that governments need has to be imported. Throughout history the really useful innovations have spread quickly across boundaries. Some spread through conquest—legal systems are a good example—and some because they caught the imagination of the public: universal suffrage spread from France and Germany in 1870, to Switzerland in 1874, Spain in 1900, Sweden in 1909, and to Britain after 1918. Others spread because they caught the imagination of governments. Income tax is a good example, introduced in Britain in 1842, then Sweden in 1861, Italy in 1864, Japan in 1867, and most of Germany in the following years. Yet others spread because governments faced parallel pressures. Social security, for example, spread from Bismarck's Germany via Lloyd George's Britain to every advanced country, encouraged in part by a common fear of the growing labour movement (pensions reform today is a similar case, though the pressures are different).

Benchmarking is now becoming a standard tool for governments, forcing decision makers to face up to poor performance, to look at who can best be learned from, particularly the 'positive deviants', the countries which are doing better than might be expected. It can also reduce the risk of copying bad policies, the ones with impressive public relations but which don't actually work.

Practical Knowledge

Much of the knowledge needed by government is not formalized: it sits in the minds of practitioners, or citizens themselves. A good example is in health, where patients with long-term conditions such as multiple sclerosis may come to understand as much about their patterns as their doctors. This is what lay behind the creation of the College of Health in the UK (where patients taught doctors about such things as pain management), and later the Expert Patients Programme in the National Health Service. Much contemporary social innovation builds on experimental practice as a better way to generate useful knowledge than formal research and pilots. The methods for doing this include fast prototyping of models, quickly putting new ideas into practice; assessing them equally quickly and adapting them in the light of experience; and pulling together 'communities of practice' to share experiences and insights. The task of researchers and theorists is then to reflect on, and synthesize, the knowledge that comes from experience.

Limits of Evidence

There are limits to the ideal of government decision-making based on evidence and objective knowledge. Some of these limits reflect the waning influence of traditional authorities in an environment where more people can offer opinions, and build up reputations (particularly on the web), without the backing of formal academic hierarchies.[9] But some of the limits to evidence derive from the nature of government. The first is democracy. In a democracy the people, and the politicians who represent them, have every right to ignore evidence. In some cases they have good reasons for being sceptical about expert knowledge, which often led them astray in the last century. In other cases they may prefer to trust their 'gut'. A good example is police numbers. Existing evidence gives little reason for thinking that more police walking the streets will be an effective way of cutting crime. But if the public sees this as a good way to spend public money and to increase their confidence, then it would be perverse of policy makers to ignore their views.

The second concerns ambiguity. Ernest Renan described nations as forged by the things they choose to forget, and all societies are held together in part by accepted ambiguities and silences. In politics, as in personal life, full revelation is nice in theory but can be deeply destabilizing and destructive of self and mutual respect, especially when different groups have diametrically opposed views or interests.

The third concerns time. Research time is different from decision-making time. The highly pressured timescales of government action preclude some kinds of testing and evaluation, and put a higher premium on quick judgements. These judgements are likely to be better if politicians and officials have internalized their understanding of how the world works, and often good government depends as much on this tacit craft knowledge as it does on explicit, formal knowledge. But time can work against knowledge. Terry Eagleton has written that 'to act at all means to repress or suspend... to suffer a certain self-induced amnesia or denial'.[10] At some point governments always have to move into action—and this requires that they suspend awareness of the ambiguities and complexities for a time.

Other limits derive from the nature of social knowledge. The most important is that all social science knowledge is historically contingent, not universal across time and space.[11] Analytical thinking of the kind that every social scientist, and every specialist, learns young also has inherent limits. It tends to deconstruct problems rather than create; it tends to look for common patterns rather than the odd exceptions which may point to the future; and it takes comfort in applying familiar methods to new problems rather than applying new methods.

How Much do you Need to Know?

Social scientists often argue that more research is needed before action can be taken. Politicians usually have an urge to act. So how much knowledge do you need before you can act? The simple answer is that it depends on the costs of inaction. The penalties for omission are less than those for commission, but it can be irresponsible not to act on the basis of partial knowledge. Clearly the costs and risks matter too: the greater these are, the more knowledge is needed. Equally, the more irreversible the action the more needs to be known. But sometimes the only way to gain knowledge is to act, tentatively, and see what happens. In any case, certainty will always be elusive. The most analytical politicians can tie themselves in knots looking for definitive answers (Bill Clinton was sometimes paralysed by knowing and thinking too much, where a more intuitive leader would have felt comfortable making a decision with 70 per cent of the data).

Fortunately governments now have access to much more knowledge. Donald Schon's account a generation ago, in which the evidence existed only in the fields that didn't matter much to the public, is no longer accurate. There is plenty of knowledge and evidence in fields as vital as unemployment, crime, health, and migration, and fierce debate both inside and outside government about its uses and meanings. But more knowledge doesn't make decision-making simpler and in any case it is often ignored, suppressed, or simply misinterpreted. That's why those involved in the creation and use of knowledge need to face outwards to the public and the media as well as inwards to government. Knowledge becomes most compelling not just when it is useful, but when its very visibility makes it harder to ignore.

Implementation: Moving from Words to Action

A COMMON vice of organizations that are good at thinking about the future is that they neglect the present. Yet every future direction has to start with changed behaviour in the present, and every serious strategy has to be as concerned with its implementation as with its logical coherence.

Many governments are good at producing paper strategies, often to impress international organizations. The countries queuing up to join the European Union in the early 2000s, for example, fuelled a healthy market in consultant-written strategies which bore only a distant relationship to reality, floating in mid-air without any pillars of money, law, or structure to support them. In other cases strategy-making is a self-contained activity. In Moscow in the early 2000s, I spent time with policy makers and Ministers. At one meeting we were presented an impressive (and very reformist) economic strategy. Only towards the end did one of the presenters confirm that the same strategy had been officially endorsed nearly ten years previously, but had still not been implemented.

The famous management thinker Henry Mintzberg (famous both for his ideas and for his ability to change his mind) once wrote that 'there is no such thing as an implementation gap in strategy and policy: only policies and strategies that are poorly designed, and that fail to take account of the realities of implementation.' In this chapter I look in more detail at how strategies are implemented, and how the realities of implementation can be absorbed into the business of designing them. In all public bodies the promise makers are not the same as the promise keepers. Ministers promise greater prosperity, better schools or a cleaner environment. But thousands of others have to keep the promise. My interest here is in how that happens.

Lines and Spirals

Implementation by central governments has traditionally been understood as a linear process:

- Politicians identify a priority and the broad outlines of a solution (e.g. in the form of a manifesto or election commitment).
- Policy makers in central government design a policy to put this into effect, assembling the right collection of tools: legislation, funding, incentives, new institutions and directives.
- The job of implementation is then handed over to a different group of staff, an agency, or local government.
- Within the agency the task is handed over by managers to more junior staff and the goal is (hopefully) achieved.

The implication of this view is that implementation and delivery are more likely to succeed if there is:

- a tight process with few intermediaries;
- simple lines of accountability;
- clear prescription to minimize the scope for fudge; and
- tough penalties and rewards on each link in the chain to perform their task.

If these conditions are in place, with the right people in the right jobs, and adequate funding, success should be assured. In some fields, and at some times, this model works. It is neat, simple, and attractive. When, as often happens, political leaders feel frustrated that their machines are not aligned with their goals, these are the obvious solutions: to align the major drivers of government, money, legislation, jobs, and rewards more firmly to a small number of objectives.

But in important respects this common story doesn't accurately describe the real world that governments operate in, and its application often leads to failure and frustration, or early successes that aren't sustained. Why is this? The basic reasons have to do with the patterns of power and knowledge described above. The initiators of strategy are unlikely to be wholly powerful or wholly knowledgeable (even though they may feel themselves to be). Even where the central state appears to be rich in both power and knowledge, implementation is never a straightforward linear process. It involves at least three closely related, but different, elements: the *implementation* of policy—for example, the introduction of a cancer screening service or a literacy programme, the achievement of *targets*—for example, an objective for waiting lists or exam results, and the achievement of better *outcomes*—for example, lower mortality or better employability. In many cases these three reinforce each other, as successive stages in a single process. But sometimes they conflict. Effective implementation of a flawed policy can worsen outcomes (for example, the initial introduction of Britain's National Curriculum for schools in the late 1980s and early 1990s, which was quite quick but led to many costly problems of adjustment), as can an emphasis on the wrong targets. Too many new policies and initiatives can wreck delivery by diverting management time—carrying out instructions gets in the way of better outcomes.

So how should politicians and officials ensure that the actions of many thousands of organizations, and the millions of individuals working in schools or police forces, are aligned with their priorities? The most influential recent answers to this perennial problem were articulated by 'public choice' theorists in the 1960s and 1970s who argued that there is an inherent conflict of interest between the 'principal', government, which wishes to achieve the maximum outputs at minimum cost, and the 'agents', the agencies, professionals, and others, who have different goals and cultures and who will tend to protect their own interests and maximize their funding. Seen through this prism it appears obvious that implementation will be helped by tough targets, precise measurement of performance (to enable the principal to judge the agent), clear divisions between purchasers and providers, and competitive markets to weed out the weak.

Strategic plans which set priorities and precise targets provide order for bureaucracies, and at their best a line of sight from the front line to the top. In the USA, the states of Texas, Virginia, and Florida have gone furthest in specifying goals. In the UK in the 2000s targets were everywhere. In health, for example, ten high-level targets were translated into around 300 lower-level targets. These provided the basis for regular stocktakes with political leaders and officials, as did data on school results, street crime, or accident and emergency waiting times. A delivery unit provided a more independent assessment of whether a couple of dozen of the most high-profile targets were on course and also helped with remedial action when they veered off track.[1]

Some targets were very successfully met. A target for cutting rough sleeping by two-thirds between 1998 and 2002 which I helped devise (with, to be honest, very little science) was met, as was a Prime Ministerially set target to halve the number of asylum applications between 2002 and 2003. Literacy results improved sharply between 1997 and 2001 (during a period when school spending was frozen). These, and the other targets adopted in the UK, were meant to be 'SMART'—specific, measurable, achievable, relevant, and timed—and not open to distortion. Few targets are ever very popular with the people they apply to. But some of these helped to motivate staff, focused attention on the poorest performers, and fitted well with what the public cared about. Target-setting has also become more sophisticated—for example, with the growing use of 'floor targets' which establish minimum levels of performance that have to be met everywhere, and a growing use of customer satisfaction targets (for example, setting the courts a target of improving the satisfaction of victims of crime).

But all target-driven systems have weaknesses. The planning system of the Soviet Union was notorious for the complex games which officials learned to play around the capricious targets of five year plans—like keeping performance down for fear that any improvements would be used as a baseline for ever more impossible targets, or 'storming'—drafting in additional resources during a period of heavy scrutiny. All planning systems produce distortions, unintended collateral consequences, and 'hitting the target and missing the point'. Departments and agencies become adept at negotiating undemanding targets or ones that were likely to be met anyway as a result of long-term trends. There are also subtler problems such as threshold effects, where the design of targets can lead to excessive attention to groups either side of the target to the exclusion of others. Prime Minister Tony Blair was embarrassed when about a fifth of local doctors met a target that any patient could see a doctor within 48 hours by preventing anyone from booking an appointment more than 48 hours in advance. New Zealand's Cave Creek disaster showed a variant of this problem in stark form when fourteen young people died because a park overlook collapsed, even though the agency had met all of its required output targets. In target-rich systems reported data is often misleading, or 'corrected'.[2] These problems can be partially dealt with by ensuring that data is collected by bodies distinct from those providing services—but that is bound to involve some duplication and cost since the latter will still need to collect their own data. Targets are also often obscure to the public and irrelevant to their concerns. In the UK the public's main concerns when they visit the doctor are that someone phones them back when they say they will, the receptionist smiles, there are toys for children in the waiting room, updates on how long they have to wait, and someone who actually deals with their problem rather than passing it on. None of these was covered by targets.[3]

Their five top priorities for improving public services included staff being more polite and empathetic, listening to consumers, and treating them more fairly. Again none of these was covered by official targets.[4]

In retrospect Britain repeated the lesson learned by many big firms and governments over the years: whipping the system harder can achieve temporary gains in performance, perhaps for two to three years (as happened in the UK with schools results), but these gains are unlikely to be sustained. Worse, if targets are set without a serious conversation with the people who have to deliver them (and many came from the Treasury, whose staff had little experience or feel for frontline services), they are likely to bite the target setter. Britain's other mistake was to substitute the monitoring of performance for performance itself when, during the 1980s and 1990s, a massive shift of roles took people out of frontline implementation and into inspection and auditing. The costs escalated, with little attention to the opportunity cost, and despite scant evidence that this would raise performance, and too often the inspectors focused on processes and rules rather than outcomes (as audits usually do), on micro issues rather than strategy, and on risk reduction rather than entrepreneurship.

There are no cast iron solutions to any of these problems—some are inherent to the unequal relationships between principals and agents. But some more sophisticated approaches to performance management and implementation are taking shape in many countries. These may involve closer involvement of practitioners in the design of policies and targets, with more provisional targets that are open to negotiation, and informed by practitioner knowledge. In the Netherlands, for example, government talks of governing from the 'second line', with framework objectives rather than very detailed rules. Quick mechanisms for taking stock also help—especially if they allow for priorities, resources, and targets to be adjusted. Other methods have taken shape to ensure that agencies keep focused on outcomes that matter, rather than intermediate targets.[5]

Simply making data more transparent can go some way to improving performance, helping managers to reflect on what they're doing wrong, their bosses to consider changing them, or their citizens to boot them out. Much data that used to be entirely secret is now in the public domain and forces people with power to justify themselves. The virtues of transparency came to me most vividly when the data for my local secondary school were made available, and showed that it was amongst the twenty poorest performers in the whole country (out of some 4,000 secondary schools). Yet local parents quite liked it, and had generally good relationships with the head and the teachers. They simply had no idea that they could legitimately expect much more from the school and subsequently, with the help of fairly draconian interventions from on high, it greatly improved.

Figure 7.1 shows some of the variations in productivity of a typical group of public services in England. The first graph shows death rates in different regions; the second shows school performance mapped against socioeconomic level; and the third shows police performance. The most striking feature of this information (which is hard to find in most countries) is the very wide variation in performance even in apparently universal public services. Sometimes these discrepancies can be explosive—for example one-year survival rates from hospitals providing heart surgery in the USA

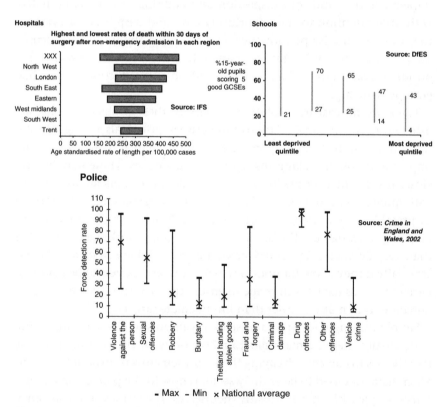

Figure 7.1.   English public service productivity

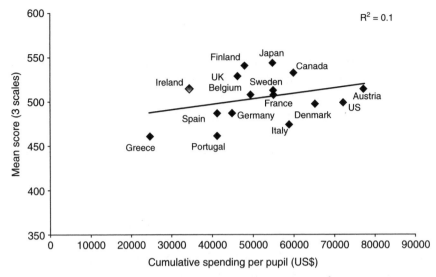

Figure 7.2.   Education spend and performance; correlation: $R^2 = 0.1$

show variations as great as from 0 per cent to 100 per cent. Often they defy assumptions. It was assumed that much of the UK data would correlate very closely with other factors, in particular levels of poverty. But plenty of schools in poor areas were doing well. Hospitals, by contrast, tended to do best in relatively poorer regions, mainly because they found it easier to attract staff. In some services money is important. Yet almost every serious assessment of the impact of higher spending on services shows at best weak correlations.

The Figure 7.2 confirms this by comparing countries according to education spend and performance. Again the correlation is weak. Singapore (not on this chart) spends less than most but regularly tops league tables. Nor do explanations of performance other than money fit the data. Finnish students study fewer hours than elsewhere but do very well. Class sizes turn out to have little impact; and nor does high pay for teachers lead to better results. Instead the critical lessons that come from the data collected by the OECD and others points to the importance of recruiting good teachers (South Korea recruits primary school teachers from the top 5 per cent of graduates); helping them to learn (Finland gives them an afternoon off each week); and acting firmly to help students who fall behind (Finland gives a third of all pupils one to one or small-group support).[6]

The accurate measurement that makes diagnoses of this kind possible remains underdeveloped in many fields, and there is great potential for systems that more automatically generate comprehensible performance information for decision makers and users. Kaiser Permanente Foundation in the USA, which is widely admired as a model of active management in healthcare, spends some 2 per cent of turnover on IT, in part to provide it with the information needed to prevent, manage, and cure disease. Data of this kind can show who is achieving the best value for money—and allow funding to be determined by the costs of the most efficient decile or quartile of performers. It can also help judgements about why some things are working and others aren't. There are many very different reasons why a target may be missed. These include: poor central management; poor local management causing wide variations in performance; poor policy design; poor design of the target in the first place; an unexpected change in the external environment; public opposition; inadequate funding; inadequate support; lack of buy-in to the vision by the main players; overambitious timescales; or overload. As will immediately be apparent, some of these conclusions will be unpalatable for higher-tier bodies, and will therefore tend to be suppressed. It follows that a good performance management system needs judgements and assessments to be separated from any position of direct power or responsibility, ideally in a third-party organization which solely exists to make judgements of this kind, and which includes people who understand the numbers and what lies behind them. And yet, because the formal management hierarchy also needs to make judgements, you risk ending up with a parallel bureaucracy. Hence the conclusion that some third-party judgements are needed, but primarily for the biggest services, or for services where there are grounds for worry.

Having made a diagnosis there are then many ways for managers to respond. They can rethink the policy, redefine the target, change the management, invest more, reshape delivery, or even change ownership and control. Much of this may appear obvious. But rigorous assessment of the options for improving performance is rare (it's typical for senior managers to blame more junior ones in the bureaucratic game of 'pass the blame parcel'), and there are substantial cultural, political, and institutional barriers standing in the way. Hierarchies are inherently bad at learning and self-criticism, though they are rather good at blame. Yet learning can be built into even the most rigid hierarchies. COMPSTAT in New York and elsewhere won fame as a system which showed police chiefs how well they were doing. In Baltimore, for example, the district commanders had to explain the situation in their area to the Commissioner, Chief, and Deputy Chiefs, as well as majors and colonels in charge of special units opposite a 12-foot high illuminated map, filled with icons. This (and its parallel projects, including Jobstat, Vendorstat, and Citistat) made performance transparent without needing formal targets, and it prompted faster learning without the pretence that the Commissioner had all the answers.

New Zealand's SKIP programme (strategies with kids, information for parents) provides a very different example of how to keep focused on outcomes without rigid controls. Rather than trying to create a new delivery machinery, the government chose instead to work with existing NGOs, 'augmenting, complementing and supplementing' them within a framework that had very clear outcome targets as well as a single brand and common materials. Evaluations showed that it achieved considerable success with relatively little money, and explained its success as deriving from the way it helped the NGOs to work together, drew on their intelligence to design the programme, and promoted fast learning, with more of the mood of a social movement than a traditional bureaucracy.[7]

In each of these examples the metaphors of delivery are misleading. Policies aren't the same as parcels. Competent public services are full of people with their own knowledge and ideas who aren't willing to be reduced to being agents for leaders who know less than them.

Embedding Continuous Improvement into Systems: The 360 Degree Model

Here we come to the more fundamental question of implementation which asks not how a particular strategy can be put into practice but rather how systems can learn to improve themselves. In what follows, I suggest that any public agency or unit is most likely to improve when top–down pressure and support (via targets and funding), combines with horizontal pressure and support (through contestability and collaborative learning, etc.), and bottom–up pressure and support (through user choice and voice as well as personal and collective responsibility).

Bottom–up Empowerment

The most important pressures to improve have to come from the bottom up, and they have to be based on power. This is as true for democratic political systems as it is for markets. When it comes to public services that power can take many forms. It can take the form of rights and entitlements to service, guaranteed in law, as well as rights to redress when things go wrong. It can take the form of rights to choice, whether for schools, hospitals, or social housing, extending to everyone the options that are usually available to the wealthy. That in turn can be helped by giving citizens power over information (for example, through electronic patient records), by advice and information (or the sort of softer information that is increasingly provided over the web by patients groups, parents groups, and the like[8]), and by funding arrangements in which money follows the user. Easy access to information is fast becoming a powerful influence on public services. In the UK 78 per cent of 16–24 year olds and 52 per cent of the whole population used navigation tools like NHS Direct in 2007 to find out about public services. By the end of the decade, data will be publicly available on surgeons' death rates joining the extensive data already available on everything from school results to crime rates.

Reinforced by access to information of this kind rights to choose provide strong incentives for providers to improve their performance, and to take seriously what the public wants. The Swedish school system is a good example. Reforms in the early 1990s gave parents the right to choose between state schools and state-funded independent schools. New schools can be set up by anyone—from parents to groups of teachers—where there is evidence of parental demand and so long as they operate fair admissions and follow the national curriculum. Although take-up has been modest (around 12 per cent by the late 2000s), there has been a significant impact on the state system. Maths results, for example, have improved fastest in state schools facing competition, and school networks that challenge orthodox methods, including the Steiner and Montessori movements, have made big inroads. Interestingly, too, the more open market has encouraged different models of organization: nearly a third of the independent schools are part of a single chain that allows them to share back-office and other costs.

In the past choice has been most demanded by the relatively affluent who also feel most confident about exercising it. Recent data in the UK, however, showed that the old and relatively poor were now keenest on choice while many of the affluent appeared to be feeling 'choice fatigue': faced with complex choices in other fields, from finance to health, their top priority was for public services simply to be reliable.[9]

Regardless of these shifting social patterns, the dynamics of choice are often complex, depending as they do on the availability of spare capacity. The very extensive literature on choice shows that it is far from being a panacea. Some expansions of choice can harm significant groups of users;

some kinds of choice can be hard to use; and some simply create confusion. For example, when in the late 1980s New Zealand introduced new 'independent state schools' with greater parental choice the effect was to significantly widen inequalities—the quality of teachers at schools in the most deprived areas declined and the most successful schools pulled in the best pupils.

The other form power takes is voice: rights to a say over decisions. This may come from elections, open meetings, officials making themselves available for scrutiny, or rights to dismiss public agencies (the negative power of 'democratic contestability', in which user communities have a backstop power to sack unelected public boards).[10] All of these too are strengthened by requirements to report on performance.

An even stronger form of empowerment gives citizens power over money in ways that go beyond vouchers for already specified packages of service. A good example is the 'direct payments' model which has allowed people with disabilities to choose for themselves how to spend money. Introduced in the mid-1990s in the UK following lobbying by disabled groups, it has shown the scope for citizens themselves to decide on the right mix of cash and professional and informal support, and is now being extended to other areas of social care.[11] In each of these cases responsibility as well as power is shared, and citizens may have to live with the consequences of bad decisions. How far this is acceptable will depend on the specifics of the situation—the capacities of the user themselves, the social implications of poor choices, and the presence of competent intermediaries (such as the personal advisers in welfare systems).[12] But these many types of empowerment together provide a constant pressure for improvement that sits alongside the feedback that comes from democracy, making it more likely that services will treat people with respect and care.[13]

Horizontal

Bottom–up pressures to improve need to be complemented by horizontal pressures and supports. The supports come from peer networks and peer reviews. The pressures come from there being competing suppliers who can displace poor performers. Competition and contestability of this kind have been experimented with in many countries over the last few decades—notably in the USA (for example, in the many southern Californian cities that in the 1960s were constitutionally prohibited from providing their own services in house), the UK, Australia, and New Zealand, as well as some north European countries. In Denmark and the Netherlands the scope for newcomers to establish schools eligible for public funding has acted as a spur on the public sector system. The research evidence now points to fairly strong efficiency gains from contestability: 5–15 per cent cost reductions in US prisons, and 20 per cent savings in household refuse collection in many countries. In Australia private and non-profit providers in the labour market cut costs by a very wide margin—while also increasing user satisfaction.

Contestability doesn't work in all circumstances: there needs to be enough private sector (or voluntary sector) capacity to provide a credible alternative; and there needs to be accurate performance information to underpin judgements about success and failure. Government has to be willing and able to become a coordinator of markets rather than a provider of services—and politicians have to be willing to cope with the political fallout of taking franchises away from existing groups of public service workers (and then taking them away from underperforming private providers). In some fields the strongest horizontal pressures may come from empowering communities to take over services. For example, in rural areas it may be more efficient for communities to take over transport services and sub-post offices, combining formal paid work and volunteer commitments in ways that are simply impossible for public agencies, let alone private companies.

Top–down

The bottom–up and the horizontal then need to be complemented by some top–down pressures and support. Central governments (and state or provincial governments in some nations), are bound to retain overall responsibility for performance if they have to raise the taxes to pay for them. Full laissez-faire can be as inefficient as full central control. There will be times when national governments have no choice but to reform whole systems, in response to public demands, and they have a unique responsibility for thinking about the system as a whole. Equity also has to remain a concern of national governments, and it has to be supported through the design of funding and entitlements. Central government, too, is implicated in designing the 'DNA' of public services, the underlying patterns of finance, pay, qualifications, and so on. These design principles can reward improvement or cut against it. They can be fragmented or joined-up.[14]

The common vice of central governments is to try to do too much: to micromanage, interfere, and then become overloaded. Here I'm describing a much more strategic approach, in which governments set the parameters for the system and provide some of its inputs (including skills and money) but leave it free to adapt and evolve.

The precise balance between top–down, horizontal, and bottom–up pressures and supports is never easy to strike. As the previous discussion makes clear, it is often misleading to think of a straightforward trade-off between centralization and decentralization. Often the best solutions combine elements of centralization (for example over standards and performance measurement) with decentralization over methods used. It may be best to centralize for brief periods when a system is changing direction, but then to devolve. The Netherlands and France have both used contracts of various kinds to commit national and local agencies to shared sets of targets towards which each contributes. In both countries national governments have periodically introduced far-reaching reforms, but their experience suggests the kind of dialogue, and helpful tension, which helps public systems avoid complacency and stagnation.

Words into Action

I've argued in this chapter that strategies shouldn't only make sense on paper. They should reflect the capacity of real people and institutions to act, and be resilient to the rough surprises of daily life. In most fields there is a messy relationship between the formal aspect of strategies (the paper document) and the real-world manifestation (which will usually be radically different). Sometimes this reflects deliberate obstruction; sometimes it reflects ignorance; but often it reflects flaws in the strategy itself.[15]

Some traditions of thinking about strategy advocated a division between the people and units doing strategy and those responsible for implementation, on the grounds that these are distinct specialisms. Much of the Fordist and Taylorist thinking which shaped twentieth-century industry was founded on similar views about divisions of labour. It's wiser to see strategy, policies, and implementation as a whole, best done by at least some of the same people working on project teams, and making full use of feedback loops including data, measurement, piloting and testing, and public responses. Rather than expecting the strategists to take account of all the realities of implementation (which is an impossible goal), strategy has to be more about conversation and negotiation, along with faster learning from the unexpected results which are bound to occur.

Positive Risks: Taking Innovation in the Public Sector Seriously

CHARLES DICKENS' novel *Little Dorrit* describes the Circumlocution Office at the centre of the government machine which decided 'what should NOT be done'. The office reliably killed any ideas which might make government better. Dickens reflected the conventional wisdom, according to which public organizations cannot innovate. Bureaucracies lack the competitive spur that drives businesses to create new products and services. Their rules squeeze out anything creative or original. Their staff are penalized for mistakes but never rewarded for taking successful risks. So while business develops new chips, iPods, aircraft, and wonder drugs, the slow and stagnant public sector acts as a drag on everyone else.

It's also often said that the public sector is bad at failure. Markets do their work by trying many things, most of which fail. Science and technology do the same (most famously when Thomas Edison tried out more than 10,000 materials before he found the right one for the filament in light bulbs). As Henry Petroski put it, 'form follows failure'—in products and businesses the forms that are taken reflect the lessons that come from getting things wrong. In public policy by contrast failure is harder to admit and certainly harder to institutionalize.

This account is commonplace, but it's not the whole story. The public sector is not short of the combination of crisis and curiosity that so often drives new ideas. Two of the most profound innovations of the last fifty years were the Internet and the World Wide Web. Both came out of public organizations: DARPA in the first place, CERN in the second.[1] NASA must rank as one of the most successful, and innovative, institutions of modern times, and is a very rare example of a public agency using competition to achieve its ends (three competing groups of employees were tasked with designing a way to land a man on the moon—the winners came up with the very lateral idea of a spacecraft that decomposed into separate units). Looking further back, business was not particularly innovative for most of human history, at least until the late nineteenth century. Instead, the most important innovations in communications, materials, or energy came from individuals, wealthy patrons, governments, or the military. The idea that businesses and markets are 'innovation machines' to use William Baumol's phrase, is a very recent one.[2]

Even today, the caricature of public agencies as stagnant enemies of creativity is disproven by the innovation of thousands of public servants around the world who have discovered novel ways of combating AIDS, promoting fitness, educating, vaccinating vast populations, or implementing new methods like intelligence-led policing or auctions for radio spectrum.[3]

Yet there are good reasons to doubt the public sector's ability to innovate. Innovators usually succeed despite, not because of, dominant structures and systems. Too many good ideas are frustrated, filed away, or simply forgotten. Public services remain poor at learning from better models—even on their doorstep—and only a handful of governments have any roles, budgets, or teams devoted to innovation in their main areas of activity: welfare, security, health, or the environment. The process of planning, and sometimes of strategy, involves using existing data and concepts and applying them to new situations: creativity by contrast involves imagining new concepts and categories.

Despite the rhetorical lip service paid to innovation, no government has anything remotely comparable to the armies of civil servants employed to count things, to inspect, and to monitor, or for that matter to support technological research and development (R&D). Nor can many give coherent accounts of how they innovate. What, for example, is a reasonable proportion of public spending to devote to innovation? Is it around 2–4 per cent, which is generally thought to be the right proportion for a modern economy to invest in R&D, or the 20–30 per cent that is more typical for a biotechnology company? Under what conditions should support for innovation be stepped up—or scaled down? Should innovation be the job of specialized units, or should it be everyone's job? What's a reasonable success rate to aim for in radical innovations: one in two, or one in ten? Should civil servants rely on politicians for new ideas—or vice versa?

Public innovation isn't always a good thing—and a world in which civil servants experimented continuously with traffic lights or taxes on pensions would be a nightmare. But the lack of seriousness about innovation is striking, and contrasts starkly with the world of science and technology. There, both the public and the private sector invest billions, and the difficult task of turning scientific insights into useful products was long ago taken away from lone inventors in garden sheds and put at the heart of great corporations and great public laboratories.[4]

Yet there are some tentative signs that this may be changing. Some of the governments that are most competent at delivery are increasingly turning their attention to innovation.[5] One pressure is rising public expectations. In the twenty-first-century economy, the biggest sectors are no longer cars, steel, or even IT. In most advanced economies much the biggest sector is health. Education accounts for 5–10 per cent of GDP. Care, both for children and the elderly, is growing fast and already constitutes some 5 per cent in a few economies.[6] These are all sectors in which government is a major player, whether as provider, funder, or regulator, and in them innovation happens in very different ways from the dominant industries of the last century.

In the public sector, as in other fields, innovation can mean many different things. It can mean new ways of organizing things (like Public Private Partnerships), new ways of rewarding people (like performance-related pay), or new ways of communicating (like ministerial blogs). Distinctions are sometimes made between policy innovations, service innovations and innovations in other fields like democracy (e-voting, citizen juries) or international affairs (prepayments for new vaccines or the International Criminal Court). Some innovations are so radical that they warrant being seen as systemic (like the creation of a national health service, or the move to a low-carbon economy).

The simplest definition is that public sector innovation is about new ideas that work at creating public value. The ideas have to be at least in part new (rather than improvements); they have to be taken up (rather than just being good ideas); and they have to be useful. By this definition, innovation overlaps with, but is different from, creativity and entrepreneurship.

Seen through this lens, governments and public agencies around the world are constantly innovating new ways of organizing social security or healthcare, online portals and smart cards, public health programmes and imaginative incentives to cut carbon emissions, congestion charges and drug courts, online tax transactions and restorative justice. Many of these innovations make little or no use of technology. Some involve new roles, like childrens' commissioners, or new rights, like disabled peoples' rights to work.

But much of the most visible innovation of recent years has come from new applications of technology. Governments have repeatedly tried to accelerate the take-up of new technologies by business and by citizens—from the 'wired city' experiments of the 1960s and 1970s, to France's ambitious Minitel programme, which tried to introduce a precursor to the Internet as a universal public service, to contemporary policies to drive down prices for broadband. Few of these efforts predicted how technology would develop. None anticipated the importance of the mobile phone, or of text messaging, and typically governments (and technologists) have underestimated the importance of people communicating with each other, as opposed to downloading information.

Around the Internet governments have steadily progressed through a series of stages that have brought them closer to more personal interactions of this kind. Most e-government strategies started with websites containing existing information. Much of this is banal but in some cases even quite modest measures—like making all health inspections of restaurants available online—can have a big impact in terms of public value. They then moved onto more active communication—for example, brigading different services together in more interactive ways; providing frontline staff such as police officers or housing repair teams with PDAs and other mobile devices to speed up response to public issues. They then extended to transactions—for example, putting financial transactions online as in Singapore (where most transactions can be performed online, including payment of fines and taxes); Australian visa services which are fully electronic from end to end; or the UK's Courts OnLine service which allows citizens to launch minor cases in a purely electronic way. Finally, in the more radical options a few have moved beyond functional transactions to enrich service delivery cultures through allowing many more comments and informal knowledge to be combined on the web.

These innovations have sometimes been spearheaded by politicians, keen to present their governments as on the cutting edge; they have been eagerly promoted by the IT industry, hungry for generous contracts, and sometimes they have been pushed forward by imaginative bureaucrats who saw how technology could help usher in new models of provision.

Alongside new technologies, organizations, and programmes, the public sector has also innovated what Bart Nooteboom calls new 'scripts'.[7] An example from the private sector was the rise of fast food retailing which created a new script for having a meal. Where the traditional restaurant script was: choose, be served, eat, then pay, the self-service/fast food script is: choose, pay, carry food to table, eat, clear up. New scripts are emerging right across the public sector, in areas like recycling, personalized learning in schools, and self-managed healthcare—and are likely to be critical to future productivity gains in public services.

There is a vast literature on technological and business innovation but much less on innovation in the public sector. Amongst the major thinkers on innovation, Everett Rogers stands out as just about the only one to consistently include public sector examples in his work on diffusion.[8] Others have looked at the traits of innovative organizations that are more receptive to ideas, the dynamics of networks involved in innovation, the rising importance of users in shaping the innovation process,[9] the difficulties of basing policy on evidence,[10] and the role of organizational milieux.[11] Some of this work has been empirical. One survey found that most innovation is initiated by frontline staff and middle managers (50 per cent);[12] is not a response to crisis (70 per cent); cuts across organizational boundaries (60 per cent); and is motivated more by recognition and pride than financial reward. Some of these research findings appear counterintuitive. For example, the most innovative local councils aren't usually the most competent but rather those with the most need to innovate—in the second or third quartile of performance.[13]

What most of the literature confirms is that in the past public innovation has tended to be patchy, uncertain, and slow, with occasional bursts of activity. It took more than a century after the invention of the telephone before governments started developing call centres to handle customer inquiries, to deal with concerns about health, or to provide general points of access to government (like New York's 311 service).

But there have been exceptions—and some cases where public service innovations evolved well ahead of the private sector. A good example was when the UK's Labour Government created a radically new kind of university in the late 1960s. Where all existing universities were based in a physical place, this one made full use of television and the telephone. Where all existing universities aimed to teach people who had just left school, this one was open to people of any age.

Most people in existing universities scoffed at the idea. There would be no demand; it wouldn't work; standards would be too low. Yet the government went ahead and today the Open University (OU) is the UK's largest provider of higher education and an acknowledged world leader in distance education (dozens of OU-inspired organizations now operate globally, from China and India to Africa). Harold Wilson, who as Prime Minister oversaw its creation, described it as his proudest achievement. In a survey in 2006 it also scored the highest marks of any higher education institution in terms of student satisfaction.[14] It has massively expanded participation in higher education through bringing in new students, adult, not necessarily pre-qualified, and part-time students. It has made full use of new communications technologies as they came along, from satellites to the web, and almost every part of its model has subsequently been copied by the private sector.

Thirty years later, another government introduced another radical innovation that was equally opposed by vested interests. This was a phone and web-based service which the public could call on for diagnoses, even at 3 a.m. NHS Direct combined three existing elements in a new way: the telephone, nurses, and computers with diagnostic software. Within a few years it was receiving many millions of calls each year (2 million people use the service each month) and evaluations showed that its diagnoses were as reliable as doctors' meeting patients face to face.

Both of these examples started off outside government. The OU was first floated in a speech by Michael Young in 1958, then put into practice through a small new organization, the National Extension College, later taken up by the Labour Party and created as a new public organization in 1969. Healthline, one of the precursors to NHS Direct (a phone and later web-based diagnostic and advisory service), was also set up on a small scale (also by Michael Young) in the 1980s with some help from BT. Neither was inherently new; rather both were hybrids, combining existing things in new ways. Both became part of the public sector but had to be built up outside existing structures. Both too benefited from good luck and powerful patrons, the minister Jennie Lee in the case of the Open University, and the Chief Medical Officer Sir Kenneth Calman in the case of NHS Direct.

In science there are well-established channels for taking ideas from basic research through prototypes to products. These are rarely as straightforward as they seem and more recent work on scientific innovation often emphasizes the loops and detours that happen along the way. In the public sector, however, there are simply no established channels and both the OU and NHS Direct took more than a decade to make the transition from conception to implementation.

Political Innovators

All ideas at some point have to pass through the two groups of gatekeepers who control power and money in the public sector. The first group are politicians. Politicians and political activists look for new ideas to gain an edge over their rivals or to keep their party in power.

Some politicians can be very open. Faced by the mass unemployment of the 1930s Franklin Delano Roosevelt said that he would try anything. 'If it fails,' he said, 'admit it frankly and try another. But above all, try something.'[15] Some political leaders are natural innovators: Jaime Lerner, the mayor of the city of the Brazilian city of Curitiba in the 1970s and early 1980s (and later state governor for Paraná), is an outstanding example. He completely refashioned his city's transport system using dedicated lanes for buses, rebuilt parks, libraries, and learning, and he experimented with lateral solutions, such as paying slum children who brought rubbish out of the slums with vouchers for transport. He was also adept at what he called 'urban acupuncture', using small-scale symbolic projects to unleash creative energies.[16]

Antanas Mockus, the mayor of Bogotá, is a remarkable recent example. Mockus used theatre and spectacle to get results. He sometimes wore a Superman costume, and hired over 400 mime artists to control traffic by mocking bad drivers and illegal pedestrians. He launched a 'Night for Women' when the city's men were asked to stay at home and look after the children (and most did) and even asked the public to pay an extra 10 per cent in voluntary taxes (again, to the surprise of many, 63,000 did).[17]

In Canada, the small state of Saskatchewan was consistently innovative thanks to a succession of creative leaders from the 1940s to the 1970s. Allan Blakeney's administration in the 1970s, for example, ran a series of demonstration projects on the risks faced by children, ranging from comprehensive school health programmes, prenatal nutrition, and postnatal counselling.[18] Some worked and some didn't, but they provided a wider menu of experience and ideas and many were later taken up at national level. In the UK, Ken Livingstone stood out as a politician who consistently championed innovations, pioneering radical models of equal opportunity, appropriate technology, and social inclusion in the 1980s, and congestion charging and green urban development in the 2000s.

Of course political innovations are not always desirable: Mao Zedong was an extraordinary innovator, but many of his ideas wreaked havoc. Few dictators have the patience to test and experiment before imposing their will on everyone else. But innovative political leaders who are willing to experiment help to make government vital and alive—energizing the society around them.

Bureaucratic Innovators

The other channel for innovations is the bureaucracy: officials can promote innovations a fair distance without much involvement on the part of politicians (and sometimes 'innovation by subterfuge' can be a good way of promoting disruptive innovations). The controversial 'broken windows' policing reforms of Bill Bratton, New York's Commissioner of Police, are a good recent example.[19] In the same city Ellen Schall, Commissioner in the Department of Juvenile Justice in the 1980s, transformed her department into a pioneer of new ideas (and has subsequently reflected insightfully on her experiences).[20]

In the UK, few civil servants reach the top as a reward for their innovations, though there is a long history of innovative public servants, from Edwin Chadwick to Geoffrey Holland, and some have continued to succeed as policy entrepreneurs, usually from a few rungs down in the hierarchy. Surestart was originally developed by a Treasury official, Norman Glass, and the Literacy Hour by an educationalist, Michael Barber. In countries like Singapore it's common for officials to become well known as innovators; Tan Chin Nam, for example, has been a consistent innovator over several decades across many fields, from economic development and education to the arts.

Alongside these relatively high-profile names, there are thousands of less visible innovators. One of the few quantitative studies of public innovation, by the Canadian academic Sandford Borins, suggested that most public innovations are initiated by middle management or frontline staff (he also suggested that most are internally driven rather than initiated in response to crisis or political pressure).[21] The work of these everyday innovators tends to be hidden from view, even when awards push some to prominence (and many countries, including the USA, South Africa, Denmark, and Brazil have introduced official awards for public innovators).[22]

The Public Sector Hinterland

All innovations must at some point gain political or bureaucratic support. But they can get there through many different routes (see Table 8.1) some in the surrounding 'hinterland' of the public sector—territory at one remove from the formal structures of accountability and control, where risks and imagination are easier, and where more radical future ideas are most likely to take shape.

Table 8.1. *Routes for public innovation*

Where	Who, how, and why	What
Politics	Promoted by politicians seeking votes, activists, think tanks	Constitutional reform, choice in healthcare, parental leave
Bureaucracy	Promoted by civil servants seeking power or recognition, helped by external stakeholders	e-government, carbon markets
Decentralization	Demonstrated by local or regional authorities seeking public approval	Congestion charging, integrated care for the elderly
Business	Promoted by business seeking profit and helped by procurement arrangements	PFI and PPPs, contact centres
Academia	Promoted by entrepreneurial academics seeking recognition for new knowledge	Cognitive Behavioural Therapy, auctions for spectrum
NGOs	Promoted through examples, campaigning, motivated by growth or recognition	Hospices, healthy living centres, summer universities

- **Decentralized systems** provide one set of channels—laboratories for new ideas. In the UK local government pioneered many of the ideas that took shape in the welfare state, as well as later innovations in contracting out, choice-based lettings, or integrated children's services. In the USA, welfare to work ideas were taken from Minnesota and Massachusetts to Washington. In Canada, business service centres (and a clutch of e-government innovations) were pioneered in New Brunswick and then copied at the federal level. In Australia, compulsory seat belts were pioneered in Victoria, and subsequently copied all over the world.

- **Business** has prompted many of the recent reforms around customer service, such as the use of contact centres and customer relationship management tools. For obvious reasons of self-interest business has also actively promoted ideas like privatization or Public Private Partnerships.

- **Universities** were where Aaron Beck and his colleagues first developed the cognitive behavioural therapy used extensively in prisons and health services, while the spectrum auctions which have generated such wealth for some governments were developed by Ken Binmore and others working on game theory.

- **Civil society** is a common source, from the growth of social housing to hospices and the neighbourhood warden schemes in the 1980s and 1990s that eventually persuaded the police in England to create a new category of Community Support Officer.[23] A common complaint from voluntary organizations, however, is that when they develop successful innovations these are simply copied by government: not only are the originators not compensated, they also risk being put out of business by competition from much better financed public agencies. A parallel example from a very different context is the Clean India project[24], launched by an NGO, Development Alternatives, in 1996, which mobilizes schoolchildren to monitor and measure the state of the environment. The programme has now spread to seventy-eight towns and cities across India, and manages a clever mix of partnership and pressure on local authorities.

Institutionalizing Innovation

Some governments have made tentative steps to institutionalize innovation and to formalize these routes.[25] Denmark's Ministry of Finance set up a unit to promote new ideas—like plans to create a single account for financial transactions with citizens. The Economics and Business Affairs Ministry has restructured itself to be based much more on projects than functions and, with two other departments, has established its own internal consultancy, Mindlab, to promote creativity.[26] In Finland, the main technology agency, SITRA, has turned its attention to public innovation.[27] In the USA, Minnesota for a time had an innovation unit, and at the federal level the US State Department had a Center for Administrative Innovation (at least until recently). In New York, the state and city partnered to support the Center for Court Innovation which helps develop, test out, and appraise new approaches, such as specific courts for drug offences and domestic violence.

Singapore has promoted innovations through its 'Enterprise Challenge' programme, run through the Prime Minister's office, which has funded some sixty-eight proposals. Examples include a 'virtual policing centre' for non-urgent enquiries to be routed through to the Singapore Police Force, and teleconferencing for prison inmates to interact with their relatives. It claims these could achieve savings ten times greater than their costs.[28]

The UK has never had equivalent champions for innovation in the public sector,[29] but has nevertheless experimented with ways of opening up the bureaucracy. There have been experiments to liberate local managers to break national rules—including the short-lived education and health action zones, and the now well-established Employment Zones. The 'Invest to Save Budget' provided a large pool of money, run by the Treasury, to back promising innovations that crossed organizational boundaries.[30] The Department for Education set up an innovation unit which supported imaginative communities of practice, and the Department of Health established an NHS Institute for Innovation and Improvement. Within individual agencies smaller innovation funds have given frontline managers a chance to try out new ideas.

In the light of these many examples of lively risk-taking, it would be easy to conclude that there is no shortage of innovation, and that any barriers are now being dismantled. Unfortunately, all of the examples cited above remain small in scale, and institutionally fragile. In the UK, the health and education zones were closed down at the first opportunity and never won backing from senior officials, and in every country the innovation budgets are tiny, certainly by comparison with public spending, or by comparison with technological R&D. The basic argument for innovation hasn't yet been engaged with, let alone won, in the great majority of OECD governments. Part of the reason is that there has been little serious analysis of when innovation is a good thing—and when it is not.

Good Reasons to Avoid Bad Innovation

There are some very good reasons why public sectors shouldn't innovate more. Few would welcome a public sector which experimented too much with ambulances or nuclear power safety arrangements. There is a lower tolerance for risk where people's lives are involved and much of the public sector is involved in far more essential services than the private sector. It is also reasonable for the public to want their public realm to remain legible and coherent. A world in which every primary school and post office was restructured and rebranded every year would be a nightmare.

Within civil services it's common to hear two further arguments *against* taking innovation seriously, both of which have more than a grain of truth. One is the traditional conservative argument that all methods and institutions which are old, tried, and tested, should be preferred to ones that are new. In its purest form this argument is unsustainable, since many methods, from police on the beat to the three 'Rs', and many existing institutions, from Central Banks to national health services, began their lives as radical innovations. But in a milder form the argument is right: even the best ideas benefit from being tested out, and adapted, in the real world.

A second, related, argument is that the public sector should be a stabilizing force, a buffer against too much change. Ideas may rain in from ambitious politicians or hustling entrepreneurs—but bureaucrats should move slowly and take the long view. This argument also has virtues and in some countries a good deal of public sector innovation and reform is driven through much too fast, in effect experimenting on the whole population rather than trying ideas out on a small scale, as is the norm in medicine or technology. Not surprisingly, experiments of this kind turn out to have many unintended consequences and high costs. Worse, they leave managers and frontline staff associating innovation with ill-thought-through top–down reforms rather than service-improving bottom–up creativity.

Bad Reasons to Avoid Good Innovation

Unfortunately these good arguments against bad innovation are often joined by much weaker arguments, as well as being amplified by structural features of the public sector which guarantee that too few good ideas make the transition from imagination to reality.

- **No one's job**: very few government departments have a board member responsible for innovation. Vast bureaucracies have grown up around performance management, inspection and audit (the annual costs of the regulators of local government alone in the UK are now over £600m).[31] Public innovation has no equivalent posts or budgets, unlike in business where innovation is central to many people's jobs and central to any process for setting budgets.
- **Risk aversion**: the environment which government operates in puts much more weight on discouraging risk-taking than rewarding it. The media will give as much weight to a small failure as a big one, to an operational failure as a strategic one; so does parliamentary scrutiny and audit.
- **Too many rules**: modern bureaucracies were designed to stop capricious and unpredictable actions. They do this by imposing rules: systematizing, formalizing, specifying how things should be done, and ensuring uniformity. Not surprisingly, innovation is squeezed out; not surprisingly too, the people attracted to working in big

bureaucracies, whether corporate or public, tend to be less creative and less at home with risk.

- **Uncertain results**: the dilemma faced by public agencies was well summarized in an influential book by Clayton Christensen which described how successful firms or organizations with established products or services attempt to maintain and improve their position by a succession of new features, steadily improving the usefulness of their product.[32] Then a new technology comes along which has the potential to be much more effective. At first it probably won't be as useful as the mature old technology (think, for example, of how much less convenient cars were than horses in the 1880s). So organizations face a twin challenge: on the one hand how to nurture the new technology when according to strict performance measures it's still not up to scratch; and on the other how to promote something new which will compete with what they already do. These problems face every innovative private company. But they are even more acute in the public sector because it is so much more visible and accountable.

- **High walls**: public sectors tend to be organized in separate silos with high walls dividing departments, agencies, and professions, or linked services like primary and acute care in health or secondary and tertiary education. The barriers that stand in the way of spreading tacit knowledge are even more of a problem than those that block formal knowledge. A high proportion of the potential innovations in the public sector, like one-stop shops or new ways of organizing data, cut across organizational or professional boundaries. But because power and money are organized in silos these are the innovations least likely to win support.

- **Unsuitable structures**: monopolistic sectors tend not to be very innovative for the obvious reason that the monopolist has little incentive to invest profits in new products and services. In highly competitive markets with lots of small players there tends to be plenty of incremental innovation but relatively little radical or systemic innovation. More radical innovation happens most often in sectors that are more like oligopolies, dominated by a small number of big companies, surrounded by a penumbra of highly competitive smaller ones which occasionally break through with a new model. Sectors like computing, retailing, software, media, and aerospace have some of these characteristics (albeit in very different forms, with much higher barriers to entry in fields like aerospace than software). The intensity of the competition provides the motive for innovation, but the scale of the major players provides the necessary resources and capacity to radically reorganize how production is done, in the way that, for example, big supermarkets like Wall-Mart or Tesco have transformed the way they do their business. Moreover, the prospect that ideas will be bought up by the big players provides a strong incentive for venture capitalists to invest in the smaller ones, just as today every Internet start-up prays to be bought up by Google. Generally the public sector has a structure almost opposite to this: in most fields there is just one monopoly overseer in the form of the national or regional department, and then a multiplicity of fairly small units—schools or GP practices—none of which has the capital or the capacity to see through really radical innovations.

Six Elements of an Innovative Public Sector

So, innovation happens—but it happens as much by chance as by design, and public innovators are usually marginalized. Nowhere does public innovation have the same focused attention that governments have given to other tasks, like raising taxes or bringing criminals to justice. The result is that many of the biggest problems facing governments are addressed haltingly if at all: adjusting healthcare or housing to a much older population; helping the unemployed back into work; or making schooling fit for purpose. Old and ineffective programmes continue while new ones have to struggle for small sums of money. Promising new ideas languish. No one knows what price the public sector pays for this innovation gap, but as Finland's SITRA recently argued it must be a key factor dragging down public sector performance and productivity.[33]

What can be done to put this right? There can be no simple formula for making governments creative or innovative. As we've seen, in the field of scientific R&D, nations have successfully pursued radically different paths, with Taiwan, Israel, and Ireland wholly different from the USA or Japan, Finland or France. The same is likely in the field of public innovation. But there are likely to be some common elements.

Leadership and Culture

Human beings are rational and, without licence from the top, few people in hierarchical organizations will be willing to take risks. Political and official leaders can establish a culture in which innovation is seen as natural. In some cases the cultures then become embedded at least for a time. The Scandinavian governments, for example, have been successful innovators for several decades. In the USA, studies of innovation at state level found that the three most consistently innovative states during the period studied (California. Minnesota, and Ohio) became more innovative over time, and the laggards more laggardly, suggesting that innovative cultures can be self-reinforcing.[34]

That has been the experience in some cities which have sustained an innovative culture over long periods of time, like Barcelona, Helsinki, and Amsterdam, or Phoenix, which won recognition in the 1990s for its embedded innovative culture.[35] These places tend to be earlier adopters of new ideas,[36] as well as better at creating their own ideas.

Policies and behaviours matter in rewarding innovation. But so too do symbols. The Cheongyecheon project in Seoul launched and completed by Mayor Lee Myung Bak in the middle of the 2000s is a brilliant example. An old 6km-long river through the city centre, which had been covered with a two-tier motorway, was recovered as a public space through an intensive process of planning, consultation, and construction, and in 2005 won the Venice Biennale prize for architecture. The newly recovered river looked spectacular and resonated with a city that has become a pioneer in software, games and popular culture as well as electronics and cars. Nothing could better symbolize a city that was willing to take risks and to see all problems as tractable.

Pulls and Pushes

While leaders support the conditions for innovation, specific innovations start with pushes or pulls. The pushes may come from a political leadership that feels a need for new ideas. It can come from crisis; each year of the two world wars probably brought a decade's worth of administrative creativity. It may come from financial necessity: like the PFI models that first grew up at a time when the public sector was chronically overspent, or the 'Block Nurse' programmes which provide home based care for the elderly as an alternative to much more expensive institutional alternatives.[37]

Sometimes the push may come from technology. Innovation in business used to be understood as a pipeline from the laboratory to the shops, with new technologies pushed out onto a grateful public. Sometimes there is a similar push in the public sector. Many governments tried (without much success) to think up uses for the new technology of smart cards in the 1980s and 1990s, and the world is peppered with monorail systems of dubious utility. More successful 'push' models include the US small business innovation research (SBIR) programme which sets aside 2–2.5 per cent of the R&D budget of agencies to finance the development and prototyping of new ideas, giving entrepreneurs the freedom to make proposals (on the basis that they will come up with more good ideas, as well as more bad ideas, than big bureaucracies).

The drive to innovate, however, comes as much from pulls as pushes. In public services that may be a need that isn't being met—like the need for care, or jobs, or housing. It may be less obvious needs like the need for protection from abuse or discrimination. Such needs emerge in complex ways, sometimes thanks to campaigners. Sometimes civil society takes the initiative in meeting its own needs, establishing hospices to care for the terminally ill, setting up small-scale recycling services, and hoping that the state will follow later.[38] Either way, the best public innovators are good at empathy and good at listening to what it is that people really want or need (Michael Young got many of his best ideas from random conversations on street corners, buses, and even in cemeteries).

Users have never had much power in public services. But they have become more organized in recent years. Parents have set up childcare schemes, mutual support groups (like Netmums[39]), or even new schools. Patients are increasingly organized around common diseases, like diabetes, heart disease, or multiple sclerosis. Through programmes like the Expert Patients Programme,[40] or 'In Control',[41] the public have won powers to initiate innovations and shape services to meet their needs rather than what professionals think they should need. In the longer term, active, demanding, and empowered users, sometimes in alliance with radical professionals, are likely to be critical in keeping public services agile and imaginative.

The other major source of pull is public procurement. For thirty years the main concern in public purchasing has been to achieve greater efficiency, for example through aggregating purchasing and achieving economies of scale. But if every procurer purchases already proven models, innovation is likely to slow. So in the 2000s several governments started to encourage purchasers to deliberately support innovations.[42]

Creativity and Recombination

If pulls and pushes create the pressure, creativity widens the range of available options. As Mihaly Csikszentmihalyi suggested in relation the arts, creativity can come from the alignment of creative people, a discipline, a field of critics, and knowledgeable consumers.[43] Some formal creativity methods, such as those developed by Edward de Bono and the consultancy What If? can help bureaucracies to think laterally and see new patterns.[44] The evidence on whether any of these work in enhancing creativity in a sustainable way is patchy to say the least, but they may at least help to make cultures more open.[45]

Seeing things in new ways can help. One method is to learn from the people most immersed in a problem: anyone seeking to find an answer to the management of chronic diseases or alienation amongst teenagers may do best by looking at how people are themselves solving their problems, and starting from the presumption that they are 'competent interpreters' of their own lives.[46]

A related approach starts with the people who are solving their problems against the odds; the ex-prisoners who do not re-offend; the 18-year-olds without any qualifications who nevertheless find jobs. Other methods try to twin different fields: airport designers with hospital managers, online bankers with victim support. Others still encourage developers and designers to engage with the toughest, most extreme customers, or the ones facing the most serious problems, to force more lateral solutions.

Every maturing technology opens up scope for public innovations. Mass television opened up new possibilities for education in the 1950s, just as mass penetration of mobile phones opened up new possibilities for front-line workers in the 2000s. Artificial intelligence in all its forms is now ripe for mining in public organizations (and is already being used with considerable success in family law in Australia).

The web is proving particularly fertile for new public service ideas. There are burgeoning feedback systems for patients and pupils. There are new means for citizens to report broken civic infrastructures that make use of online maps. There are time banks—'slivers of time' networks that make it easier for welfare claimants to offer hours of work to prospective employers. And there are networks linking up children whose parents are going into care and networks comparing data on carbon emissions.

Every public service throws up many possible innovations, the brain-children of police officers and nurses, aggrieved citizens and pressure groups. Most never get much beyond a conversation over a cup of tea. Some briefly find backers but then fade away when the barriers turn out to be insurmountable or the idea turns out not to be so good after all, perhaps because it is too expensive, too dependent on a few individuals. One key to success is to ensure that there is as wide as possible a range of choices to draw on. As Linus Pauling (who won Nobel prizes in chemistry and peace) observed, 'the best way to get good ideas is to have lots of ideas and throw the bad ones away.'[47]

Prototypes and Pilots

Innovation depends on creativity, but creativity is a necessary and not a sufficient condition. The next stages of innovation require different structures and mental styles because few ideas emerge fully formed. Instead they need to be tried out, tested, and adjusted in the light of experience. Tinkering and trial and error contribute to all kinds of innovation. In the social sector (and in some industrial design and software) this often happens through people trying out new ideas on a very small scale.

The public sector tends to demand rather more formality and organization and so this stage involves specifying what the idea is; turning it into a prototype; and then testing it out either in a controlled environment or in the real world. Pilots are one way of doing this. A new model is specified in detail and then tested out in practice with measurements of baselines and results achieved, control groups to compare with and various methods of evaluation. Piloting is mainstream in medicine, and has been increasingly used in welfare, policing, and education. But piloting isn't always the best way to organize innovation: it may freeze a model too soon, when it should be evolving; it's usually slow, and certainly slower than political cycles.

As an alternative, governments have made more use of pathfinders and trials that embody learning-by-doing, allowing iteration rather than treating an innovation as an inviolable scientific experiment. In the case of the moon landing, for example, a carefully planned series of stages paved the way for Apollo 11, but each learned from the ones before. In very different policy fields new models have been tested out in a stepped way, initially covering, for example, 5 or 10 per cent of the country. Recent examples include the UK's New Deal for the unemployed and Surestart, the programme for under-5s. In both cases, the early adopters were closely watched and linked together to share experiences. Other recent examples include the EU emissions trading system (an unusually large-scale experiment) and experiments in hospital choice.

Some prototypes are essentially adaptations of successes elsewhere around the world. Few public sector tasks are unique to any one country, and a great deal of time and effort can be saved by learning from countries which are doing particularly well. 'Welfare to work' models developed in Scandinavia influenced the UK and Australia, which in turn have influenced the rest of continental Europe. A very different example is the successful community-based programme to cut heart disease pioneered in north Karelia in Finland in the early 1970s, which has subsequently been adapted all over the world, from China to the USA, with help from the World Health Organization. It's rare for a model to be precisely copied: instead new prototypes draw on experience elsewhere but adapt it to local cultural or political conditions.

The prototyping and piloting phase can be hard to manage. As with technology, early expectations often rise too far only to be knocked back when things go wrong or projects are delayed. Anything genuinely innovative is almost certain not to go quite according to plan. It's vital to have some measures of success, but judgement and experience count for as much as the numbers: people who have seen the trials and tribulations of past innovations are much better placed to make judgements than generalist officials or ministers. After all, as Rosabeth Moss Kanter put it, every success looks like a failure in the middle.[48]

This is also where the generally welcome mantra of 'evidence-based government' can be misleading. Pilots and prototypes rarely generate unambiguous evidence. There may be 'Hawthorne effects'—the label given to changes in organizational behaviour which result not from the innovation or pilot itself but from the fact that the innovative or piloting organization (or relevant part of it) has been the subject of focus or attention.[49] There may also be 'Ashenfelter dips', named after the academic who showed that workers who entered training programmes had often experienced a fall in earnings beforehand.[50] So when their earnings then went up they were in fact on a rebound that would have happened anyway (just as many of the patients who were subjected to leeches in the nineteenth century went on to make healthy recoveries). Equally, 'learning curve' effects may lead evaluators to underestimate how well a model will work in the future.

A classic example of the pitfalls of evaluation is the experience of the High/Scope Perry pre-school programme and similar programmes launched in the USA in the 1960s. For ten years or so, the evaluations of these programmes were generally negative. It was only later that it became clear that they could achieve impressive paybacks in terms of better education and lower crime.[51] The same may be happening to the UK's Surestart, whose first evaluation was equally ambiguous.[52] An even starker example is welfare to work. One of the most influential policy evaluations ever done was a study of the GAINS programme in California which used random assignment—choosing people at random to benefit from different policies and comparing them to a control group. The research showed that the offices which placed welfare recipients into jobs achieved better outcomes than those that put them into training.[53] The 'work first' message went on to have a very big influence on policy in both the USA and UK. Yet when researchers studied what had happened to people nine years later it turned out that although the 'work first' group had initially done better, in the long run those who had gone into training ended up earning more.[54] So evaluation needs care, and certainly needs to be done differently for new and mature programmes. Nor should failure always be seen as a disaster. Sometimes it can be instructive and can make future success more likely.

Scaling and Diffusion

If the pilot or prototype broadly works, the challenge then is to launch the innovation on a larger scale. Only a small proportion of ideas and pilots deserve to be replicated. But having decided that something is worth replicating, governments are well placed to scale up innovations. They have at their disposal the power and the money to spread ideas, good and bad. They can command people to do things (for example, telling all schools to adopt a new national curriculum). They can provide generous incentives or use the stick of penalties.

But many public innovations can't be spread in this way. There isn't enough political capital around to impose many new ideas, and there isn't enough money around to bribe people to adopt them. Instead, much public sector innovation depends on willing adopters—people who become convinced that their lives and work will be improved by doing things differently.

This is where the public sector often falls down. When someone builds a better mousetrap the world doesn't automatically beat a path to their door. In fact, innovations are slow to spread, partly because the incentives for adoption are weak. Few managers are taken to task for failing to keep up with best practice in their field. Local authorities, hospitals, police forces, and social services teams can be remarkably ignorant of demonstrably superior practice even when it is happening on their doorstep. Most services simply lack a culture of rigorous learning and benchmarking— and as with so much of what is being discussed here it's rarely clear whose job it is to identify what works and to promote it.

Cultural and cognitive barriers also get in the way of diffusion. Even where strong networks have been put in place to promote diffusion, the results have been disappointing. Different professions may simply have a different view of what counts as success. Innovations may threaten demarcation lines and power structures, particularly if they cut across organizational boundaries. When diffusion does happen successfully, it's often because of effective champions; because of strong networks (including within the professions); plenty of hand-holding; and last but not least some financial inducements.[55]

Sophisticated Risk Management

The final element of any innovation system is sophistication about risks. The most common justification for blocking innovation is that it's too risky—with political or media pressures usually identified as the chief culprits. Right from the start, even a small-scale pilot may be interpreted as a signal of where government wants to take policy. If it fails, ministers will be called to account for wasted money. If lives are damaged, voters will justifiably be angry.

So any programme of innovation has to be smart about risks and how they should be managed. Generally it will be easier to take risks when there's a consensus that things aren't working (a 'burning platform' makes the status quo seem even more risky than trying something new). It will be easier if government is honest that it is experimenting with a range of options, rather than pretending that all will succeed. It will be easier where users have some choice (so that they can choose a radically different model of school or doctor rather than having it forced on them), and it will be easier where the innovation is managed by an organization at one remove from the state, a business or NGO, so that if things go wrong they can take the blame. But the key is to be explicit about risks and how they should be managed.

Organising for Innovation: Exercising the Innovation Muscles and Cultivating Hinterlands

If these are some of the likely elements of an innovative system how should they be pulled together? John Kao has written that the most important characteristic of an innovative firm is that it has an explicit system of innovation which pervades the whole organization, which is visible, known about, generates a stream of new ideas, and is seen as vital to creating new value.[56] No public agencies have anything quite comparable. But such a system is what many governments need, working with the other organizations that contribute most directly to collective intelligence, including universities, business and NGOs. Doing this requires that they balance innovation-friendly internal structures, processes, and cultures with sufficient porousness and permeability to make the most of innovations that come from outside. In other words, public sectors need to exercise their own 'innovation muscles' *and* cultivate their hinterlands.

Doing that requires that internal institutions of governance regularly assure that there is an adequate flow of potential new ideas, ranging from high risk and high impact to ones which are relatively low risk but also likely to be low in impact. It requires that there are teams and networks dedicated to organizing innovation. These need to include people to scan the world and other sectors for promising ideas (and in some cases governments may be wise to prioritize effective following rather than original innovation—what Paul Geroski and Markides Constantinos called the 'fast second' strategy).[57] They need people to map current pilots and pathfinders and assess which ones are worth building up; and to design new innovations, incubate them, and then launch them. Experience suggests that these teams generally work best with a mix of skills, experience, and contacts, combining civil servants, social entrepreneurs, designers, and practitioners. That may be easiest to organize at arm's length through units combining 'insiderness' and 'outsiderness' or through 'skunk works'.[58] Some people need to be explicitly employed to act as brokers and intermediaries—making links between emerging ideas and changing needs. A high proportion of teams and networks of this kind then need to be organized across organizational boundaries, reporting directly to central departments like the Cabinet Office or Treasury, or Chief Executives' departments in local authorities. These may be focused on problems (for example, the rising incidence of Alzheimer's or gun crime) on groups (like migrants with poor English language skills), or places (like depressed seaside towns). These brokers can play a vital role in protecting innovators outside the state who are bound to be attacked by threatened vested interests.

It's then essential that the main processes encourage and reward effective innovation, including audits and inspections. Any regular strategy or spending reviews should take stock of which policies are working, where new priorities are emerging, and which promising innovations should be adopted or adapted—and should ensure that enough money is set aside to finance innovation. There is no science of what budget allocations are right. But there are few circumstances where the figure should be less than 1–2 per cent of turnover, and in fields of relative failure the figures need to be higher. These can then be allocated through departments and through cross-cutting budgets. From there, money can be directed either to individual projects or, more fruitfully, to teams with good track records and to intermediary organizations. It can be offered to local authorities to encourage them to play a more explicit role as laboratories for national policy,[59] to user groups to engage them in commissioning innovations, or to networks of collaborators.[60]

Teams for innovation are bound to benefit from including people who have proven track records of public innovation, but such people are often prickly, ill-suited to conventional careers and management structures. So alongside recruitment and development policies that don't squeeze out creative people, and training courses that acclimatize officials to innovative processes, pay arrangements also need to be designed to encourage risk taking (for example with bonuses when ideas are taken up). New hybrid positions may also be needed—for example, keeping innovators on the civil service payroll so long as they can find willing departmental paymasters for at least half the year.

For the public sector as a whole, diffusion and the adoption of innovations matters even more than invention. There are also many other devices which can help diffusion, ranging from performance management systems which put pressure on managers to keep up with best practice, through prizes and honours to promote successful innovations, to training which straddles organizational boundaries.[61]

Public sectors are often poor at innovation from within, and poor at learning from outside. They contain many innovative people but aren't good at harnessing their talents and imagination. They too rarely cultivate a plurality of alternatives and too often impose ill-conceived innovations on whole regions or countries. Innovation is an integral part of being strategic—recognizing that all strategies need to create new knowledge as well as using existing knowledge. It's also a tool for helping public organizations return to the underlying motivations of public service, which should be not only about doing good, but also about always striving to do better.

Negative Risks: Strategies for Resilience

IN the summer of 2007 David Walker, the head of the US Government's Accountability Office, warned of a future that could include 'dramatic' tax rises, an explosion of debt, slashed government services, and the large-scale dumping by foreign governments of holdings of US debt. He talked of 'declining moral values and political civility at home, an over-confident and over-extended military in foreign lands and fiscal irresponsibility by the central government'. He claimed to have warned about these in the past but now wanted to 'turn up the volume' on problems, some of which were too sensitive for others in government to 'have their name associated with'.

He was living up to one of the responsibilities of his role as Comptroller General, which was to take a long-term perspective and face up to unpalatable possibilities. Yet the sheer gravity of his warnings confirmed how hard it is for governments to deal with risks—and to decide which warrant a strategic response and which can be ignored.

Strategies are usually designed to achieve something positive—a stronger economy, or a better environment. But being strategic also involves readiness for the unexpected and resilience in the face of an uncertain future. Governments are held to account for failing to prepare adequately for disasters, for programmes going awry, and crises that appear as if from nowhere. The contemporary contract between governments and the public requires them not just to keep their people safe from invasion, crime, or epidemics but also to deal with many other risks that individuals, families, and communities cannot handle on their own. The growth of modern governance has come as individuals and families have trusted governments to handle risks that in the past they would have coped with themselves—old age, sickness, migration. People expect risks to be controlled rather than being effects of fate or random chance and they expect to hold institutions to account when things go wrong.

The assumption that knowledge has replaced random fate (or God's will) with human control profoundly colours people's expectations of government. Not much more than a century ago even child mortality was assumed to be an act of God. Today most social, economic, and environmental phenomena are seen as having consistent and knowable causes, so that they are at least potentially amenable to action or regulation. This view of knowledge explains why the public in wealthy countries have come to expect fewer external risks (to health, physical security, and financial security) while also wanting to be able to choose to take more risks which they themselves control. This leads to apparently contradictory demands—for more regulation and less, more control and less (a UK poll in the mid-2000s found that 62 per cent agreed that 'government does not trust ordinary people to make their own decisions about dangerous activities' and 61 per cent agreed that the government 'should do more to protect people by passing laws banning dangerous activities'). Behind both sets of views lies a greater faith in knowledge: what is at issue is whether the state or the individual is better placed to use that knowledge to manage risks.

What people want to be protected from reflects how the world has changed. The biggest new source of risk is science and technology. New knowledge has also created new knowledge about its dangers. Regulators have to judge the balance of benefit and risk across a huge range of technologies—from genetically modified food and drugs, to industrial processes, nanotechnology, or cloning methods. At one extreme easier access to 'weapons of mass destruction' has prompted governments to run simulations of biological attacks on cities, and to tighten security. At the other extreme there are the much less proven risks associated with ubiquitous technologies like the mobile phone or food additives.

The other new source of risk is the greater connectedness of the world which has rendered us all more vulnerable to distant events—from economic crises on the other side of the world, attacks on IT networks, and diseases carried by air travellers, to the indirect impact of civil wars and famines. Some of the biggest risks that come from a connected world are invisible. Most twentieth-century pollutants were experienced as toxic, but potentially the most dangerous in the twenty-first century, carbon dioxide, is not. This is why, as Benjamin Friedman put it in his book *The Moral Consequences of Economic Growth*, CO_2 'is the one major environmental contaminant for which no study has ever found any indication of improvement as living standards rise'.[1]

Risk, Power, and Knowledge

To make sense of risk I return to the framework set out previously. Risks matter when they have the most potential power to do damage; and they are hardest to handle when there's least knowledge about their likelihood or character. How risks can be handled also depends on the context of power and knowledge. If a government has untrammeled power, and full knowledge, it has little to fear from risks. Such omniscience and omnipotence is impossible but much of the progress that has been achieved in government has come from greater knowledge of how to handle risks— from public health to unemployment. Investment in knowledge can reduce levels of risk even if its side effect is also to make people more aware of risks that might previously have been obscure. Governments now benefit from large volumes of statistical and time series data which help them predict which risks matter: economics knows enough to warn when an economy is overheating or a house price crash is imminent, and demographics is (just) reliable enough to warn when pension contributions are likely to be inadequate for an ageing population.

But in many fields not enough is known. Risk is just one way of describing a lack of knowledge about what will happen—it may be defined as 'probability times outcome' but probability is a misleading concept in relation to most of the changes that affect government. Few have happened with sufficient regularity to make the idea of probability meaningful: more often governments are dealing with degrees of uncertainty rather than calculable risks.

Even where the knowledge is firmer it creates collateral uncertainties if it takes governments into morally novel territory. This is particularly true in the field of crime. Statistical analysis of crime patterns allows the police to make fairly accurate predictions of which offenders are likely to offend, or to go on to commit murders, simply on the basis of past arrest patterns. Civil libertarians object both to the collection of this data (in the USA police can only use data collected from convictions, not arrests, which is much less predictively reliable), and to the very idea of preventive action which appears to punish people for crimes they have yet to commit.

Knowledge about risks doesn't always translate easily into action for other reasons too. George Tenet, then head of the CIA, said that in the summer of 2001, just before the attack on the twin towers, the indicators were flashing red, but nothing was done; the information wasn't brought together; the significance wasn't communicated to the people at the top. The 9/11 attack was one of many events that have cast doubt on security agencies' conceptions of their role. In the past they believed their role was to protect territory from invasion. Now their enemies are not primarily other states but rather non-state actors, networks, and networks taking advantage of other networks. And so their role has shifted its focus to ensuring the security of functions, capacities, and systems, many of which are not territorial.

So how should governments improve their resilience? How should they manage risks which range from the predictable to the unknowable? To improve their chances, governments need to make judgements about risk in five main areas:

- What could happen (identification of risks). In every area of government regular reality checks are needed, with rigorous assessment of trends, possibilities, dangers, and their likelihood and impact. Often this needs to involve people without a direct stake in the specific area of work itself to ensure objectivity. It needs wide networks, and informal channels as well as formal ones (some of the worst disasters have arisen from overdependence on formal, hierarchical information channels). The UK government, for example, now has a matrix of the major threats faced by the country, weighted according to impact and probability, which guides such decisions as stockpiling of vaccines or simulation exercises, as well as the allocation of resources to flood defence. Like some other governments it has institutionalized awareness of risk through networks, committees, and procedures, and through creating safe spaces where senior officials can speak openly to ministers about potential threats, and where they in turn can share concerns about their departments' abilities to respond. Non-executive directors in government departments and agencies can play a role in this, making the most of their relative detachment from decisions.[2]
- What matters (assessment of risks). Having established what could happen, governments need to make judgements about how important, or desirable, different outcomes are likely to be. A catastrophic fall in the gold price may be less important than a catastrophic fall in the price of microchips; an epidemic amongst cows may be less important than one amongst people.
- What can be done (action). Having established what matters, governments need to work out how to avoid the risk; or, if that is impossible, how to mitigate or contain it.
- What has happened (review). Every action needs to be followed up with an assessment of whether it had the intended effect, whether the assessment was right, or whether different actions are now needed.

The language of risk management implies a neater process than is possible in reality. In economics and game theories risks are analogous to those faced in playing cards, or a casino: they are quantifiable and definable. But most of the risks surrounding government are more opaque than this: they combine knowns and unknowns, the calculable and the incalculable. They pose the challenges of 'Signal Detection theory'—the theory of how observers judge what is relevant information and what is only noise, and what an appropriate ratio of 'false positives' to 'false negatives' is in different fields. Governments need to be somewhat paranoid, but not so paranoid that they cannot act. How they strike this balance will vary across the three main ways in which they act on risks—as regulator, steward, and manager (though in each case, as the great French scientist Louis Pasteur put it: 'chance favours the prepared mind').

Regulating Risk

In modern liberal societies governments do not generally intervene when individuals take risks on voluntarily and others aren't affected. The most that the state can do is to ensure people are aware of risks—for example, when hang gliding or mountaineering—and allow them to shape their own resilience. There are many borderline cases—such as driving without a seatbelt or smoking in one's own home—and there are relatively few behaviours that have no effects whatsoever on others (even a single adult's decision to engage in dangerous sports may impact on an elderly parent who risks losing a future carer).

Governments generally act when voluntarily taken risks have direct or indirect consequences for others—for example, drunk driving, or passive smoking—and they follow a general principle that the costs of externalities should be borne by their creators—through taxes on pollution, for example. The courts provide a backstop, whether for individual claims or class actions (as in the case of smoking in the USA). Greater knowledge about how actions affect others is likely to expand this role for government. More sophisticated knowledge about how particular emissions affect health, or about the genetically based vulnerability of a minority of the population, could prompt more detailed regulations to govern what actions are permissible and at what cost. An example is the food industry, which is being subjected to ever more stringent rules and constraints as knowledge about the interactions of diet and well-being grows, and the wider costs of fried chicken or cocktails of additives. A more knowledgeable society is bound to be more conscious of risk—and more concerned to see risks managed.

But governments have to be careful not to go too far in protecting their citizens from risk. Children's lives in many countries have become tightly constrained with well-meaning rules: playgrounds covered with zero risk materials (despite the fact that child fatalities are almost unknown); health and safety rules that make it impossible for children to be taken on school trips or outward bound courses; parental fears that keep children indoors. At the extreme, in the UK, children have been fined for drawing chalk pictures on pavements, arrested for building a treehouse, and banned from rough games, all in the name of reducing risk. These do harm because children need to learn how to navigate the risks of the outside environment. No one would want their child to die on a school trip. But no policy on risk should be shaped by the experiences of the most unlucky.

Government regulation of the private sector has to strike a similar balance between freedom and control. The crises that affected Enron and other companies in the early 2000s revealed managements that were out of control and barely accountable to their boards. The managers had too much power; the people they were meant to serve had too little knowledge. The result was a sharp swing of the pendulum towards more systematic— and often bureaucratic—management and reporting of risks. Yet within a few years it was widely believed that these were disproportionate. Governance concerns of this kind move in cycles: scandals and failures lead to calls for much tighter scrutiny and regulation; but these in turn end up constraining entrepreneurialism and effective action, which leads to a scaling back of regulation; this in turn creates the conditions for more abuses.

Many governments have sought an objective calculus for risk, a single metric which could guide decisions about how much to invest in road safety or preventing a disease. Some use standard measures of the money that's worth spending to save a putative life, but very different figures are used in practice (ranging from 0 to £60m in one recent UK study, with a typical figure used in transport of around £1m per life).[3] These figures, which are incorporated into cost–benefit analyses, turn out to be difficult to use. No sane public agency uses them except as a very broad guide. In any case public perceptions of risk are only partially rational and quantifiable.[4] We tend to be much more frightened of visible and dramatic threats than we are of slower, more everyday ones. We gamble in the face of very unfavourable odds, but exaggerate low probability extreme outcomes. In the year after the 9/11 terrorist attacks many Americans took to their cars rather than travel by plane. This resulted in 1,595 more deaths on the roads, six times as many as the number killed on the hijacked aircraft.

At a deeper level, too, attitudes to risk are embedded in cultures, and can't be reliably quantified. In the USA, thousands are killed with handguns every year. For one group of citizens the right to hold firearms is a fundamental liberty. For another it is an insanity. It is not hard to analyse the easy availability of firearms using methods of risk assessment and cost–benefit analysis. But these are of little help. When shootings take place in American schools one group argues that the solution is to arm teachers so that they can act more decisively if a pupil brings weapons into the school. For their opponents such incidents are yet more proof that the availability of firearms is bound to lead to their use. Risk is rarely objective—it is also a cultural matter, about how we view the world (and these views are radically different amongst the various groups analysed in more detail in the last part of Chapter II). These complexities don't make it impossible to analyse risk, or to use measurements: but they make it essential to view risk as plural, with decisions based on judgement rather than standard formulae.

Stewardship of Risk

Some risks, such as the risk of disease, flooding, or global economic recession, cannot be attributed to any one individual or agency. In these cases governments have traditionally acted as the poolers of risk—either through social insurance schemes or more directly through general taxation to fund such things as flood defences, job creation schemes, or public health. Economists have documented in great detail why individual purchase of healthcare through insurance markets can be inefficient and unjust. In other cases governments have tried to persuade the public to insure themselves against risks as an alternative to pooling, for example through personal pensions or private insurance, against unemployment. Most societies combine pooled risks and risks that individuals handle for themselves (for example, responsibility for personal safety) or through commercial contracts (for example, buildings insurance, or life assurance as a condition of a commercial mortgage). Where there is a risk that an activity may cause serious harm to others, but those taking part can't cover their liabilities, governments often require them to pool their risks by taking out insurance first. The requirement to take out third party motor insurance is an example. Similar principles apply to critical services provided by business, such as energy, water and telecommunications, where the effects of service failure on the wider public are severe. In some cases there may be requirements to maintain buffers, reserves and stocks to reduce the risk of crisis, since markets typically underestimate the impact of low probability but high impact events.

Managing Risk

In relation to its own business, the risks facing governments include IT failures, delay, or unbudgeted expenditure, overload or policy failure. In these fields questions of power and knowledge become particularly acute. Governments often appear to have more power over their internal processes than they really do. They may face obstructive or misleading internal advice, vested interests that try to cover up mistakes or problems, as well as legitimate resistance to bad ideas. Where services are contracted out, things get even worse since governments remain responsible for the overall outcomes but lack the means to deliver them. In principle contracts can specify who bears what kind of risk; but for this to happen the risks have to be predictable and the other party has to be able to bear the risk. In practice governments remain the bearers of risk in the last resort (if a private contractor goes bankrupt, for example), and many attempts to transfer risk have failed. As a rule, risks are easier to transfer in clearly definable capital projects, where outputs can be clearly defined and where timescales are not too long, than in long-term service delivery. While it is relatively straightforward to transfer financial risks to a third party, it is more difficult to transfer reputational risk, as the public rightly expects government to be accountable for services delivered on its behalf. When essential services go wrong, people still look to government to put them right, even where these services are provided privately. The power generation crisis in California in 2000–1 led to the bankruptcy of Pacific Gas and Electric and the public bail-out of Southern California Edison. The failure of the privatised railway company Railtrack in the UK led to it effectively being returned to public ownership. Each of these examples confirmed just how much governments retain ultimate responsibility.

The Three Levels for Handling Risks

Government needs to handle risk at three levels: strategy, programmes, and operations. At the strategic level, what's at stake is the government's political contract with the electorate and the coherence of its overall programme. Here the crucial decisions involve how strategic objectives are formulated, how money is allocated, and how policies change in response to successes or failures. A generation ago the key concerns included the performance of nationalized industries or exchange rate crises. More contemporary examples of setbacks that threatened the government's contract with the electorate include the aftermath of the Bush administration's war in Iraq, the UK's ignominious exit from the European Exchange Rate Mechanism in 1992, and the demonstrations which forced the French Prime Minister Dominique de Villepin to reverse labour market reforms in 2006. On rare occasions the very legitimacy of the state is at stake. In the UK this happened in 2000 when a group of lorry drivers briefly blockaded power stations in a campaign against rising fuel costs. For a short time it looked as if government was losing control over the basic functioning of society, and ministers took fright. Government prepared to negotiate and readied the army to take over critical pieces of infrastructure, and then, to immense relief, the blockades crumbled. During a strike in 2002 the Venezuelan government went a step further and sent the military to take over fuel distribution centres and oil tankers.

At the programme level come the detailed policies—how plans will be implemented and by whom. Here the risks include major overspends; lack of attention to the operating environment; resistance by powerful stakeholders (for example, professional trade unions in public services). The organization of government in functional departments has made it harder to deal with cross-cutting risks at this programme level. BSE—the disease which struck British cattle, and later others across Europe, in the 1990s— was a classic example. The British departments blamed each other, responded in contradictory ways, and fuelled public uncertainty. Similar problems emerged when an outbreak of foot and mouth disease erupted in 2001: the only contingency plans turned out to be nearly forty years old, and no one had thought through the impact of such an epidemic on tourism as well as farming. The combination of new science (to model how the disease would spread), and draconian action with the military (including mass culls) got the disease under control, but only after the normal procedures had proven grossly inadequate.

An example of a programme risk was the imaginative, but doomed, policy to give people individual learning accounts in the UK. This was meant to pave the way to a radically different way of funding education, effectively providing citizens with accounts that they could use to purchase learning from any supplier, with funds provided both by the state

and by individuals and employers. But the ways in which it was implemented made it far too easy for spurious providers to set themselves up
without proper checks. Ambitious targets encouraged rapid expansion
without attention to quality. Within a few months the programme had
to be shut down because of abundant evidence of fraud. The department
itself concluded that although there were measures to manage risks these
were 'focused too heavily on the risk of failing to meet programme targets',
and not enough had been done to simulate how others would respond to
the new policy.

At the project and operational level, decisions will be concerned with
technical issues, managing resources, schedules, providers, partners, and
infrastructure. Here the common problems include lack of contingency
planning and lack of fallback plans, overoptimistic timescales, and so on.
An example at this level was the very public breakdown of the UK passport
issuing system in 1998, resulting, like so many government disasters, from
failures of IT and flawed contracts with suppliers. In this case the National
Audit Office highlighted 'insufficient contingency planning' and ten general lessons for public bodies which included: the need for robust forecasting of service demand and contingency plans to deal with surges; formal
risk assessments for all new computer systems; and good communications
about service problems to reduce public anxiety and relieve the conse-
quent pressure on services from extra enquiries.

At all three levels governments can choose whether to muddle through
or whether to systematize their approach to risk. Perhaps the most important question for any government is whether it is bringing the right people
to the table to make decisions about risks: that should mean people with a
strong feel for how things really work—whether what's at issue is vaccinating animals, the competence of an agency charged with implementing
a policy, or fixing computer systems. It's a universal experience of government that the most important decisions are made without the presence of
anyone who really understands what impact they will have—seniority and
political status trump direct experience. It's no wonder so many unnecessary disasters happen or that so many cures are worse than the disease.

A genuinely strategic government doesn't shy away from risk: it faces up to
the facts that surround it, and puts in place systems to spot and prepare. In
extremis it needs to be ready to step in, whether to run essential infrastructures or to bail out collapsing financial systems. But for systems to be resilient
the capacity to understand risks and respond to them needs to be widely
distributed, grounded in real-life experiences of failure and adversity. Too
much centralization, and too much reliance on the formal machinery of risk

registers and audits, renders systems less able to respond to unexpected shocks. Similar considerations apply to critical infrastructures. One of the important lessons of the twenty-first century is that these are more resilient if they can be disaggregated: so energy infrastructures based on local combined heat and power (or anaerobic waste) will be more resilient than national grids based on a few mega power-stations, just as communications systems are more resilient if they don't depend on just a handful of Internet gateways.

In the UK I helped to create a set of fairly centralized institutions to deal with risk, including a horizon-scanning committee for all departments that kept a watch out for disruptive events, a civil contingencies team to deal with crises, and much more systematic processes for handling risk within departments. These worked reasonably well, and in the years after they were created the UK was spared the traumas that had accompanied BSE and Foot and Mouth (probably thanks to luck as much as design). They were there in part to manage risk explicitly and honestly. But they were also there to cultivate a mentality in which all strategies were tested against many possible futures and not just the ones we hoped would happen. And they worked more because they encouraged people at every level to think harder about resilience than because they gave the centre of central government an accurate view of what lay ahead.

10

Joined-up Government

ALL large organizations face the same problems of coordination: how to cajole and encourage agencies, departments, units, and professions to point in broadly the same direction, and how to align incentives, cultures, and structures of authority to fit critical tasks that cut across organizational boundaries, such as urban regeneration, protecting the environment, or enhancing competitiveness.[1]

These problems are difficult because real states are neither monoliths nor pyramids. They are more like flotillas of boats, sometimes sailing in roughly the same direction, but always competing for the wind and the sun, the favour of the flagship. Within bureaucracies the successful leaders are the ones who can not only command but also influence, inspire, and cajole disparate agencies to work to the same ends. But the most successful systems of all are the ones that are structured in ways that make it easy for people to collaborate.

I coined the phrase 'joined-up government' in a speech written for Prime Minister Tony Blair to launch a new unit to deal with social exclusion.[2] We wanted a simple label for an idea that is anything but simple. Although some aspects of joined-up government are new—particularly the impact of the Internet—others are very old. They faced all the big imperial bureaucracies whether Roman, Ottoman, or Chinese and every military command attempting to coordinate complex forces. In Britain similar problems led to the creation of multi-functional local government in the late nineteenth century as a joined-up alternative to the separate boards for sewage, water, gas, and education. In France (echoing ancient China) they prompted the creation of ENA as a tool for forging a 'joined-up' administrative elite. In business companies have continually wrestled with the problem of horizontal coordination, and some, like Shell, have overcome the substantial managerial challenge of implementing fully fledged matrix structures.

Governments opted firmly for functional departmentalism during their great expansion in the late nineteenth century. A functional division of labour, with large vertically organized departments for finance, education, defence, housing, colonies, trade, or transport, made sense not only for governments but also for large firms and city administrations in an era when communication and the management of knowledge were costly, and best organized within institutions and professions. Funds were then voted by Parliament for specific ends, with tight monitoring to ensure that they were spent correctly. The departments could then develop close relationships with particular professions: health with the doctors, education with teachers, the Home Office or Ministry of the Interior with the police, in line with the argument of R. B. Haldane, one of the British civil service's architects, that the knowledge base was the best determinant of how organizational boundaries should be defined.

From this could be derived the classic architecture of a modern state, with neat lines of accountability up through agencies and departments to a Prime Minister or Cabinet (see Fig. 10.1). This model for dividing government up by functions was efficient for getting homes built or developing national education and health systems. It prevented corruption and waste. It ensured clear lines of accountability and was in line with John Stuart Mill's prescription (in *Representative Government*) that 'any executive function, whether superior or subordinate, should be the appointed duty of some given individual. It should be apparent to the world who did everything and through whose fault anything was left undone. Responsibility is null when nobody knows who is responsible.' Moreover it didn't always lead to fragmentation: in many countries either presidential power or collective Cabinet responsibility ensured some coherence.

There is much to be said for clarity (and as I suggest later the biggest challenge for joined-up government is to avoid responsibility being dissipated). But over time, the weaknesses of this model became more apparent. The 'tubes' or 'silos' down which money flows from government to people and localities are part of the reason why government is bad at solving problems which don't fit departmental boundaries. Vertical organization by its nature skews government efforts away from activities like prevention—since the benefits of preventive action often come to another department. It tends to make government less sensitive to groups whose needs cut across departmental lines (the elderly are a classic

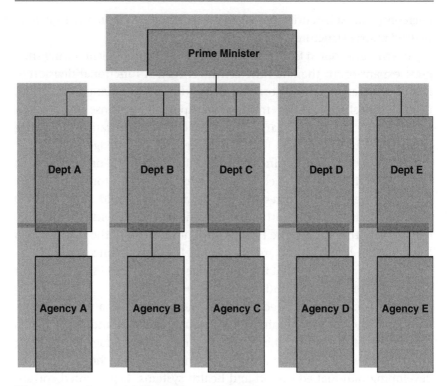

Figure 10.1.   Accountability in the modern state

example). At worst it incentivizes departments and agencies to dump problems onto each other—like schools dumping unruly children onto the streets where they become a problem for the police, or prisons dumping ex-prisoners into the community without adequate job preparation or housing to become a burden for social security. Over time it reinforces the tendency common to all bureaucracies of devoting more energy to the protection of turf than to serving the public.

Departmentalism also makes it harder for governments to see the connections between things. For example, in the UK by 2005 there were more people out of work because of mental health problems than were on the official unemployment register, yet the departments responsible for the two issues had no tradition of cooperation. Another example is the link between trade and aid: the world spends some $300bn on trade protection, six times as much as is spent on development aid, and many governments contain departments whose policies effectively cancel each other out.

In public administration there is a long history of concern for the 'wicked issues' and tangled knots which cut across organizational boundaries and take up an inordinate amount of time and energy. In some cases there may be little reliable knowledge about what should be done. The influential thinker Donald Schon used to compare a high ground of solid knowledge based on research and soluble problems and a swampy low land of complex, wicked problems not amenable to straightforward solutions (which are, unfortunately, the ones that matter most to people). These issues and problems cut across departmental boundaries, as do some of the tasks of government, like efficient purchasing or IT.

Many reformers in the past have tried to grapple with these problems. In the early twentieth century governments experimented with alternative design principles, like shaping government around problems (a ministry for public safety, for example) or particular parts of the population, such as a ministry for farmers (see Fig. 10.2). Almost every government has set up cross-departmental committees, of varying degrees of effectiveness. Some created super-ministers—like the UK Prime Ministers Edward Heath in the 1970s and Winston Churchill in the 1950s (who called them 'overlord' ministers). Some streamlined their bureaucracies—like Scotland, which in 2007 reshaped all of its departments into six clusters, each with its own

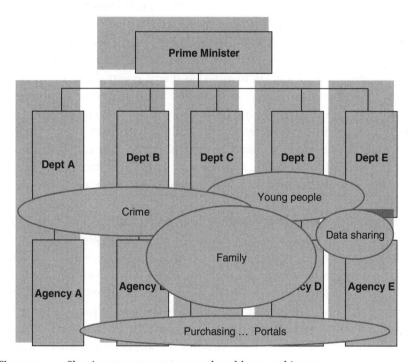

Figure 10.2. Shaping government around problems and issues

lead minister and official. In many countries governments have provided funding for projects that produce more than one service (such as foyers tackling homelessness and unemployment). Some have supported case managers in health and social care and more recently welfare, building on a long history of attempts to create bridges between health and care professionals. Almost every government has supported some physical or virtual one-stop shops to make it easier for people to access information or help.

The smaller-scale reforms have been more successful than higher-level attempts at cross-departmental working. Super-ministries can simply worsen the information overload at the centre and they require super-ministers to make them work. Many attempts at cross-cutting arrangements—such as those on social policy in Britain in the 1970s, or on family policy in Germany in the 1980s—failed because of insufficient political will, inadequate buy-in by departments, or unclear goals. On their own, interdepartmental committees and task forces have relatively little effect on behaviour, without substantial investment of time and political capital by top ministers. The same considerations explain why there is often frustration with partnership working even amongst its strongest advocates. Literally thousands of ostensibly joined-up partnerships proliferated during the 1980s and 1990s in the UK and in much of North America. Although many did good work, too many diverted energy and confused responsibility because they lacked the power or knowledge to act decisively (and some in the UK involved as many as fifty different organizations).[3] Another lesson—that is confirmed again and again by studies of cooperation—is that people are more likely to act in a collaborative way if they expect to have many future dealings with each other, whereas one night stands are more likely to be exploitative. For collaborations to work they need to be stable, and not subject to capricious restructuring. Yet this is a field where national governments have been inveterate fiddlers.

During the 1990s and 2000s some tried to go further. The new public management of the 1980s had successfully encouraged government to be more focused, more organized around targets and performance, and more governed by market forces. But breaking issues down into their component parts is the opposite of what's needed for complex problems, and tends to worsen 'dumping' of problems across organizational boundaries. Another factor is rapidly growing evidence on the interconnectedness of problems. Social scientists have steadily accumulated evidence on such things as the extent to which social exclusion is bound up with risk factors and protective factors in early life, the extent to which crime is influenced by family influences and economic conditions, and the fact that barely a quarter of health improvements come from health services. Horizontal government has also been encouraged by technology—cheaper IT and communications make it much easier to organize activity in networks, partnerships, or project teams. The US Department of Justice, for example, used a dozen different and incompatible case management systems not to mention incompatible systems for purchasing and administration, and has commissioned more collaborative IT networks to simplify and integrate the way its many agencies worked.

Collaboration isn't right for everything. It's most likely to be necessary when individual public agencies lack either the power or the knowledge to deal with a complex problem. It's then most likely to be feasible when the different agencies' goals, planning, and delivery can be aligned. Because cooperation isn't natural, all the main drivers of behaviour within government have to be aligned to cross-cutting tasks. That typically means:

- reforming how money is allocated—to ensure that it goes to specific problems, areas, or client groups rather than to functional bureaucracies;
- reshaping how career rewards are organized—rewarding those who act corporately or collaboratively with promotions, honours, and bonuses;
- designing targets that are shared across agencies;
- influencing the day to day cultures of the professions to reward collaboration;
- ensuring that information and knowledge are shared better at all levels;
- ensuring clear leadership and responsibility for joined-up tasks; and
- designing structures in which people learn to collaborate through mutual favours and reciprocity.

Most important of all, joined-up government has to be aligned with political realities. That means strong 'ownership' from the top to override vested interests, as well as kudos for ministers—giving them horizontal as well as vertical responsibilities, enabling them to use these to produce political capital, and promoting those who do them well.

Over the last twenty years many governments have experimented with new models.[4] In the UK, nearly a third of targets are now shared across departments, alongside pooled budgets linked to goals like conflict prevention overseas or early years development at home. Units have been established that cut across departmental boundaries on social exclusion or climate change. New structures have also been established to implement policy—seconding in people from different agencies and merging budgets. Ministerial jobs have combined vertical and horizontal responsibilities. Local structures have been reshaped to bring together all the agencies with a role to play on such things as cutting crime or regeneration in 'Local Strategic Partnerships' that can now negotiate 'local area agreements' which allow money to be pooled. Some internal corporate functions have also been joined up—for example, giving the head of IT a 'double key' power to approve new IT systems so as to promote easier communications and common standards.

The Social Exclusion Unit exemplified these new approaches. It sat at the centre of government, reporting directly to the Prime Minister. Its staff included secondees from many departments as well as from voluntary organizations, universities, and business. It operated openly, publishing surveys of the state of knowledge before coming up with policy proposals.

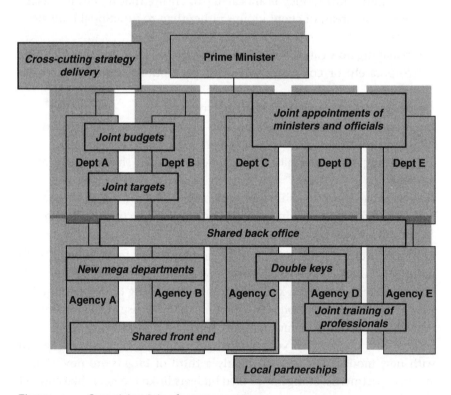

Figure 10.3. Organizing joined-up government

Its recommendations were then taken through Cabinet so that they could be published as statements of government policy, in some cases with budgets attached. Many of the recommendations were implemented by existing departmental structures, using some of the staff who had worked on the strategy; but in other cases new teams were set up to implement them in a similar spirit, focused on results rather than processes.

Figure 10.3 summarizes some of the many options for organizing joined-up government. A good example of joined-up implementation was the Rough Sleepers Unit set up to cut street homelessness. It took a distinctive approach, led by a specialist practitioner, using a hand-picked group of staff from inside and outside government, and a style of work which started with the people being helped and redesigned services working backwards from their needs, with clear goals and a limited time to achieve them. The unit pooled budgets from several departments and had the authority to take risks—including challenging many of the NGOs in the field. But it achieved its goals.

In other countries more radical steps have been taken (see Fig. 10.4). Under Prime Minister Paavo Lipponen Finland reshaped its government in the early 2000s around a small number of high-level strategic goals—with political authority and budgets oriented around these. His successor, Matti Vanhannen, has kept the broad approach, and each priority area has a lead minister and a lead programme manager. In the USA the new Department of Homeland Security attempted to coordinate the often competing agencies that were seen to have failed in protecting the USA from terrorist attack. In Australia the state of Victoria went further than anywhere else in implementing networked governance for communities, shaping itself around places and people rather than programmes, and finding subtler ways to link organic communities into formal governance structures. Many countries have tried to implement a 'no wrong door' principle—so that wherever people enter the system they will be directed to the right place.

Some of the policies for joining up are simple and practical. Sweden's FAROS programme for disabled people aimed to reduce the number of handovers between agencies, and cut by a factor of ten the proportion of people who were sent between agencies. Portugal's 'On the spot firm' made it possible to create businesses through a single office, and faster than in any other EU country. In the 1980s France's Prime Minister Édith Cresson promised to cut the time it would take to set up a company from nine months to three months; Portugal managed to get it down to one hour. Other countries have focused more on the inner workings of the

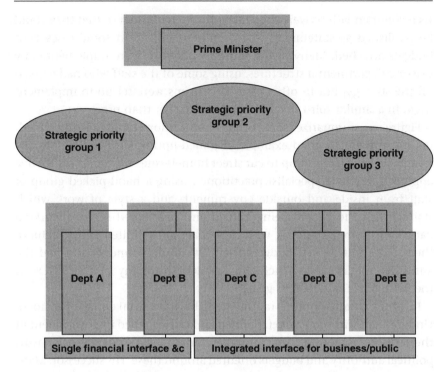

Figure 10.4.   Strategic joined-up government

bureaucracy, providing overt incentives for ambitious officials to look after the interests of government as a whole rather than just their own bit of it. The province of Ontario was one of the first to introduce explicit rewards for horizontal collaboration. At the beginning of each year, the goals of departments and individuals are agreed and at the end of the year when performance is assessed this has to take account of how much staff have helped other agencies as well as how well they've achieved their own direct targets. These horizontal considerations are even more important for the discretionary awards made by the Secretary to the Cabinet.

Joined-up government should make it easier to act preventively and pre-emptively—dealing with problems before they become too acute and costly. Many fire services have turned their attention to prevention, advising householders and businesses, to cut the number of fires they have to put out. The Federal Emergency Management Agency (FEMA) under administrator James Lee Witt shifted from solely responding to crises and towards a 'life-cycle' approach to disaster management, with more emphasis on prevention, working with states and NGOs to prepare evacuation plans, and with the construction industry to build houses that were more resistant to hurricanes. By the late 1990s FEMA's reputation had markedly improved.[5] The Bush administration squeezed its budget and put in place political appointees who showed little interest in good administration. Hurricane Katrina in 2005 destroyed its reputation, revealing the incompetence of an organization which only found out that thousands were in the New Orleans Superdome by watching the TV news.

Some global institutions have been enthusiastic advocates of joined-up action. Since the 1980s the World Health Organization has promoted the idea of healthy cities, and, more recently, 'Health in all policies'—looking at every field from planning to schools to consider their impact on health. Since research shows that health is strongly shaped by social determinants, this made obvious sense, not that it's easy to shift resources away from hospitals. In the environmental field, climate change has forced governments to look across the board in the same way. The UK's Climate Change office set up in 2007 was given wide-ranging powers to review and shape policy, from transport to regulation. In both fields impact statements have been a tool for change: health impact statements have been pioneered in British Columbia, Quebec, and New Zealand, and environmental impact statements have become mainstream not only in governments but also in business.

When government can't join things up, external organizations can. The commercial managed care companies in the USA (like Kaiser Permanente and Humana) have pioneered more effective ways of helping patients navigate their way through a care system, providing continuity of care to compensate for the failures and fragmentation of health delivery. Their sophistication in using data to tailor care to the individual's needs, to track their likely risks, and their use of proactive coaches, 'motivational interviewing', and other methods to encourage behaviour change so as to prevent costly health problems are proving influential with public health systems. NGOs and social enterprises also often provide joined-up services to compensate for the failures of public agencies.

Strategic Audits

Joined-up government works best when the whole of government shares a common understanding of what needs to be done and why. A good way to do this is through regular strategic audits or reviews. In the UK variants of this were carried out in 2003, and then again in 2005/6 and 2006/7, commissioned by the Prime Minister. The first of these started halfway through

Tony Blair's second term of office to help revive and renew his adminis-tration—and reverse the risks of complacency and stagnation. Describing it as an 'audit' helped to make it sound suitably anodyne and bureaucratic. But it was really about stimulating government to think in ways that would prolong its life. The process was carried out by a team within the government's Strategy Unit, with secondees from across government and from outside. Its elements included:

- detailed analysis of hundreds of international indicators to show how the UK was performing compared to other countries, and to show which were doing better and might offer useful lessons;
- honest reviews of key areas of policy to see which were working and which needed change (e.g. showing up the dire state of transport policy);
- a detailed survey of how different parts of the population were faring. This showed, for example, that low-income middle-aged women were doing particularly badly by some measures, perhaps not surprisingly since they were poorly represented in political and media argument; and
- futures exercises, with some attempts to clarify when different issues might arrive on the political radar.

The most intriguing strand consisted of anonymized interviews with all senior officials and ministers (including the Prime Minister) to elicit their confidential perspectives on which policies were or weren't working, where the big challenges were likely to lie, and how well they thought the leadership team was working. Most of these were scheduled for an hour—but some went on for much longer, clearly providing vital therapy for ministers who could rarely discuss their views openly (some were painfully honest: I ensured that only two people knew who had given which interview). In retrospect this may have been the most valuable part of the whole exercise: the main findings were presented back to the whole leadership group, which was able to reflect on its own thoughts in ways that would have been impossible in open discussion.

The material was then used for a series of discussions with ministers and officials which led to broad conclusions about strategy as well as many more specific policy ideas. It also drove a programme of policy reviews; helped shape the budget setting process; and, perhaps most importantly, provided the framework for the governing party's next manifesto (in 2005).

Not all of the conclusions were acted on. The reviews argued for a moratorium on health restructuring, for more modular IT projects, and for beginning a much more open public debate on finance for long-term care—none of which in the end found favour. Other governments have done very similar exercises, including several states in Australia. They seem to be most useful either at the beginning of a term (as in the Australian government's 2020 programme which involved 1,000 people in thinking about future priorities in 2008) or when a governing party has completed its first wave of tasks but needs to renew itself and redefine its overall direction.

Where Next?

Joined-up government has been most successful where there have been clear objectives, political commitment, and viable joined-up structures at lower levels, with strong cultures of collaboration. Equally important, success has depended on the key drivers of behaviour[6]—money, kudos, career rewards, and targets—being aligned.[7] Joining up can be encouraged top–down—but it can also grow bottom–up. Charles Sabel has written of how federated organizations decompose 'complex tasks into simple ones [and create] search networks that allow actors quickly to find others who can in effect teach them what to do because they are already solving a like problem.'[8] In an era of cheap communications and smart computers this more organic approach to collaboration is an attractive alternative to waiting for the formal structures.

These methods are reminders that joined-up government is about more than structure. It also depends on relationships. The emerging tools of social network analysis help to reveal how well these relationships work, for example surveying the many people involved in a field like crime reduction in a region or city. The maps that result show who connects to whom; who is helpful to others; and which junior staff glue the system together.[9] They diagnose organizations that are clustered too tightly together, or that are too loose. Figure 10.5 for example comes from Karen Stephenson's work analysing the networks in Philadelphia: each point represents a person.

These relationships are likely to be stronger if they're underpinned by a share view of how the world works. Systems thinking provides one shared view, as well as a theoretical lens for thinking about how shared views come about. It has never quite become a core skill for government, despite the pioneering work of figures like Geoffrey Vickers and Stafford Beer. But its ideas continue to provide insights that aren't available from other

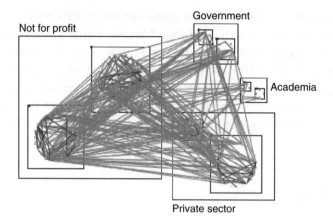

Figure 10.5. Social network analysis in Philadelphia; each underlying data point represents a person

disciplines on how complex systems really work, whether on the often counterintuitive dynamics of feedback or the role of variety in helping systems to adapt.[10] The training for civil servants in most societies still misses out on these skills, and the specialists in particular disciplines, economics, statistics, or sociology, may spend a lifetime giving advice without engaging with the higher-level systems thinking skills that are needed to make sense of their specialist knowledge.

What will the future bring? Are we at the early stages of a fundamental transformation of government, or will joined-up government turn out to be just another fad? Although governments are quite conservative institutions, the pace of change is unlikely to let up if only because the factors described earlier show no signs of receding. But it is unlikely that government will ever be predominantly organized in horizontal as opposed to vertical structures. If it was, there would be as many boundary problems are there are today. Instead the future shape of government is likely to involve a combination of vertical hierarchies, particularly for carrying out long-standing tasks with clear lines of management and accountability, and horizontal structures for determining strategy and carrying out shorter-term tasks. In effect that would mean government evolving further in the direction it is already taking with:

- more work becoming project-based, with teams created for time limited periods drawn from many different agencies;
- more policy making done in a cross-cutting way, and with the close involvement of practitioners;

- a larger share of budgets tied to outcomes—and then allocated across departments and agencies according to how much they can contribute to outcomes;
- more vertical functions passed out to agencies, leaving behind slimmer but more integrated central staffs;
- a greater emphasis on shared knowledge management as the glue holding central government together;
- an expectation that civil service careers will move across and beyond government;
- use of the integrative power of the Internet to organise access to services according to people's needs rather than producer convenience; and
- a greater emphasis on professional formation across boundaries.

Longer-term more radical options may also be feasible, for example with responsibility for whole systems—like the criminal justice system, transport, or children's services organized in an integrated way, potentially with purchaser–provider splits, rather than, as at present, divided between many different agencies and professions each with their own budgets, structures, and targets. Other ideas to encourage joined-up behaviour include 'blind' strategy sessions, where prospective ministers invest time in devising and agreeing strategies prior to the allocation of ministerial posts.

In most contexts evolutionary approaches work better than big bangs. But over time the biggest gains will come from moving beyond the relatively modest joining up of the late 1990s and 2000s to more fundamental systems redesign. I have already spelt out many of the reasons for this. One other concerns bureaucratic motivations. Contrary to the claims of the public choice school, most bureaucracies do not seek to maximize their resources or turf. Instead what they often value as highly is autonomy, that is to say relatively undisputed jurisdiction. Moves towards joining up that reduce this autonomy for all players are almost certain to be resisted, and are likely to be ineffective. By contrast moves that create new structures and powers, or that give existing agencies greater autonomy to tackle a cross-cutting problem, stand a far higher chance of succeeding.

The barriers remain substantial. Harold Seidman's ironic words remain a healthy warning to all reformers. The quest for coordination, he wrote, 'is the twentieth century equivalent of the medieval search for the philosopher's stone... if only we can find the right formula for coordination we can reconcile the irreconcilable.'

There is, of course, no such formula. But this should not be a counsel of despair. Joining up in all its forms has happened, is happening, and will happen even more in the future. It may rarely if ever be perfect. But governments that can think and operate in 360 degrees will over time prove better at solving problems and meeting needs than governments that remain trapped in the vertical hierarchies that they have inherited.[11]

Changing Minds and Behaviour

MUCH of government is about changing people's minds. Even more of it is about changing their behaviour—cutting water use or drink driving, or cultivating a sense of national identity. The UK health regulator NICE determines which treatments are cost effective and measures them in terms of costs per QALY ('quality adjusted life year'). The available research shows that smoking cessation programmes cost around £500–1,000 per QALY, compared to over £20,000 for Tamoxifen for breast cancer prevention and anything up to £800,000 for beta interferon for multiple sclerosis.[1] Clearly the right actions to change behaviour can achieve remarkable results and at relatively low cost (for NICE any treatment needs to cost under £20,000–30,000 per QALY to justify introduction within the NHS).

Yet changing behaviour is a delicate subject. No one wants to be told that there's something wrong with their behaviour. When I worked in the UK government I asked each department what it knew about behaviour change and commissioned a programme of research on what was known. It proved hard to track down who knew about the field, and what lessons had been learned. But even when the work was completed I felt wary about putting any of our conclusions into the public domain for fear of the scope for misunderstanding—deliberate or not. On the day that we eventually did publish a background paper the London *Times* ran a front page story misquoting a passage from the paper as proof that government was about to introduce a 'fat tax' to penalize the obese. Mild hysteria descended on the spin doctors and the health department (fortunately Tony Blair was always much more calm about the silliness of the media than many around him).

These sensitivities have not gone away. But strategies to change behaviour are becoming less controversial. Many of us have driven too fast, drunk too much alcohol, or dropped litter. But we want to live in societies without too much speeding or drunkenness and where streets are clean. Governments have many ways of changing behaviour, from the soft to the brutal and hard. They can introduce prison sentences or heavy penalties for drunk driving. They can catch more people who break the law with speed cameras for cars, or closed circuit television for litterers. They can raise the taxes on drinks, or wrapping paper, or highly polluting cars. They can make speeches or run advertising campaigns to frighten us, or persuade us to change.

There are few fields where governments aren't trying to shape behaviour. Crime and antisocial behaviour are strongly influenced by people's willingness to restrain themselves and to restrain others around them. Education can never simply be done to passive pupils (though some teaching methods have appeared to try): it also depends on students' willingness to work and learn. Cutting levels of waste depends on householders' willingness to separate their rubbish; cutting levels of traffic congestion depends on persuading people to use trains, buses, bicycles, or trams rather than cars.

An ideal society might be one where people automatically policed themselves—saving governments the bother of fines and enforcers. Yet that is easier said than done, and it might make for a sadly anxious society. Instead the only alternative options lie in different mixes of sticks, carrots, and persuasion to encourage people to take greater responsibility and do the right thing.[2] In the field of welfare, successive governments have tried to persuade people to do more to find jobs and to acquire new skills rather than becoming dependent on benefits. In health it has become increasingly apparent that once the threat of infectious diseases is contained better health depends more on the lifestyle and behaviour of citizens (diet, exercise, smoking, drinking) than it does on the quality of healthcare. Banning smoking in public places has done more for life expectancy than many billions spent on pharmaceuticals.

Economic considerations have forced policy makers to take seriously what might have been considered soft or marginal issues. The UK government's review of long-term health funding in the early 2000s concluded that the public's willingness to take responsibility for their own health would dramatically alter future funding pressures, and concluded that much more effort should be made to influence it.[3] But strategies to change behaviour enter delicate philosophical territory. The appropriate division of responsibility between the individual, community, and state has always been contested. In past decades there were furious arguments over whether the state should provide fluoride in the water, enforce the wearing of car seat belts, or force children to stay in school up to the age of 16. For many traditions of social and political thought greater personal responsibility is a good in itself because it enables society to function with a less coercive state and judicial system and allows public goods to be provided with a lower tax burden. The exercise of responsibility strengthens individual character and moral capacity, and greater personal responsibility—in terms of restraint and support for others—enhances the quality of life of the whole community. But for others any suggestion of using state power to enhance personal responsibility smacks either of a conspiracy to pare back essential public services or of an excessively paternalistic desire to control people's lives.

Many of the issues in this territory are strongly shaped by perceptions of fairness. It seems fair to impose the costs of a harm onto the person most responsible for producing it—so that smokers should pay more for the health needs of passive smokers and big companies should pay more for the pollution they cause. These judgements depend in part on perceptions of how much moral responsibility the perpetrator really has: a child is viewed differently from an adult, and someone suffering from a genetic disorder will be seen in a more forgiving light than someone who has no excuse for their behaviour.

Public perceptions of what's fair, and of the right balance between paternalism and responsibility, change over time. For example, the vast majority of the British public believe that it is the state's responsibility to provide healthcare for the sick, but less than a third think that it is the state's responsibility to provide a job for everyone who wants one. Many more now believe that the state has a responsibility to protect children or to punish domestic violence than in the past. Conversely more people expect to be able to buy or own their own house, or to choose their own pension.

Most governments have traditionally relied on two sets of tools to shape behaviours. One set are the tools of law, prohibition, and coercion: forcing people to behave in a particular way because of the pain or harm that would result from penalties. Coercion works much of the time: it stops people from stealing, killing, and raping. But prohibitions can notoriously fail, as happened to the US' prohibition of alcohol use in the 1920s and the prohibitions of hard drug use that did little to stem rising demand from the 1960s to the 2000s.

The other set of tools are economic: incentives to reward one kind of behaviour over another. These are effective in some circumstances—for example in encouraging people to shift to more ecologically benign cars.

The World Bank claims that in developed countries a 10 per cent increase in cigarette prices reduces smoking by about 4 per cent.[4] Price signals have been used successfully to shift people onto unleaded petrol and to cut alcohol consumption. In the USA, high sales taxes on snack foods have also been shown to cut consumption.[5]

But incentives are often ineffective. Better incentives to save should encourage people to save more. Yet the available evidence suggests that while they encourage shifts between savings vehicles, from less to more tax efficient, they do little if anything to affect aggregate savings rates. Sometimes incentives can have perverse effects. For example, in order to reduce the number of parents dropping their children off late at an Israeli nursery, fines were introduced for late arrival. But rather than reduce lateness, the fines led to a marked increase in the number of children dropped off late. The fines led parents to feel that they were entitled to drop their children off late, since they were now paying for it.

An alternative approach lets government set the defaults for behaviour—rendering it as easy as possible to make choices that suit the individual's interests and the communities' interests, while not removing the freedom to make another choice. This has been particularly favoured in fields like pensions—with default state-guaranteed options that citizens can choose to opt out of—or health, where a doctor's prescriptions come along with some freedom to choose differently (the phrase 'libertarian paternalism'—setting default options in the interests of the public but enabling them to opt for alternatives has been used to describe these options).[6] These work in part by creating new social norms. A small-scale but impressive example is the Irwell Valley Housing Association's 'Gold Service scheme' which rewards tenants who pay their rent on time (and abide by various other commitments to good behaviour) with quicker emergency repairs, discounts on home insurance, and faster access to improvements. The scheme has brought down costs, evictions, and voids, and has worked by rewarding good behaviour and making this the norm, rather than through penalties.[7]

There are many more rounded views of how human behaviour really works, and a rich literature that's full of insights.[8] One school of thought emphasizes conditioning—how people are shaped by rewards or punishments that follow closely on a particular behaviour. So speed cameras that reliably catch speeding drivers and make them immediately aware that they have been caught literally condition changed behaviour. Experimental evidence shows that the most difficult behaviour to change is that which has been learnt through a programme of increasingly intermittent rewards. This helps to explain puzzling phenomena, such as why people stay with abusive partners—the relationships were originally rewarding, but the intervals between the positive experiences gradually became larger (and may even follow episodes of abuse).

The very different ecological view looks at how individual choices are affected by interpersonal relationships (of people close at hand) as well as by broader social pressures and encouragements.[9] Young people are more likely to take up smoking if their peers do—one study found a 1,000 per cent increase in smoking if two peers smoke, compared to a 26 per cent increase if a parent does.[10] Robert Cialdini has shown that people are twice as likely to litter if their environment is dirty because of the powerful impact of perceived group norms. Similarly if you want to persuade people to cut their air travel, don't warn them that if everyone carries on flying the environment will collapse: instead try to persuade them that everyone else is taking fewer flights. Social marketing approaches draw on these ecological theories to change either the individual or the environment around the individual, or both. The changed behaviour of individuals and changed environment, then, hopefully interact, gradually establishing new social norms.

Other approaches exploit people's desire for cognitive consistency. Where there is a clash between their actions and their values, people often resolve the discrepancy by changing their values or attitudes rather than their behaviour. For example, if someone agrees to take on a boring task for a very limited reward, there is a dissonance between their behaviour (doing the task) and their reasoning (they would only do a boring task if there's a decent reward). One way out of this dissonance is to stop doing the task by changing their behaviour. Another is to convince themselves that the task is actually quite interesting.[11]

Policy tools that exploit this aspect of human nature encourage people to make public commitments and then put pressure on them to live up to their commitments. These may be commitments to learn, to help their children with homework (in Parent–School contracts, for example), to diet, or to help others. Studies of the level of activity in 'staged' crime scenes show that individuals who agree to 'watch over' someone else's property become over 400 per cent more likely to attempt to prevent a theft than those who are aware that something is being stolen but have no such prior commitment to protecting it.

Another set of methods go with the grain of the heuristics, or mental shortcuts, that people use to make decisions.[12] People assume that events that they can easily call to mind, or that are easy to imagine, are more frequent and therefore likely to happen. Hence they tend to be more nervous about flying than driving because airplane crashes are easy to recall (even though hundreds of airlines have never had a fatality). Similarly, the larger the jackpot in a lottery, the more tickets are bought, because the consequences of a large prize attract more attention and are easy to imagine. Policies that emphasize individual success stories (such as disabled people who have triumphed in their careers) or that highlight dramatic risks (such as the violent effects of driving while drunk) are exploiting these heuristics. There is good evidence that people value things differently depending on whether they are gaining or losing them. Loss tends to be felt more keenly than gain. Messages stressing the potentially negative consequences of ill health tend to be more effective than those that phrase the benefits in terms of potential gains. Warning people that they stand to *lose* money if they don't get more educational qualifications works better than promising that they could earn more.

Daniel Kahneman has shown that in making judgements of this kind everyone discounts the future but in very different ways.[13] So people living chaotic or impoverished lives apply especially high discount rates as a result of their immediate circumstances—making it less likely that they will commit to longer-term investments in their health, welfare, security, or education. Hence policies that try to influence individuals' investment in their future (e.g. promoting personal pensions or adult education) tend to widen inequalities as those with high discount rates fail to take up new opportunities.[14]

Another set of approaches take advantage of the social context of behaviours—and try to influence those around the individual. To persuade sexually active teenagers to use condoms they need to know what type of condoms work best and how to use them properly; to believe that potential sex partners won't reject them because they want to use condoms; and to have the confidence in themselves to state their wishes clearly before or during sex. *Self-efficacy* refers to people's confidence in their ability to take action and to persist with that action.[15] Bandura's research shows that self-efficacy can be increased by setting and rewarding small incremental goals, along with very overt monitoring and feedback. This works well for things like training patients to manage their own care. Surprisingly simple methods can have a big impact: recovering depressives who record on a daily basis the good things that have happened to them and what they owe to others get better much more quickly than others.

This last example is a reminder that humans are social creatures. Reciprocity is a powerful social force. We respond to being placed in some sort of debt, even if unwillingly. This is the technique used in direct mail when a pen or pre-stamped envelope is supplied with a request for money. Wine tasting at vineyards works on a similar principle—a little is given free, but a lot is realized in return—though without a formal contract. It has been argued that the strongly generational pattern of civic behaviour in the USA resulted from the GI bill—the public funding of free college education for Second World War veterans—which triggered a cycle of reciprocity that lasted a lifetime. There may be ways in which similar effects can be achieved through 'social gifts' such as educational bursaries, or publicly subsidized children's trust funds, rather than couching such public expenditure in terms of 'rights' to services.

The importance of social interactions explains why face-to-face actions can be so much more powerful than impersonal ones delivered by letter or email. For example, individual face-to-face approaches have encouraged people to make greater use of alternatives to the car. In Perth in Australia door to door visits combined with peer pressure encouraged people to use their cars less. Some schemes asked volunteers to keep a travel diary to help them think about which journeys could be made by other means. Similar results have been found in terms of civic and political behaviour. A randomized experiment with 30,000 voters in the USA to see how voter turnout might be increased compared the effectiveness of leaflets, telephone campaigns, and face-to-face reminders of a forthcoming election, all using a non-party political message highlighting the importance of voting.[16] Leaflets had a modest effect, boosting turnout by around 2.5 per cent. Telephone calls had, if anything, a negative effect. But face-to-face contact—someone turning up at your doorstep to remind you in advance—boosted turnout by around 10 to 15 per cent.[17] Despite its relatively high cost, face-to-face contact was ultimately more cost-effective. Other methods take advantage of the extent to which people look for social proof (i.e. that others are changing their behaviour in a similar way) or to the influence of an authority figure, the doctor, judge, or policeman.

Some recent policy directions have used these insights and theories. The welfare to work programmes pioneered in Scandinavia introduced much greater conditionality into welfare and took advantage of aversion to loss (the threat that benefits would be removed), psychological discount rates (giving extra emphasis to immediate consequences), the authority of personal advisers, and a sense of societal reciprocity. In health there has been much discussion over the years about making personal responsibility for health and the responsible use of health services more explicit by adding conditions, penalties, or rewards alongside patients' rights. Even modest compacts can take advantage of a similar sense of reciprocity, especially if they encourage patients to make visible commitments about future behaviour and reinforce the sense of new social norms taking shape.

These devices can balance the powerful psychological forces that stop us taking care of our own health. Discounting makes us disinclined to change our behaviour now for a long-term gain in health or longevity (rather the drink or burger today than the extra year tomorrow). Asymmetry of losses versus gains makes us disinclined to give up our current satisfaction (smoking) for a potential gain (feeling fitter). And our psychological defences and attributions make us feel that early death and morbidity are things that happen to others, not us.

A good example of how psychology can be exploited is Thailand's success in reducing the transmission of AIDS and other sexually transmitted diseases. This was achieved by a sustained, multilevel attempt to change social norms concerning condom use. The campaign combined consultation with national information campaigns, active engagement of at-risk groups (*commitment* and *consistency*), severe penalties for brothels not following safe practices (*economic sanctions*), and practices that empowered prostitutes to insist on condom use (*self-efficacy*). But perhaps the most important aspect of the programme was that together all the elements created a sense that habits were changing (*social proof*) and fostered the emergence of new social norms.

There are many other examples. Graduation incentives that pay a young person to stay on in school (such as Educational Maintenance Allowances in the UK) have shown that a positive conditionality can be more effective than the conventional negative forms. Restorative justice models in which offenders are held directly accountable to victims, and sometimes have to restore the losses they suffered, have also proven effective. They make the human harm and suffering caused more real and salient for the offender (*availability* and *simulation*), and they empower the victims by giving them an opportunity to express their feelings (*self-efficacy* and *closure*). Restorative justice creates opportunities for 'reintegrative shaming'—the offender is given an opportunity to apologize and make up to the community the harm they have done, while the community can in turn forgive them; together these help offenders re-establish a more positive image of themselves both in their own mind and for others. Parenting classes have been found to be extremely effective both at changing parents' behaviour and impacting on child behaviour—effects that are rapid and sustained.

Antisocial behaviour has been reduced by 30 per cent where parents of offending adolescents have attended parenting classes.

Changes in the physical environment can also influence the norms that affect crime. Even minor changes to street lighting can have an impact.[18] People are also influenced by how others are behaving. The term 'broken windows' was coined in New York for a style of policing which aimed to change social norms of acceptable behaviour by tackling visual signs of disorder, such as broken windows and burnt-out cars. These methods are given credit for cutting crimes as diverse as 'threatening behaviour' and 'drug-dealing'. Finally, neighbourhood characteristics and community behaviour also influence how individuals behave. Work in the USA has shown how neighbourhoods with higher levels of 'collective efficacy'—where more neighbours know each other and are more likely to intervene in minor incivilities (such as children playing truant or teenagers hanging around)—suffer significantly lower levels of crime.[19] These positive effects are found even after controlling for socioeconomic factors and prior levels of crime, suggesting the effect is causal.

Behaviour change isn't yet a settled science. But the best behaviour change strategies draw on careful analysis of what is shaping behaviour to devise detailed interventions tailored to the very different motivations that people have. Crucial to this is detailed market research, quantitative analysis, and qualitative research using psychological profiling techniques to segment the population. To influence obesity, for example, populations have to be segmented not only according to their health status and current behaviour but also according to their capacity and willingness to change. Then, targeted strategies can be introduced for each group, combining the right mix of incentives and peer pressure, individual encouragements and group encouragements, alongside reinforcing messages from opinion leaders.

Psychologists do not yet have a prominent place in policy design. But looking to the future, these methods are likely to loom ever larger in the world of policy makers and strategists. Behind all of them lies the simple insight that dreams rest on habits: the freedoms that people aspire to depend on the habits that they and millions of others follow day by day.

Motivating Public Servants

I've focused so far on changing the public's minds. But successful strategies have to win over the hearts and minds of the people charged with putting them into effect. Many have foundered from a failure to understand their motivations. Others have succeeded in achieving their declared goals, but were seen as failures because the frontline workers responsible for implementing them felt so disempowered that they became anti-ambassadors for their service (at one point in the UK the more people had friends or family working in the NHS, the more likely they were to oppose what was happening to it).

There have been many influential analyses of the interaction of structures, policies, and motivations. Richard Titmuss's work on blood donation is a classic example. He showed that markets and payments could damage the altruistic desire to make a gift of blood and thus damage the public interest. Introducing payments for blood risked reducing both the quantity and the quality of the blood that the public provided. Many, like Titmuss, see public service as an essentially altruistic act. The people who choose to work as teachers or doctors, police or officials, are seen to have sacrificed more lucrative alternatives because of their love of service. This makes them willing to work longer hours, to take less pay, and to put up with more demanding roles. It follows that exhortation and support, and appeals to values, will be the best way to motivate the implementers of new policies. Certainly many public organizations talk to themselves as if they are guided by the highest ideals.

But from the other side of the ideological spectrum, it's been argued that if public workers are not treated *as if* their default is to cheat, maximize power and monetary reward, society will end up with sub-optimal results: lazy, self-serving, power-hungry agencies, and poor quality services. To succeed, any strategy has to be coldly realistic, and it's claimed that the behaviour of real public servants and agencies, belies the rose-tinted picture of altruism. In practice public servants are often paid very well, especially when perks are taken into account (like long holidays for teachers or early retirement for the police) and they benefit from high levels of job security.

These conflicting ideas have a long history. In the English tradition, Hobbes was a seminal influence who argued that power is the primary human urge, overriding everything else. We are all driven, he wrote, by 'a perpetual and restless desire of power after power that ceases only in death'. This drive comes from our frailties and vulnerability, the brute fact that we cannot protect our lives and guarantee our well-being, and even the power we already have, 'without the acquisition of more'. Not all of the effects of this drive for power and recognition are bad. It can motivate people to create great art or to be generous with their charity ('there can be no greater argument to a man of his own power', Hobbes wrote, 'than to find himself able not only to accomplish his own desires but also to assist other men in theirs', a comment with obvious relevance to public sector professionals). But any designs have to assume the worst of human motivations, and fear of punishment is likely to be a more powerful motive for pro-social behaviour than any alternative. The other consistent influence has been David Hume. He wrote that 'all plans of government which suppose great reformation in the manners of mankind are plainly imaginary' and he advised that 'in contriving any system of government every man ought to be supposed a knave and to have no other end in all his actions than private interest.'

Seen from the vantage point of the twenty-first century neither view—the one emphasizing the will to power, the other emphasizing material acquisitiveness—looks realistic. Hobbes's vision requires a potentially limitless quantity of inspection, audit, and policing to hold greedy and megalomaniac officials in check. Hume's argument likewise implies high costs—mainly through significantly higher levels of pay to match the private sector and so motivate people to work in public services. But it is striking that many reforms are still designed *as if* Hobbes and Hume were essentially correct, either imposing severe performance management regimes, inspection, and audit, or using financial incentives to solve problems such as the unwillingness of doctors to work in inner city areas. Yet as Julian Le Grand put it: 'Philosophers, social psychologists, economists, evolutionary psychologists and scholars from a wide range of fields have all tackled issues of motivation without achieving much by the way of consensus. There is controversy in the meaning of terms such as self-interest, altruism and the extent to which either can be found in the real world'. We could also add there is controversy over the broader issue of work motivation, which crudely divides into whether happier employees work better, or whether stress, fear, and unhappiness can be functional.

So should public strategists assume that the people they are working with want to do the right thing? Experiments surveyed in the psychological and economic literature show very clearly that people contribute more to the provision of public goods, and to the public good, than is easily explained by pure self-interest. People do not exploit freedoms to cheat; they are willing to sacrifice their own resources to punish others acting unfairly; and many types of altruism are common. Even though altruism can sometimes be explained in self-interested terms (that is to say, people behave altruistically to gain future credit with others), often it cannot.[20]

There has been much research in recent years on the dispositions of the people who become public sector employees. Most of the work has been directed to *stated* dispositions and this paints a fairly consistent picture. A comprehensive survey of the literature in the USA found that public sector employees claim to have a greater concern for serving the community and helping others than people working in the private sector.[21] Similarly a UK study which surveyed public, private, and non-profit sector managers found considerable evidence of altruistic service motivations in the public sector and much more than in the private sector.[22] Out of sixteen possible goals that managers were asked to rank, the first for public service managers was to provide a service to the community. This did not appear in the top ten goals of private sector managers. Research on the health sector found similarly strong stated commitments to public service,[23] as has research on eldercare provision. One survey investigated the motivations of independent providers (profit and non-profit) of residential care and domiciliary care for elderly people.[24] The highest motivation was to meet the needs of elderly people (85 per cent), 87.5 per cent cited feeling a responsibility towards society as a whole or a particular section of society. Other motives included professional accomplishment (76 per cent), developing skills (67 per cent), satisfactory level of personal income (58 per cent), independence and autonomy (40 per cent), income and profit maximizing (8 per cent). In terms of priority the needs of the elderly (41 per cent) clearly trumped professional accomplishment (15 per cent) and income (14 per cent).

It would be unwise to take people's stated views at face value—some of these are necessary for a profession's self-image. But actual *behaviours* suggest these are not wholly cosmetic. Research investigating pricing patterns adopted by both for-profit and non-profit providers of residential care for people with mental health problems found both were not as high as they could or should have been to maximize profits. Not for-profit organizations had lower markups than for-profit companies.[25] A later study also found evidence of altruistic behaviour: case workers tasked with placing clients in jobs took on harder clients when their financial interests would have been better placed by accepting more easily employable ones.[26]

So the research suggests that public service workers not only claim to be altruistic but also are, though to a lesser extent. But these dispositions are only dispositions and they can come into conflict with other dispositions—such as wanting better pay or an easier workload. Thresholds, levels, and doses matter a lot. People are altruistic only up to a point, and they require other rewards (like recognition) to sustain their altruism. As we shall see, the same applies to monetary rewards. Beyond a certain level rewards can be counterproductive because they implicitly call into question that part of the employment contract which is a gift relationship. But, up to a point, pay undoubtedly matters both as direct motivator and as a signal of recognition. So although surveys show that public sector workers work harder and produce more output when they have a financial incentive to do so,[27] they also manipulate the quality and timing of what they do to maximize their rewards, with effects that the organization may neither intend nor want. One study, looking at medical practice in the USA, Canada, Denmark, and Scotland,[28] found that those paid on a fee for service basis provided more services than those paid by salary or capitation. A survey investigating the impact of financial and non-financial factors on teachers found that relative earnings compared to alternatives had a marked effect on teachers' decisions to leave teaching, on graduates' choice of occupation, and on ex-teachers' decisions to return to teaching.[29]

Performance-related pay, which has been introduced into public agencies in two-thirds of OECD countries, has turned out to be an unreliable tool. It can upset rather than motivate people, fuelling conflict and jealousy. Team-based PRP can overcome some of these limits, but depends very much on the boundaries of the team. Much also depends on transparency: the single best predictor of a person's satisfaction with their salary is their knowledge of how much others are paid in the organization: hence the conclusion that pay should be kept secret. The motivational power of money is relative, not absolute. There is also some evidence from the USA of relationships between pay differentials and poor product quality; baseball teams with wider pay differentials have lower winning percentages and gate receipts than more equal ones, though again these are all matters of degree.

What works best will depend on the characteristics of the work being done. Where the tasks involved in a job are broadly standardized and replicable, easily monitored or assessed, then pay related to performance, transparent performance management systems, and promotion based on evident merit are more likely to work. But where the tasks are more varied, involving subtle judgements and changing contexts, these tools are much less likely to work well. So in public services there is some role for pay as a motivator and a signaller—but it has to be used with great care; relativities have to not be too visible; and there needs to be the right balance between recognition for the individual and recognition for the team.

Another important boundary issue here is whether volunteers should be paid, for example, the 500,000 plus who volunteer in the British National

Health Service. The payment of volunteers has received some support from research so long as it does not cross a threshold which challenges the voluntary nature of the work. When pay becomes too formalized the research shows that there may be an increased amount of work but less effort. Carers do not provide care for strangers solely for the money—but few would have done it without any payment.[30] Many feel that being paid is more important than the level of pay; being paid the market rate matters less than having their unavoidable 'expenses' covered. Carers want to do what they feel clients need irrespective of payment. But the 'dose' matters—if the sacrifice involved is big then some compensation is needed; but if the compensation rises too high at some level the moral content of the sacrifice is diminished.

Other rewards can also help to motivate public servants. Some public organizations have made much of their more family-friendly employment policies—and used this to improve both recruitment and retention. In some surveys the fit with life seems to be quite an important motivator, linked to the localness of many public services which are embedded in a community. It's likely to be less motivating to provide a service to strangers than to people you know, although some public services have traditionally employed people in communities different from the ones they live in (police, for example).

What of control and audit? Autonomy clearly matters for job satisfaction: the self-employed tend to earn less than the employed but are consistently happier. More intensive audit and performance management send an implicit message that professionals and frontline workers aren't trusted: not surprisingly, they can corrode motivation. For people who have committed their lives to a skill or vocation, any moves which force them to 'go by the book', following formulaic procedures, will be resented. Too much control also diminishes any aspect of the implicit contract which is a gift. Teresa Amabile's work has shown that the intrinsic motivation of jobs influences creativity and innovation too.[31] Extensive research on excellent municipalities in the UK pointed in a similar direction. It found that key factors were not pay, working hours, or friendly colleagues but rather the opportunity for staff to influence their job plans and their chances for initiative, which in turn correlated with satisfaction at work. In principle there should be some optimal trade-offs between intrusive control, which provides a guarantee that a good job is being done, and motivated autonomy for the employee. Some styles of audit may be experienced as stretching in a good way, while others may be experienced as entirely negative.

The appropriate level of control will vary according to the context. For example, if a profession has become stuck in bad habits it may benefit from a period of more intensive control to rebuild habits of excellence. Chile's teaching profession is a good example. It is well paid and benefits from generous investment. Yet overall performance is poor, and much worse than it should be for a country of Chile's prosperity. There has been little if any performance management and no moves to replace inadequate teachers. Some inspection and audit would probably be beneficial; but once the service is again performing well, intrusive methods of audit and intervention may start to have counterproductive effects.

Finally there are the messages sent from within professions, and from outside, by stakeholders, politicians, and the media, which have a direct bearing on motivation. An example is social work, which was denigrated as a profession in the UK to such an extent that recruitment became extremely difficult, with barely one applicant for each vacancy. Relative pay also fell. By contrast, during the same period medical consultants were showered with esteem and financial reward.

A ten-year-long project at Harvard has looked at what makes work good, and how tasks can be better aligned with broader ethical and public interest considerations. Howard Gardner, who has led the project, describes good work as coming 'about when the principal stakeholders are in agreement about the importance of the work being carried out and the way in which it is currently being pursued'. Through asking people about the mission of their jobs, and whether they are embarrassed by their roles or proud of them, the project has found which sectors have the best alignments between values and actions, personal motivations and those of the field. The early work of the project focused on the media, biotechnology, and business and found particularly low levels of alignment in journalism, where people felt bad about their work, and often felt under pressure to compromise their values. Attitudes to work and its 'goodness' are clearly influenced by many factors, including social norms. But the available evidence suggests that it can move quite sharply. The ISSP survey of job values across the OECD found that the percentage saying that it was very important for their job to be useful to society remained flat for women between 1989 and 1997 (25.4 per cent and 24.3 per cent) and for men slumped from 22.1 per cent to 16.8 per cent. Yet from 1997 to 2005 the figure for women jumped to 31.6 per cent and to 25.7 per cent for men.[32] How much these shifts reflect deliberate attempts by governments to influence social norms remains unclear, but these data disprove any notion of a one-way trend towards greater selfishness.

So how should policy makers think about the people who ultimately have to implement their ideas? In the past policy has tended to oscillate between broad brush assumptions about public service workers' motivations: 'knights and knaves' in the words of Julian Le Grand; power maximization or humility; greed or generosity. This oversimplification has often led to mistakes. Sometimes the mistake has been to assume that public servants are more benignly motivated than they really are, which leads to poor performance or at worst to corruption. On the other hand assuming that they are venal can be equally problematic. The available empirical evidence—which is far from definitive—suggests that the best policies mobilize a combination of motivations rather than just one, and that they need to be calibrated (i.e. enough pay but not too much; enough audit, but not too much).

In the case of teaching, for example, a combination of measures was introduced in parallel in the UK in the 1990s and 2000s which roughly fit this schema. Recruitment put a significant emphasis on finding people with stronger dispositions to teach. The Teach First programme adapted from the USA to recruit top-level graduates into teaching with a strong ethos of service is a good example. Some changes (though not enough) were also introduced to change the nature of teachers' tasks to improve satisfaction. There was substantially higher base pay and a significant performance element. More audit and inspection was introduced, shifting in time to more risk-based audit and inspection. There were stronger professional messages about the importance of teaching, mass advertising on their unique qualities, and visible public appreciations (e.g. Oscars and honours, including knighthoods, for teachers—'Sirs for sirs').

Some of these measures were undermined by the mixed messages coming both from politicians (who still sometimes talked about teachers as if they were the conservative enemies of reform) and the teachers themselves (whose unions liked to threaten strike action, and showed little concern for children's welfare). But the package of measures did change the status of teaching and showed the sort of diverse strategy that's needed to shift motivations.

Influencing Cultures

The third perspective on behaviour change looks through the lens of culture. Many of the mistakes made in government are essentially mistakes of cultural understanding—just as most mistakes in international affairs come from misunderstanding how the world looks to the other side.

Fortunately a lot is known about the dynamics of cultures. The surprising continuities that can be found in institutional cultures were best theorized by the late anthropologist Mary Douglas. According to her theory, which has been widely applied within organizations and to the work of policy-making, there are four main ways of organizing human social relations which can be understood with the help of a simple two by two matrix shown in Table II.I. On one axis is what she called the 'grid'; the extent to which behaviours and rules are defined and differentiated, for example by public rules deciding who can do what according to their age, race, gender or qualifications. Examples of high grid would include a traditional corporation, or a traditional agrarian society. On the other axis is what she called 'group'—the extent to which people feel an identity with, and obligation to, a larger social group. The more people do with a group of other people, the more they experience testing trials or the more difficult the group is to get into, the higher this sense of group will be. These two dimensions come together to provide a simple matrix: high grid and high group is hierarchy; low grid and low group is individualism; high group and low grid is egalitarianism; low group and high grid is fatalism (for example, the culture amongst long-term prisoners).

This very simple model has turned out to be an extremely powerful tool for understanding social relations, and how people see the world. Within a hierarchical culture the world is seen as controllable so long as the right structures and rules are in place. Most governments tend towards hierarchy. It is the natural world view of civil servants, political leaders, and of most of the consultants working in and around big business and governments. To every problem there is a solution, so long as it is firmly enough implemented by a sufficiently powerful leader or elite team.

In an egalitarian world view the problems usually arise from too much hierarchy and inequality, and not enough bonding and solidarity. More

Table II.I. *Ways of organizing human social relations*

	Low group	High group
High grid	Fatalism	Hierarchy
Low grid	Individualism	Egalitarianism

discussion with more people is seen as an unmitigated good, and any measures which widen inequalities are to be resisted. In an individualistic world view the answer to problems is more freedom: let people determine their own choices and things will come right. Dissent is to be celebrated; rebels are heroes, and the world is made, and remade, by the imagination and energy of individuals. The fatalistic world view is most common amongst people with little power and little experience of power.

What is striking about these four world views is that they can be found at every level of human organization, from families and streets to global companies and the UN. They are constantly in tension with each other, but also need each other. Hierarchies need to re-energise themselves with the creativity of passionate individuals, and they need some egalitarianism to reinforce their sense of common purpose. Egalitarian cultures need some hierarchy to resolve disputes and make decisions. Individualist cultures need some hierarchy to enforce the rules, and some egalitarianism to encourage people to care for each other. All, perhaps, need some fatalism to get by and avoid a constant state of rebellion.

In their recent book *Clumsy Solutions for a Complex World*, which applies Mary Douglas's ideas to the world of public policy, Michael Thompson and Marco Verweij use the example of climate change to show how these different perspectives can shape a strategic argument.[33] For egalitarians climate change is a consequence of the profligacy of the rich north. A rapacious capitalist system has led to widening inequalities and the destruction of the shared environment. The flaws of big government and big business have wrecked the world. The solutions therefore lie in a return to smaller-scale institutions, closer to nature, free from gross inequalities, and in a simpler and more sustainable lifestyle.

From a hierarchical perspective climate change can only be solved with strong rules and strong enforcement to cut CO_2 emissions. That will mean binding treaties that go well beyond Kyoto; new organizations—perhaps a World Environment Organization—to enforce it, and equivalent laws and regulations within nations. Scientific knowledge, collected by the IPCC, has provided the world with an authoritative truth about the climate that now needs to be taken seriously.

From an individualist perspective, both of the other groups are scaremongers, using unproven science to impose unnecessary burdens on the world. Past experiences show that, given enough freedom, people and markets are sufficiently adaptive to avoid disaster. New technologies will arise from competition to cut emissions if that is what is needed, and in any case the solutions proposed by others are likely to be worse than the problem they are seeking to address.

All three stories are plausible; all are strongly held by different groups; and all are remarkably resistant to disproof by any new evidence. Similar patterns can be found around other issues. Take migration. For individualists immigration is a good thing; there should be as much mobility as possible. Given the freedom to do so, migrants will contribute to their new society and economy and overcome any barriers. For egalitarians too, migration can be a good thing, but needs to be supported by strong rules against discrimination. For hierarchists, on the other hand, migration is more likely to be seen as disruptive, and if it does occur needs to be accompanied by active social engineering to ensure that migrants are properly socialized and integrated.

Each cultural world view is good at ignoring the others, and people wanting to achieve change tend to adopt only one perspective. When it comes to policy this risks failure. As their book shows through a rich range of examples from school segregation to hydroelectric power, strategies that rest on just one culture tend to backfire. Too much command and control turns people into rebels. Too much individualism corrodes the social glue that makes societies hold together.

Michael Shapiro coined the term 'clumsy' to describe what he saw as the good properties of strategies that can accommodate multiple cultures. Ones that fail to do this include much of the repertoire of public policy— from cost–benefit analysis to neoclassical economics. Many of us learn in life that overly neat and rational solutions don't work in practice. Much of what works in human societies is inconsistent and apparently irrational. This is perhaps not a new insight. But it is rare to find it in any discussions of public policy.

Successes combine expert analysis and design; widespread deliberation and partnership between many players; markets and other arrangements that tap into individual motivations. The World Wide Web is an outstanding example which has fed off all of these, even if the Internet was originally imagined as part of a classic command and control system for the US military. The Kyoto protocol is an example of relying on just one—top–down bureaucratic regulation of activities, but without much realistic prospect of implementation let alone effective monitoring. Yet in practice combating climate change will depend on the interaction of many cultures—some regulations and penalties combined with market forces favouring energy efficiency and renewables, and egalitarian cultures driving people to adopt more sustainable lifestyles and to take responsibility for the future of the group, in this case humanity.

How should governments use these insights? They are warnings against using any one set of tools as the definitive answer to such complex things as human societies. But they are very powerful tools for thinking about any strategy to change the world. Bluntly, if it doesn't contain some room for all of the cultural frames then it is likely to fail. Perhaps this was what F. Scott Fitzgerald was hinting at when he commented that 'the test of a first-rate intelligence is the ability to hold two opposed ideas in the mind at the same time, and still retain the ability to function'.[34]

So, for example, public service reforms based only on incentives are as doomed to failure as strategies to cut antisocial behaviour that rely only on coercion. Strategies that don't turn enemies into fatalists will face powerful resistance. Wise strategies mobilize all of the cultures and avoid excessive linearity. The message is opposite to Occam's razor. Neat strategies which offer a simple model of causation can work for very simple tasks. But for more complex tasks, that include most of the big tasks facing governments, they don't work well.

We can also draw another conclusion: cultural literacy may be as valuable a skill as the more common skills in administration or economics. Many of the hardest issues of the twenty-first century concern culture and identity. These tangled knots of attachment and resentment can tear countries apart, and are rarely reducible to logic and reason. Yet even the most vicious cultural battleground can be brought to peace. A good example is France's abortion controversy. Like many other countries France was divided in the early 1970s by incompatible views, with one side seeing abortion as murder, disgusting, and an assault on fundamental rights to life, and the other seeing it as a fundamental right, and entirely private. The culturally skilful shapers of France's legislation succeeded, however, in finding a way to neutralize the argument, through a 1975 law which gave women in the first ten weeks of pregnancy a right to an abortion so long as they could certify that it was needed because of distress or an emergency sufficient to overcome the foetus's right to life. Only the woman could decide this—but, if she did, the abortion would be delayed for one week while she received counselling on the opportunities available if she changed her mind and kept the child.

This example is a case of deliberate and careful cultural compromise, which allowed both sides to see their values respected in the outcome.

The same is true of the many 'asymmetric' deals which have been done to maintain harmony in diverse societies—like permitting Sikhs not to wear motorcycle helmets, or allowing prayer rooms for Muslims in public offices, while also enforcing strict laws in relation to such issues as forced marriage. In each case the solutions do not derive deductively from a single set of principles. Instead they are constructed out of divergent views.

Winning (and Losing) Public Trust

A RECENT survey put it starkly: 'except for the Netherlands...from the 1970s until the mid-1990s all of the other advanced industrialized democracies recorded a decline in the level of trust their respective governments have enjoyed.'[1] The USA is typical: trust in government peaked in the 1960s, and since then, although it's bounced up repeatedly (in the mid-1980s and again in the early 2000s after 9/11), on each occasion it rose to a lower level, and then fell further than before.

Trust is both an effect of good strategy and, in many cases, a necessary condition for it. Ambitious goals depend on the public giving governments the benefit of the doubt. But the combination of external pressures and misguided politics can do as much to destroy trust as to build it. Politics is constantly buffeted by commentators, cynics, and sceptics working on short time horizons, whether in talk radio or newspapers, polling organizations or lobbies. In some countries the media coverage of politics gives little incentive to politicians to do the right thing, dramatizing minor issues and ignoring major ones, playing at accountability rather than doing it for real. How politics is shaped in turn shapes what governments can do. For example, international evidence shows that countries with adversarial party politics have high prison numbers in part because politicians feel the need to respond to media pressure for higher sentences, while countries with more consensual politics have found it easier to pursue strategies that address the causes of crime.[2]

The influence of public opinion, and the relative weakening of party structures, has raised the status and power of professionals schooled in marketing, polling, packaging, and spin, and promoted models of politics in which party members become largely irrelevant, with the great bulk of political resources spent on mass advertising or targeted messages, shaped by focus groups.[3] Spin is usually at odds with strategy, presentation with substance. The media's short attention span does little to aid public understanding and can penalize slow and steady achievements.[4] But public strategies are political things. They need to communicate and they need allies, and it is not easy to separate off their design and implementation from the political methods used by elected politicians to lock in support, win adherents, and influence swing voters.

Within every system there are dividing lines—some clear and some blurred—to distinguish the appropriate roles of politicians and officials. In Westminster systems officials are there to provide advice on how to implement policies, including advice on what is proper, what will protect the government's reputation as well as affordability and effectiveness. It is their responsibility to deliver and implement policy; explain how policy works (for example to parliamentary select committees); defend the policy—explaining why ministers thought it right in the circumstances; publicize the policy. The lines they should not cross include offering praise for the policy; criticizing the opposition; or offering advice on fundamental philosophical options (high v. low tax, authoritarian v. libertarian).

But even in these environments it's vital that officials are highly politically attuned, whatever their personal views, and it's particularly vital that they understand the dynamics of trust. As strategies are developed, the handling of their political dimension has to be treated as seriously as any other dimension: how to frame public arguments, how to neutralize, bypass, or buy off enemies; and how to build momentum (though for the responsible official these should all be means to the ends of achieving better results for the public rather than just the survival of a particular administration).[5]

Public strategies depend on trust to work; but governments can also pursue deliberate strategies to cultivate trust. This is territory where philosophy and principle intersect with craft skills—the practical tools for involving large numbers of people in complex decisions. Some of that craft is well grounded in experience. So, for example, many cities around the world have grappled with the problem of where to locate unpopular facilities like incinerators, or prisons, or facilities for the mentally ill. Few issues are as likely to mobilize a community as a proposal to locate a new facility—such as 'special needs residential facilities'—in a residential neighbourhood. Proposals of this kind are almost bound to make residents fearful that they will be more at risk of crime, or that their property prices will fall, and many will be easily persuaded that they are being forced to bear an unfair burden.

Yet experience around the world has shown that fairly simple measures can substantially mitigate these fears. One is information: publishing reports which show the location of existing and planned facilities usually reassures neighbourhoods that they are not bearing an unfair share (as New York has done). Another is involving the community early—before it appears that a decision has been made. A third is to hold small rather than big public meetings, so that there is a real chance for dialogue. A fourth is to avoid places with a high proportion of long-standing residents who, other things being equal, will be more resistant to change.

These lessons are neither particularly complicated nor difficult to implement. But they are part of a growing body of knowledge about how governments can best secure and sustain their legitimacy, often by making what John Milton called the 'mists and intricacies of state' more transparent.[6] I suggested earlier that legitimacy is the goal that lies behind every other policy and strategy. Yet it is surprising how often governments make elementary mistakes that unnecessarily alienate the public, and I've seen at first hand some striking failures. Tony Blair's administration promised greatly to increase investment in public services, and then to deliver better services and better outcomes, such as lower crime and better education results. Yet when he departed from office in 2007 after a decade as Prime Minister he left behind a remarkable and paradoxical position. Many of the targets the government had set itself had been achieved. Waiting lists, and times, were much shorter. Exam results had sharply improved. Crime was down. The number of frontline public servants was well up. When asked about standards of service locally most of the public agreed that things had got better and they were generally satisfied with what they received from local schools, hospitals, and police forces. But few believed the government's claims to have achieved its targets and few believed that standards in the whole system had improved. Most assumed that their own direct experiences were atypical.

There were some obvious reasons for this mismatch. Some were external to government, like the influence of histrionic media which amplified every public service failure and ignored most successes. But some were under its control, in particular a style of reform that alienated professionals and public servants, and appeared sceptical of their motivations and their competence.

So what's happened to trust? Has it gone for good? And is it amenable to influence? It's easy to romanticize the past: there never was a golden age of pure trust. In 1944 at the height of the Second World War the British public were polled by Gallup and only a third of them believed that their political leaders were motivated by the good of the nation (a third thought they were serving their party and a third that they were acting for themselves). But there are some secular trends which suggest that trust may be more fragile. The psychoanalyst Eric Eriksson described 'basic trust' as something that is learned early, when children put trust in a carer's hands and, through this, learn to trust others and themselves.[7] In some societies this basic trust has declined over time—levels of interpersonal trust in the UK fell from over 50 per cent in the 1950s to under 30 per cent in the 2000s. Trust in major institutions has also fallen over thirty years and in many countries trust in elected politicians has fallen well behind trust in other institutions—from NGOs to armed forces (see Fig. 12.1). Another common pattern is a divergence between trust in institutions, which has fallen, and trust in the frontline workers of public service, teachers, police, and doctors, which has remained high. This divergence between institutional distrust and personal trust has prompted many governments to reshape themselves so that citizens' contacts with the state are more personal, 'one to one': through family doctors, or personal advisers in welfare offices, or named police officers responsible for a neighbourhood, rather than impersonal bureaucracies.

In some parts of the world, however, even the front line of the state is untrusted. When a 2007 Gallup poll in eighty-six countries asked whether it was likely that a neighbour, the police, or a stranger would return a lost wallet or valuables, 96 per cent of Norwegians and 93 per cent of New Zealanders trusted the police, and 94 per cent trusted neighbours in

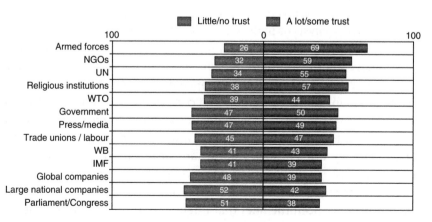

Figure 12.1.   Trust in institutions (%).

Source: Gallup, Environics International, 2002; 36,000 respondents from 47 countries.

both countries. But in most countries people trusted their neighbours more than the police (in Jamaica and Azerbaijan only a third had confidence that the police would do the right thing) and in some people trusted neither: just 24 per cent trust their neighbours in Cambodia and Laos. The overall picture is of people who are reluctant to trust, and probably with good reason.

In some countries interpersonal trust has risen—for example, Denmark and Sweden, and some institutions have managed to win back trust that they had lost. The reasons are complex, and at odds with conventional wisdom.[8] Distrust is often attributed to individualism, or disengagement from communities, yet levels of volunteering have not fallen. It's sometimes attributed to generational change. But cohort studies have shown that young people's trust and engagement with politics increases as they get older, and matches the levels of previous generations'. It's true that young people are less likely to join political parties. But overall the levels of civic activism—how many people have taken part in a demonstration, a consumer boycott, or a petition—are much higher than they were in the supposedly more activist 1960s.

An alternative explanation for distrust is that public expectations are too high and therefore bound to be disappointed. But survey data shows that people are realistic about government's ability to deliver and that differences in trust are not linked to differences in expectations about the ability of government to deliver. Nor do higher levels of education explain distrust—perhaps because better informed electorates are less easily duped. In fact higher levels of education are associated with higher levels of political trust, not lower. And over time political trust has fallen faster amongst the least educated rather than most educated groups.

These are good reasons to be cautious of sweeping generalizations. The more detailed analysis of nations and institutions shows a more interesting, and positive, picture. Some nations have managed to raise levels of trust, as have some institutions. Broadly speaking the successful ones have performed well in their core tasks. Competence matters, particularly when it comes to managing the economy. But competence isn't enough. It's also vital to be seen as honest and working in the public interest, or for moral causes, rather than for vested or private interests. The more trusted institutions have admitted mistakes quickly and dealt with them (when things go wrong, trust is rebuilt more by showing how the same mistake will not be repeated rather than paying restitution). And often the most trusted institutions have been the ones that interact most often with the public, from police forces that regularly communicate with the public to parliaments that allow the public to directly petition for issues to be debated.

These common patterns found amongst high trust institutions are mirrored by the common patterns of trust decay. Governments lose trust when they are seen as out of touch; when they go stale, recycling old rhetoric and ideas; and when they become so pragmatic that they appear to have no principles left. Political party funding has been a particularly common enemy of trust in the Western world: the scandals associated with dubious donations from rich individuals or corporations have stained many reputations, and in most countries the political class has underestimated how much needs to be done stave off crises. Corruption too is utterly corrosive of trust,[9] as is incompetence during crises, particularly crises of economics or defence. During these periods it's vital to be in control and to be seen to be in control, and governments need to follow principles almost opposite to the inclusiveness prescribed above when events are moving very fast. Trust is likely to depend on decisive and commanding action, and highly centralized communication that stops conflicting messages coming out from the different parts of government.

Whether promises are seen to be kept or broken also influences trust. A simple principle that was briefly attempted in the UK was that announcements of major new services should always wait until at least 50 per cent of the population could receive them: 'under-promise and over-deliver' is a good principle, even if it's one that ministers in a hurry find very hard to abide by. This is where the style of politics matters too. Governments need self-restraint if they are to preserve trust: fewer announcements, fewer claims, avoiding the temptation to cover up, and sticking to a tone of modesty.

The evidence on public disconnection has prompted many governments to work harder at staying in touch. In the words of one minister, they have to retain the mentality of 'insurgents rather than incumbents', outsiders who happen to be in power rather than insiders who assume their right to rule. The same urge to strengthen their relationship with the public has also encouraged governments to innovate new approaches to governance. These include stricter rules on behaviour and codes of conduct.[10] Others have tried to widen the channels of communication to decision makers. In the US city of Phoenix, which is often seen as a model of good management, tight control over spending is combined with active input from hundreds of volunteers who sit on committees to keep leaders informed on the public mood.[11] Participatory budgeting, pioneered in Brazil, involves the public directly in decisions about spending. Citizen juries which have been used in many countries, give a representative sample of the public the chance to engage in issues in-depth, while deliberative polls do the same on a larger scale, sometimes with the involvement of the mass media.[12] Striking recent examples include British Columbia's citizens assemblies which recruited 160 random members of the public to advise on electoral reform, and AmericaSpeaks engagement of 5,000 New Yorkers to deliberate on what should replace the Twin Towers in Manhattan. Most of these methods have left the public with a sounder understanding of the issues and choices, and a more adult relationship between governors and governed, which is honest about the limits of power and knowledge and open about the possibilities.

But their methods can be costly and don't guarantee trust, not least because they can't easily influence the people who don't take part. Mismanaged consultations can leave people more hostile and distrustful (especially if they're cosmetic and the decisions have already been taken, or if they're not honest about when elected politicians will still ultimately decide). Some engagement methods can raise expectations faster than they can meet them. Others simply don't animate people enough. Chicago's energetic efforts to engage the public on community policing and public education in the late 1990s, for example, only attracted around 5,000–6,000 city residents to meetings out of a population of several million. Pôrto Alegre in Brazil engaged a much larger proportion of the public in its participatory budget-setting (rising to over 30,000 each year from a city of about a million, with a disproportionate involvement of women and the poor). But in 2004 the Workers' Party (PT), which had led the initiative, was voted out of office.

The methods that have worked best have complemented representative democracy rather than offering an alternative to it. This is wise, since only a small minority are willing to commit significant time, except on the rare occasions when fundamental interests are threatened. A common pattern is that only about 1 per cent of any population become very active (for example, this is the ratio of viewing to uploading videos onto YouTube, or of active members of political parties to voters).[13] Their engagement can greatly improve the quality of policy-making: but it can't substitute for mass communication and mass voting. Some of the most successful experiments have either been very visibly advisory—letting elected politicians explain why they do or don't accept the advice that's given—or have focused on issues that are on the margins of party politics. In fields such as nanotechnology or genetically modified crops such inclusive processes have taken the sting out of acute controversies. So too have long-term commissions that take controversial issues out of politics (albeit with great difficulty in competitive party systems where no party has much interest in denying its freedom to act or oppose). These are easier to pull off in consensual political cultures. The Netherlands, for example, applied the consensus-building lessons learned from religious conflicts to industrial relations, and later to policy development. In one author's words, the growing confidence the elite gained from using these models became 'a self-reproducing path...involving substantial increasing returns to learning'.[14]

Wider engagement doesn't always make it easier to get to the right decision. The risk of wider conversations is that they may mobilize opposition. It was, for example, an irony of the European Constitution that was formulated in the early 2000s that the more it was debated the more it catalysed opposition, often from contradictory viewpoints. Where there are profoundly opposed underlying values, or conflicting interests that cannot be easily squared, more open dialogue can simply provide opponents of change with more time to organise and mobilize. In other cases the public may simply want government to decide: when Arnold Schwarzenegger held a mid-term poll in California on a clutch of disparate policy proposals, turnout was low and all of them were rejected.

This is where the craft of politics overlaps with the craft skills needed by modern officials. Good politicians learn early on how to judge the critical wants and fears of the people they are trying to influence or represent. They learn about the words that matter most to them and the interests that lie behind them. And so they learn how to craft arguments to pre-empt as many likely objections as possible; they think in terms of winners and losers; and they demonstrate the costs of inaction as well as the benefits of action. So, for example, a strategy to introduce national road pricing can justify itself as:

- a responsible step to prevent inevitable congestion that is in no one's interests;
- a fair move to spread the costs of mobility more evenly across the population;
- an act of moral responsibility to help mitigate the trends towards climate change; and
- a policy of comparative advantage—helping the nation to get ahead in an important new set of technologies.

The importance of these stories, and how they reach the public, hardly needs spelling out to modern public servants. In Europe since 1970, the percentage of citizens of democracies who read a newspaper every day has grown by 67 per cent and the percentage of people who watch television news daily has increased almost 50 per cent. This attentiveness to the media is sometimes blamed for mistrust but the story isn't so simple. Even controlling for education, European citizens who take an interest in the news know more about politics, as well as everyday social and health matters, than those who do not. People attentive to news are no less (but also no more) trusting and confident in government than the inattentive.[15] Individual news outlets may, and often do, distort their views of the world around them, but as a whole media do not.

In societies rich with information, communication has become one of the essential skills of public officials and public strategy. Messages have always played a decisive role in the biggest strategic successes. Clement Attlee was once asked what Winston Churchill had done to win the war (Attlee had been his deputy Prime Minister during the Second World War and became Prime Minister after it). His answer was: 'talk about it'. This is sometimes interpreted as a gentle put-down. But his ability to talk and persuade his fellow Britons to fight on despite the disasters of 1940 was critical at a time when a more rational leader might have felt that the war was unwinnable and that the national interest lay in negotiation.

Yet communication is rarely easy for officials who are used to operating out of the limelight and few are skilled in its arts. We know that the public tend to trust public institutions more when they feel well informed about what they do, yet many do little if any active communication. We also know that clever communication helps to create a sense of momentum or inevitability and that it can win over the opinion formers with one set of arguments while providing a more demotic version for conversations in the cafe, pub, or kitchen. But this requires very careful work to provide the decisive frame through which events and actions will be interpreted, a 'word picture' that sticks in people's minds. So, for example, the politics of any review of energy policy depends on which frame is dominant. If the dominant frame is affordability—bringing down excessively high prices— one set of policies will tend to win out; if it is security of supply (becoming less dependent on unstable areas of the world), the results will be very different, and likewise if the primary frame is ecological (how to shift to renewables and low carbon solutions). These frames become powerful through the to and fro of political argument, and they work if they tap into existing structures of feeling and thought. Thorough analysis of the numbers and technological options is of little use if the wrong frame has become fixed in the public mind.

Active trust-building has become part of the day to day work of government, at all levels. It is no longer enough to rely on the formal political channels of political parties, occasional elections, and parliaments to sustain public trust and legitimacy. Some conclude that declining trust is just in the nature of things. But there are many things which governments can do to earn and keep trust, and some public agencies have made the transition from low to high trust by the right combination of competence, integrity, and communication. There is a rapidly growing literature on the dynamics of trust, with important lessons for public agencies, and how they can work with the grain of human dispositions to reciprocity and cooperation.[16] Perhaps its most important message is that being strategic about trust means much more than getting the right words or images into the newspapers: it means seeing government as a relationship, a dialogue not a monologue, and being willing to earn trust not just once but again and again.

13

Metrics: Measuring Social and Public Value

ALL public strategies aim to turn the public's hard-earned money and freedoms into something more valuable: for example, security, better health, or more education. Over the last decade much work has gone into trying to make sense of this value,[1] with metrics and targets that have shifted attention onto outcomes rather than outputs or activities. Until the 1990s international accounting conventions assumed that public sector productivity never improved. Yet in a period of greater public pressure for results, and value for money, that position became untenable, and considerable effort has gone into working out not just what public interventions cost but also what value they create.

Better metrics do not of themselves deliver better outcomes. You can't fatten a pig by weighing it. But if you don't have some means of weighing it you may find yourself unable to persuade others that it's as fat as you believe. Many methods try to put a price on value. The idea that the value to be gained from a new training programme can be directly compared with the value from a health screening programme or water conservation is immediately appealing to busy bureaucrats and ministers. The methods which try to monetize public value usually draw either on what people say they would pay for a service or outcome ('stated preference methods') or on the choices people have made in related fields ('revealed preference'). There are also methods which try to adjust the cost of public services with reference to quality—for example comparing school exam results, or the success of operations. Other new methods compare public policy actions by estimating the extra income people would need to achieve an equivalent gain in life satisfaction. One imaginative study of a regeneration scheme, for example, showed that modest investments in home safety which cost about 3 per cent as much as home repairs generated four times as much value in terms of life satisfaction.[2] Analyses of this kind are at the very least instructive, particularly when they point to surprising results.

But paying too much attention to monetary equivalence can lead to bad decisions. The different methods used to assess value generate wildly different numbers, and they often ignore what people turn out to value most. Revealed preference and stated preference methods are notoriously unreliable, and in the example above the urban regeneration project was found to have achieved an improvement equivalent to £19,000 per person of working age, yet 'willingness to pay' studies came up with a figure of only £230 per year.[3] As I will argue all methods of this kind are useful only to the extent that they help inform the negotiations between providers of services and their users, or between public agencies and the citizens who pay for them.

These conversations and negotiations are bound to involve qualities as well as quantities, values as well as value. As many commentators have pointed out, there is an analogy with the electromagnetic spectrum. Although radiation can take many forms, only a narrow range of frequencies are visible to the naked eye in the form of light. Similarly money focuses attention on only some of the features of the world around us and obscures others. Since many of the features it obscures matter a great deal to the voting public, it's not surprising that the simpler attempts to monetize public value have failed.

More sophisticated thinking about value tries to mitigate this common optical distortion by analysing what really matters to the public. In this chapter I set out an approach to value that tries to make the most of useful metrics without falling prey to the many pitfalls.

I first became interested in the idea of public value when I read a remarkable book called *Relevance Lost*.[4] A history of management accounting is not likely to be a gripping read. But this book tells in a lively way the story of how over two centuries successive generations of business leaders, technicians, and management accountants devised new ways to track value in everything from railways and steel to aerospace and software. It reveals that value is rarely easy to grasp and is never an objective fact. The economists' accounts of managers equating marginal costs and marginal returns turn out to be fanciful. Instead, even within firms, value is constantly being re-estimated and re-allocated in the light of changing priorities and changing production technologies.

It seemed likely that the same would be true in the public sector where the dimensions of value are even more complex than in the world of business, for which profit and loss provide at least a rough and ready measure of success.

There are many methods for trying to make sense of value in the public sector and providing a bridge between the complex patterns of public demands and needs, as expressed through political and other processes, and the changing production systems that keep people healthy, educated, or safe. Cost–benefit analysis has been the most widely used, mainly in transport (where in recent years it has been integrated with environmental appraisals) and for big projects (where they are notorious for underestimating costs).[5] There are also the many theories and applications of public sector welfare economics; the burgeoning field of environmental economics which has spawned methods for measuring everything from wetlands to emissions; and the lively thinking that has surrounded social accounting over the last thirty years. Social accounting matrices and satellite accounts supplement GDP with additional measures of activity and value. QALYS and DALYs (quality and disability adjusted life years) have become a common measure for judging health policies and clinical interventions. In education 'value added' measures assess how much individual schools 'add' to the quality of pupils they take in—some schools might achieve very good exam results simply because of the quality of their intake. Social Impact Assessment methods have been in use since the 1960s, trying to capture all the dimensions of value that are produced by a new policy or programme. All estimate numbers to guide the hunches and assumptions of politicians and officials who need to decide whether a new road, a hospital, or protecting an endangered species will add or destroy value for the public they serve.[6]

The more ambitious methods try to be inclusive and exhaustive, capturing every direct and indirect impact of an intervention. In principle they can justify actions now that will save money in the future, showing how helping ex-offenders into work, investing in young children, or promoting health will lead in the long run to higher tax revenues or lower prison bills. Detailed methods have been in use for several decades to estimate the direct costs of an action (e.g. a drug treatment programme), the probability of it working, and the likely impact on future crime rates, hospital admissions, or welfare payments. Analysis of this kind can be very powerful. In the USA, for example, researchers identified what they called 'million dollar blocks' where the costs associated with criminals topped the million dollar mark: in principle, good preventive actions targeted at the people living in these blocks might save far more than they cost if they diverted some people from a life of crime. A recent study in the UK found that using a mix of drug treatment, surveillance and behavioural interventions instead of prison could deliver cost savings per offender of as much as £88,000 for the taxpayer only and up to £200,000 if savings to victims were included.[7]

These analyses can be made highly sophisticated. They can, for example, be adapted to reflect income distribution, on the principle that an extra dollar, or an extra unit of utility, is worth more to a poor person than a rich one (since 2003 the UK Government's Green Book has required all appraisals to include distributional effects).

But all measurements of complex effects are inherently hard. The benefits tend to become more dispersed over time, affecting ever more agencies in ever more uncertain ways. Social science isn't robust enough to make any hard predictions about what causes will lead to what effects—there are usually far too many variables involved. Meanwhile standard cost–benefit models apply discount rates to these gains, usually based on prevailing commercial interest rates, which renders a benefit in a generation's time much less valuable. An even more fundamental problem is that these analytic methods presume that everyone agrees on what counts as valuable. But in many of the most important fields for government action— like childcare, crime prevention, or schooling—the public are divided over values as well as value. For most people, for example, there is an intrinsic virtue in punishing criminals regardless of the costs and benefits of alternatives to prison. This is why the economic models for thinking about public goods and externalities, though informative, are often inadequate to the real choices faced by policy makers and out of sync with public attitudes and politics.

Developing a Model of Public Value

At the beginning of the 2000s I commissioned a programme of work, within the Cabinet Office Strategy Unit,[8] to flesh out the idea of public value.[9] We started with a few simple principles.[10] One was that something should only be considered valuable if citizens—either individually or collectively—are willing to give something up in return for it. Sacrifices can be monetary (i.e. paying taxes or charges); they can involve granting coercive powers to the state (e.g. in return for security), disclosing private information (e.g. in return for more personalized services), giving time (e.g. as a school governor) or other personal resources (e.g. giving blood). Some idea of 'opportunity cost' is essential for public value: if it is claimed that citizens would like government to produce something, but they are not willing to give anything up in return, then it is doubtful that the activity really is seen as valuable.[11]

Another principle was that the different dimensions of value should not automatically be treated as commensurable. Economics has traditionally treated all values in this way: anything can be traded off against anything else, and turned into a monetary value. But many of the currencies governments deal with are not like this. Laws ensure that such things as votes, body parts, and freedoms can't be sold, and the public turn out to have very clear views about which kinds of exchange or trade-off are legitimate and which ones aren't. This is one reason why the many attempts to coerce different types of value into single numbers (as has happened with standard economic measures, as well as many environmental measures, CBA, and some methods used for estimating Social Returns on Investment) have often destroyed relevant information rather than helping decision makers. Useful methods of valuation need to cope with varied types of value, with differing degrees of certainty.

A more challenging principle is that any measures of value should be comprehensible and plausible to the public. It's not enough for a measure to make sense to specialists. If it doesn't help to educate the public about choices, and to enrich the democratic process, then it's likely at some point to be rendered irrelevant by raw politics.

Many things that governments do are valuable to the public, but they roughly fit into three main categories. The first is the value provided by services—like well-maintained roads, or hospitals. Services can be relatively easy to analyse in terms of value. In some cases there are private sector benchmarks, and in others people can be asked how much they would be willing to pay for different levels of service—for example, evening opening of a library, or retaining a very local post office. The second category of value is outcomes—like lower crime, or security from invasion. Again, through democratic argument, or through surveys, people can place a rough value on these. One of the outcomes they often value is equity. In the UK 79 per cent of people (a figure that hardly varies across social groups) agree with the statement 'public services should be targeted at those with greatest need', suggesting that they are not interested only in their own experience.[12] Whether people use privately funded alternatives to public provision has surprisingly little impact on their propensity to support higher state spending (there is a slight decrease in support for state spending on health and transport, but none in education),[13] and 66 per cent of people refer to their relationship with public services as being that of citizens or members of the public compared to only 30 per cent who think of themselves as customers or users.[14]

A third category of value is trust in its widest sense, which includes whether the work of government is seen as just and fair. A recent study in Michigan, for example, found a significant link between perceptions of procedural justice in government services, as distinct from outcomes, and trust in politicians.[15] There are many examples of reforms which apparently improved efficiency but ruptured this relationship and therefore damaged the legitimacy of government.[16]

Social Value: Effective Demand and Effective Supply

Value is never an objective fact. It arises from the interplay of supply and demand, and through processes of negotiation and argument. In consumer markets value is determined by the shifting decisions of individual consumers and how these interact with the supply of goods and services. In the public sector it's refracted through political argument and the interplay of what I call 'effective demand' and 'effective supply' (see Fig. 13.1). Effective demand means that someone is willing to pay for a service, an outcome, or a change in trust. That someone may be a public agency, or it may be individual citizens. Effective supply means that there is a capacity to provide that service, outcome, or trust: a public agency, NGO, or business.

In some fields there are mature links between supply and demand: for example public willingness to pay through taxes for policing or primary

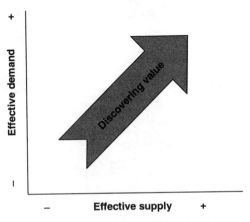

Figure 13.1.   Social value in terms of effective supply and demand

schools connects to government's ability to supply in familiar ways. In other fields the links are missing. There may be available supply but insufficient demand—because the public or politicians don't see the need as sufficiently pressing (in some countries drug treatment or sex education would fall into this category). In other cases there may be demand but inadequate supply at a reasonable cost (for example of methods for cities to cut carbon emissions).

Both sides of the equation may be complex or fragmented. In many areas of social policy demand for the results that come from more holistic approaches is split across many different public agencies, from welfare to prisons. Equally the supply may be similarly fragmented, depending on the contribution of many different agencies, for example providing therapy, alcohol treatment, skills, and housing.

In these cases value has to be discovered, and a critical role will be played by a 'social market maker' who brings together supply and demand (see Fig. 13.2). This could be a local council or a national government (and in rare cases a foundation). To do this well they need to help both sides of the market clarify what they want and what they can provide. On the demand side public agencies need to work out what they are willing to pay for lower crime in five years' time or lower welfare payments. On the

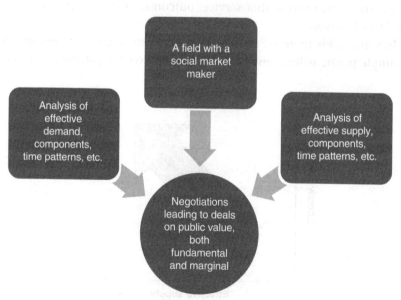

Figure 13.2. Creating deals on public value

supply side, analysis needs to show what can plausibly be expected from different mixes of actions. For this some of the existing Social Impact Assessment or Social Return on Investment methods can be used. Then a series of negotiations can take place to commission activities and services, with the 'social market maker' working to ensure that no agencies try to freeride on others. These processes are likely to work best when they can be disaggregated as well as aggregated, that is, when commissioning agencies can directly specify what they want from provider agencies.

Horizons in Time

To be strategic is to take the future seriously, and to resist the myopia that particularly affects institutions facing intense pressures to be accountable for present actions. Many institutions try to formalize their relationship to the future through devices to compare future values with present ones. Governments use discount rates to judge when to make investments, since a sum of money in five years' time is less useful, and less certain, than an equivalent sum of money now. Typically annual discount rates are around 5 per cent. These try to reflect both time preferences and, in the more sophisticated versions, to take account of the fact that extra income in the future will be worth less than income today because future populations will be richer (the UK Treasury currently applies a 1.5 per cent rate to reflect time preferences and 2 per cent to reflect these income effects).

A strict application of discount rates from the private sector radically reduces the attraction of investments in the future. A 5 per cent discount rate values $100 after thirty years at $35.85 today, and after fifty years at $7.69. Even the lower discount rates sometimes applied to health (like the 3 per cent usually applied to QALYs in the USA) still render years saved in the distant future much less valuable than years saved now. But these 'exponential' discount rates are at odds with how people think and act. Much of our behaviour reflects an implicit 'hyperbolic' discount rate that starts off high but declines, putting a higher value on distant outcomes than exponential rates. In our own lives we generally regret past decisions that applied a high discount rate to future gains, and there is some evidence that people apply different 'mental accounts' to their choices (for example with a different way of accounting for investment in their own education, housing, pensions, or their own children). Most governments also apply quite different discount rates to different phenomena, which is why they are willing to invest in future defence, education, or infrastructures. Their behaviour is closer to that of a guardian or steward who is charged with sustaining or growing capital, rather than the strictly rational consumers of economic theory who always value present consumption more than future consumption.

Environmental economics has been riven by arguments over the appropriate discount rate to apply to issues like climate change. Nicholas Stern, author of an influential UK government review, argued that the 'inherent discounting' of economists such as William Nordhaus (who advocated a 3 per cent discount rate as a measure of future uncertainty in the costs and benefits of action on climate change) was ethically questionable because it devalued the future. His analysis applied a zero pure time preference and compared benefits today and in the future by comparing percentages of income (rather than cash), weighting income for the poor more than the rich, and for today's citizens more than future ones since, whereas current average global income is around $7,000, his forecasts projected average world income in 2100 at around $100,000.[17] But in all of these analyses economics has clearly reached its limits. It cannot explain some basic contradictions like the very wide gap between equity returns and returns for bonds (which calls into question the idea of a single market discount rate). And it cannot explain much of what's been observed in human behaviour in relation to the future.

Sociology may offer additional insights. If we dig deeper we find that attitudes to time generally reflect the intensity of social bonds and commitments. Very strong commitments eliminate the difference between the present and the future, even though there is still the same uncertainty as in commercial markets. Parents may commit all to their children's future; aristocratic landlords commit to passing on richer estates than they inherit; and for a committed NGO or social movement it is simply inappropriate to devalue future rewards—the cause is everything. Similarly where fundamental rights are involved it is inappropriate to devalue the future. Assessments of QALYs in a rights-based healthcare system might be expected to treat a year of life in 2050 as equal in value to an extra year of life in 2020: if they didn't they would build in a profound bias in favour of the old and against the young. The application of standard discount rates turns out to reflect the values of highly individualized market economies and sectors. It is, in fact, quite culturally specific.

These apparently arcane issues are very relevant to questions as diverse as climate change and childcare, both of which involve profound moral commitments. They suggest that assessments of social or public value need to take account explicitly of how public attitudes and morality affect time preferences. These attitudes are likely to show a very different view of time in those parts of the public realm which are most like private consumption (for example, air travel) as opposed to those which are touched with moral obligations of stewardship or mutuality.[18]

Public Value in the Built Environment

The built environment of cities provides an example of how these ideas can be applied. Buildings are self-evidently things of value, and they can last for a very long time, far beyond the horizon of standard discount rates. They also provide a range of different kinds of value, to owners, users, residents, and passers-by.

There are many dozens of methods already in use to measure aspects of value in the built environment.[19] Some of these are relevant to thinking about public value in any field while others are very specific. Some are designed to guide investors, including income capitalization methods as well as methods focused on profits, residuals, and replacement costs; methods using multiple regressions and stepwise regressions; methods using artificial neural networks and 'hedonic' price models (which attempt to define the various characteristics of a product or service); spatial analysis methods; fuzzy logic methods; and, for the eager, 'auto-regressive inte-grated moving averages methods' and 'triple bottom line property appraisal methods'. The different methods in use serve different interests—the devel-opers concerned with asset values and income streams, other landlords and the public who may benefit from new parks or canals, municipalities which may benefit from growing tax revenues, and the wider public who may benefit from lower crime. Each also has different strengths and weaknesses: hedonic methods, for example, ignore the value of buildings for which there is no market; multi-criteria analyses provide little help in allocating resources; and contingent choice methods reduce the value of the poor.

What none of these achieves is a method for handling the wide range of *different* types of value which are involved in urban developments, including not only the reasonably measurable world of asset values, rental streams, and tax revenue streams, but also less tangible things like the value of good design or aesthetics, and the impact of design choices on crime, health, and the environment. There is strong evidence that the urban environment affects health both directly and indirectly (e.g. through availability of leisure time); it also affects people's feelings of safety as well as objective levels of crime. Any major urban development

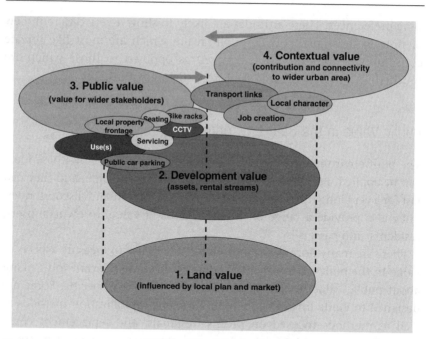

Figure 13.3.   Analysing the value in the built environment

can not only create private and public value but also damage value, whether through shutting off lines of sight, weakening the cohesion of communities, or cutting fitness levels if walking and cycling routes are replaced with roads for cars.

This field is a good one for thinking about value in that there are many tools in use around the world for capturing what's sometimes called 'planning gain', the surplus which results from conferring planning consent on a developer. This means that there are often very overt negotiations trading off private values against public values, for example, requiring a developer to provide affordable housing or childcare facilities. Effective supply and effective demand come together in negotiations of this kind.

How they come together will depend on the underlying structure of value, which varies greatly in different fields. In the case of the built environment (see Fig. 13.3) value has a roughly four-level structure:

- **The underlying value of land**—usually seen as a common good (since it is scarce, and socially defined, by planning decisions which can at a stroke increase land values a thousand-fold, for example when agricultural land is redesignated for office development). Much of the theoretical work on development over the last century has focused on how to capture economic rents associated with land.

- **The market value of buildings**—including rental streams, property values, as well as tax revenues—in proposed developments.
- **The other kinds of value** that can be created or destroyed—including indirect effects on other property values but also various types of public value, including crime reductions, design and aesthetics, health effects (e.g. fitness), merit goods, environmental goods, etc.
- The relationship between a development and **the broader context** for the city—its connectivity, contribution to economic growth potential, etc.

Good planning processes ensure that economic rent on land is not captured by developers but directed to public good: in other words the surplus on level 1 is used to subsidise value at level 3. Local governments try to measure and capture this value through betterment levies, development land taxes and planning gain supplements (and a clutch of other potential devices), in order to finance public services or environmental improvements.

To put numbers on value there is a limited range of methods to use. As we've seen, some ask people how much they would pay for a new service or a different kind of building. 'Stated Preference' methods estimate what non-users might value, whether through *'altruistic use'* (knowing someone else might like it); *'option use'* (having the opportunity to do something if you want); *'bequest use'* (leaving something for the future), and *'existence use'* (satisfaction that things exist even if you don't enjoy them personally). All methods of this kind are notoriously prone to distortions and have to be 'triangulated' with other methods. The most important of these look at real choices that people have made. These 'revealed preferences' are more reliable but gathering relevant data about how people respond to real choices is bound to be hard. 'Travel Cost Method' is one example which looks at the time and travel cost expenses that people incur to visit a site as a proxy for their valuation of that site. Because travel and time costs increase with distance it's possible to construct a 'marginal willingness to pay' curve for a particular site. Then there are methods which enable people to change their views through discussion, such as 'Planning for Real' exercises which enable the public to generate alternative options rather than being solely ex-post methods. In the future many more of these may be correlated with evidence on life satisfaction, using before and after surveys to find out what exactly makes people happy.

These many methods provide insights into structures of value, and in all fields of public activity there are distinctive structures of value too. For example, in education some value accrues directly to the learner (in the form of future earnings), while some accrues to the family or the wider community. Several decades of research has tried to distinguish individual and social returns from different types of education. Vocational education has a different structure to generic skills. Some skills may be not only specific to an industry, but also to a location (e.g. particular language skills). A programme providing intensive support to a chaotic drug user will have a more complicated structure of value, creating some value for the individual (both financial and in terms of well-being) as well as value for a wide range of public agencies (from hospitals whose emergency services will be less used to police, prisons, and welfare agencies). To all of these can be added the complexities which come from data on life satisfaction, which tell us that it's not just absolute gains that matter, but also changed relative position. In other words, even if our position improves, if others around us improve more we may end up less happy. The general point here is that value is not one-dimensional, commensurate, quantifiable, and comparable. Instead its specific character and context needs to be understood.

Any model of public or social value becomes useful only if it can inform processes for making decisions that bring effective supply and effective demand together. In the case of the physical environment this will include developers proposing plans through to approval, building, and subsequent monitoring. In other fields the critical stages may include budget bids and planning, and subsequent allocations by finance ministries and cabinets. Using these methods earlier and upstream in decision-making helps to ensure that a range of options can be assessed rather than only one. Negotiations can then consider a rich range of options on the margins (e.g. everything from building heights to tenure mix to construction of childcare centres, street architecture, and bicycle racks) as well as more basic trade-offs (for example between the interests of the elderly and families with children, or between cars and the environment).

Lessons for Social and Public Value

These examples bring out some important general lessons. First, measures of value are only useful to the extent that they support negotiations and arguments about what needs to be done. They are useful if they bring choices and trade-offs to the surface, useless if they disguise them. Second, more creative ways of handling value generally depend on a guardian or social market maker who takes responsibility for bringing demand and supply together. In a democracy, that has to involve democratically elected politicians whose constitutional role it is to distil and represent public preferences, even if sometimes they also have to challenge the public's beliefs. In relation to urban developments municipalities can play this role, and they can be reasonably neutral between the competing stakeholders (by contrast, the use of public value measures by public agencies primarily to legitimate themselves is inherently more problematic, and risks being self-serving). Third, value is an aspect of the relationship between states and citizens rather than an objective fact. It is shaped by what each considers desirable and important and then becomes more precise through conversation and negotiation.

In any real-world situation trade-offs have to be struck between the cost and time involved in more detailed assessments of value and the need for urgency. But more systematic methods of mapping public and social value make assumptions explicit and allow an honest discussion between stakeholders about what they want and about what they can realistically get, helping technocrats avoid what Oscar Wilde described as the vice of knowing the price of everything and the value of nothing.

14

Persistent Leadership

IN one of the Monty Python films King Arthur addresses a group of peasants as their king. But it turns out that they are members of an anarcho-syndicalist commune. One says: 'I didn't vote for you.' Another complains that 'strange women lying in ponds distributing swords is no basis for a system of government.' In the end the angry Arthur has to leave.

Ruling depends on complicity. Leaders can only lead if followers are willing to follow and strategies can only become real if people are willing to abide by them. As one Kiowa Plains Indian Chief was reported to have said in answer to a question about how he knew he was a chief: 'if I'm going to the prairie with my bands and I turn left and they turn left I'm a chief. But when I turn left and they turn right, I'm not a chief.'

But what kinds of leadership are needed for strategies to succeed? Many of the qualities needed have been described already: leaders need to understand the importance of priorities, how to synthesize disparate types of knowledge, and how to persuade and inspire others. They need self-knowledge, as well as inner strength. To carry through demanding strategies they need the wisdom and the resilience to bounce back from the inevitable crises and disappointments that accompany any fundamental process of change. Indeed the most common personality trait found in studies of leadership is persistence, and this is certainly vital for seeing through a difficult strategy (and is particularly problematic in organizations with short job tenures: little of any use can be achieved by someone who's in a leadership job for less than two years).

The paradox of leadership is that leaders rarely do anything directly. All of their successes depend on others who fight, cure, teach, or invent. There is a great deal of difference between strategies which assume compliance and those that assume that others will act as leaders too, taking responsibility for their situation and its outcomes. These ambiguities are reflected in the roots of the everyday words we use to denote leaders, and the people who carry out their instructions. Some of the words emphasize their first status (Premier, Prime Minister, Head, Chief), or their role in a group, presiding as President, chairing as a Chairman. Then, a layer down, there are chief executives and executives (who strictly speaking 'follow out'), directors (whose primitive Indo-European root *reg* meant to 'move in a straight line', and also gave us the word regal). Further down, come the managers (from *manus*, 'hand', the people who handle situations), and then the officials (from *officium*, bringing together work—*ops*—and doing—*facere*), bureaucrats and administrators (who 'minister', a word meaning service, literally by the lesser person). There are plenty of parallel hierarchies (for example in the military, or the many meanings of the word secretary, which can range from the head of government to the most junior assistant) and parallel lexicons (like the word 'entrepreneur', which means undertaking, bringing things together, acting as a broker).[1]

These words capture the ambiguity of leadership—that it simultaneously puts leaders ahead of others, but also demands that they serve others. The phrase 'prime minister', for example, is strictly speaking an etymological oxymoron—combining the sense of being first with the sense of being the lesser person. So is the phrase 'chief executive', combining being first with following.

Some of these words draw on metaphors that are about doing things to people; others are about travel, moving in a common direction. The roles higher up the hierarchy have greater power and discretion, but also often involve greater risk and vulnerability. The courage to gamble has always been recognized as a mark of greatness. Marshal Foch was once seen as a paragon for his famous comment 'my front is attacked, my flanks are attacked, my rear is attacked. What do I do? I attack.' But failed gamblers are the worst leaders and in early societies leaders were routinely tossed aside if they failed. Kings were killed if they suffered military defeats; others were sacrificed if the harvests failed. Today the risks are more modest—dismissal, demotion, or public humiliation—but no less real.

So what kinds of leadership are most likely to help strategies to succeed? Leadership clearly matters, but as Jim Collins wrote, 'every time we attribute everything to leadership we are no different from the people in the 1500s who attributed everything they didn't understand (such as famine and plague) to God.'[2]

In modern democracies leadership will always have at least two dimensions: the political dimension of carrying out mandates, persuading public opinion, and sustaining majorities, and the bureaucratic dimension of planning, execution, and motivation. But in either dimension it can be concentrated in a single leader, or dispersed. It can be quiet or charismatic. And while some systems separate thought from execution, and turn the great majority into agents, others empower many (like the tens of thousands of mayors of communes in France).

The traditional recipe for strategy is to identify a very visible leader who can be held responsible, to give them the power and freedom to act, and then to hold them to account. The traditional qualities they are expected to have include vision, valour, vigour, and virtue (and not the vices of venom, vengeance, vacillation, venality, and vanity).[3] Stamina is also all-important: one of the common features of people who rise to the top is reliable health, and the ability to survive without much sleep.

But the sheer variety of styles of organization and government challenges any claim to rigid prescription. Every virtue of leaders can turn into a vice. Persistence can become obstinacy. The infectious optimism that characterizes so many leaders can easily turn into the giddiness with success that then makes them overshoot, or assume that they're lucky. Courage can become folly.

Switzerland changes its Prime Minister every year by rotation—yet remains one of the world's most competent governments. Some countries for cultural reasons like very visible leaders—France, the USA, and UK—while others are more at home with collegiate leadership teams, including the Netherlands or Japan, making it hard to generalize about what works best. In some otherwise hierarchical organizations (from the US military to Toyota) deliberate work is done to encourage bottom–up leadership and the ability to 'swarm' in response to a problem.[4] In societies that have gone through internal conflict a higher premium is placed on encouraging leaders to mediate, negotiate, and calm fears.[5] A leadership quality in one context may appear to be its antithesis in another. One of Britain's most successful Prime Ministers was seen by many as devoid of leadership qualities: Winston Churchill remarked that 'an empty taxi arrived at 10 Downing Street and when the door was opened Clement Attlee got out.'

Many public services cultivate leadership skills and many universities and business schools seek to train it and run lucrative programmes to do so. But there is little that could honestly be called a science of leadership; there are no clear lines to distinguish it from management; and there is remarkably little hard evidence about what works. Over ten years ago Gary Yukl's wide-ranging review of the literature on leadership effectiveness concluded that 'most of the theories are beset with conceptual weaknesses and lack strong empirical support. Several thousand empirical studies have been conducted but most of the results are contradictory and inconclusive.' Leadership may be an example of what John Dewey called the 'pedagogical fallacy': the wrong assumption that anything which needs to be learned can be taught.

The weaknesses and contradictions of the different theories of leadership reflect conflicting views of what it means to be a good person. One set of theories focus on people's qualities, seeking qualities that can be identified early and that will then predict whether someone is likely to become an effective leader. These traits, or 'unseen dispositions', vary in number from the 18,000 established in one early review, to the shorter lists that are favoured today, for example: Self-Confidence, Empathy, Ambition, Self-Control, and Curiosity. Supporters of these approaches emphasize that leaders are selected rather than developed— so the key to getting a strategy effectively implemented is simply to put the right sort of person at the top. In much of this literature the critical quality that is often emphasized over any other is charisma—the ability to inspire and engage.[6]

Recent years have brought a proliferation of tests and methods to judge qualities and traits, partly to help recruit leaders and their teams. The Myers–Briggs Type Indicator remains one of the most widely used methods in this field (drawing loosely on Jungian principles). It certainly can help teams to be more aware of their styles, and of their potential weaknesses. But many psychologists are sceptical about whether people's personalities are so easily defined, or whether they are stable (embarrassingly many people taking these tests find that they 'come out' with different personalities each time).

An alternative set of approaches focuses more on how to cope with varied situations rather than on the exceptional qualities of a few individuals. In this view leaders should develop a repertoire of skills and styles that can be deployed to suit the particular situation, or the level of skill or motivation of the people being led.[7] Within all public systems it is possible to find the full gamut of leadership styles from the highly coercive ('do it or else') through very soft styles ('people's feelings before everything else') to styles of leadership that are more like coaching ('helping and supporting others to develop'). Most people involved in leadership roles, and many of the academics who have studied leadership, have a strong preference for one set of styles, which usually has more to do with their values and tastes than any objective evidence. Yet what we do know suggests that context is all-important. A nation suffering imminent defeat needs very different leadership from one that is cruising successfully.

An organization that has lost public confidence needs very different kinds of leaders from one that is growing fast. Similarly the styles needed to drive through change or improve performance are different from those needed for a team that's been through a traumatic crisis.

That may be why one of the few strong findings of research into this area is that the most effective leaders use a range of styles in dealing with different situations. So, for example, analysis of a subset of the most successful head teachers in English schools showed that the heads from high-achieving schools demonstrated many more leadership styles than the ones from failing schools who tended to rely too much on coercion. More generally, it is clear that behavioural characteristics rather than cognitive or technical skills tend to be more important in determining success. This is why leadership courses that help people to reflect on their own leadership styles, their motives and responses, can help people to be more effective, and to carry through the different phases of a strategy—from coalition-building through to tough assertion against resistance.

Another strand of thinking on leadership is exemplified by Ronald Heifetz, who has been highly influential in recent years. He emphasizes the role of followers: leaders achieve things only because others are willing to act. They can succeed best by helping people to think and see in new ways—rather than by offering themselves as the omniscient problem solver. In his work he distinguishes between situations that require mechanistic responses—which he calls 'technical' issues (often called 'management' elsewhere to distinguish it from 'leadership')—and those that require 'adaptive' responses. Part of the leader's role in these more complex situations is to share the problem-solving with others—and resist the temptation to present themselves as a magician or shaman—not least because without constructive dissent and challenge errors are much more likely.[8] In this view leadership is not solely about the very top of the hierarchy. For any radical change to succeed its ownership needs to be widely spread—and the many thousands of local leaders may be more important than the visible politicians or officials at the very top.

Thinking about the role of leadership in making strategies work has also been shaped by greater awareness of the emotional styles of managers and teams. Howard Gardner provided a framework for thinking about these issues when twenty years ago he suggested that there are eight or nine key intelligences which we are born with to different degrees, and which help us to get by, and which educational institutions and bureaucracies cultivate and sometimes crush. Some leaders may be very able in relation to logical analytic skills—but hopeless at interpersonal skills or the intrapersonal skills of self-knowledge. Others took the argument in complementary directions. 'Emotional intelligence' was the name that Peter Salovey of Yale University and John Mayer, of the University of New Hampshire, used for the personal, emotional, and social abilities that they were trying to measure when they began their research some ten years ago. Reuven Bar-On described EQ as 'an array of personal, emotional, and social abilities and skills that influence one's ability to succeed in coping with environmental demands and pressures' and suggested in his preferred model five domains: Intrapersonal Skills, Interpersonal Skills, Adaptability, Stress Management, and General Mood.

Daniel Goleman has achieved great renown with his adaptation of Gardner's theory and has proposed a theory of EQ that is performance based and which relates EQ to twenty competencies in four clusters of general abilities: Self-Awareness, Social Awareness, Self-Management, and Relationship Management. Each of the four clusters is seen as distinct from cognitive abilities and from each other. The Self-Awareness cluster is defined as knowing what one feels. The Social Awareness cluster encompasses the competency of empathy and the ability to read non-verbal cues. The Self-Management cluster relates to the ability to regulate distressing emotional responses and to inhibit emotional impulsivity. Relationship Management, the fourth cluster, is defined by one's ability to understand or influence the emotions of others.

These capabilities are not solely innate. Although it is easier for organizations to recruit people with leadership qualities, these qualities can also be learned, whether through coaching or systematic self-reflection during the course of a career.[9] This has certainly been the view of many military organizations which in the past took leadership more seriously than other public organizations. This list summarizes the UK Ministry of Defence view of the nine essential features of leadership which it aimed to nurture amongst its officers:

- inspiration—ability to enlist the active and committed involvement of a critical mass of followers;
- empowerment—ability to devolve power and authority to take action to others in pursuit of outcomes;
- personal strength and sensitivity—self-discipline, high self-awareness and robustness, combined with empathy for others situations and feelings;
- recognition and support—loyalty, capacity to show and voice appreciation of others' contributions and provide the backup they need to contribute effectively;

- team building—capacity to form and maintain capable, focused groups (leaders succeed by helping their teams and groups to achieve results);
- articulate vision and values—ability to see and communicate a clear and well-judged purpose and the values that inform it;
- innovative challenge—ability to see the flaws in existing policy and processes and ways to do things better;
- example—ability to set an example and display the values and behaviour required of others (includes integrity, courage and commitment); and
- decisiveness—ability to make timely, clear decisions consistent with values and vision.[10]

A very different list to the one provided by the Ministry of Defence comes from William Edwards Deming, the evangelist of continuous improvement who did so much to transform first Japanese industry and then American industry too. This is a list for managers but he addresses it to anyone in a position of leadership. All, he argues, need to have a 'System of Profound Knowledge', consisting of:

1. appreciation of a system: understanding the overall processes involving suppliers, producers, and customers (or recipients) of goods and services;
2. knowledge of variation: the range and causes of variation in quality, and use of statistical sampling in measurements;
3. theory of knowledge: the concepts explaining knowledge and the limits of what can be known;
4. knowledge of psychology: concepts of human nature.

These skills can be learned, both through pedagogy and reflection, and they provide a good analytical basis for leadership even if they say nothing of ethics or responsibility.

However, such generic lists can be misleading because different styles of leadership are required in the many different types of role that play a part in public strategy. Political leadership will always put a higher premium on communication, empathy, brokering, and negotiating skills, and connecting with the 'emotional rudders' which help to guide decisions in conditions of uncertainty. Official leadership within public services requires much less of these types of skills: indeed too much charisma can corrode relationships with political masters. The most successful are therefore generally quieter, more collegiate, more willing to adapt and adopt the changing demands of their masters. Invisibility can be a virtue as these leaders create credit for others. Agency heads are different again: the more that they have direct responsibility for the oversight of large groups of staff the more they may need to be visible, leading by example, and 'walking the talk'. Members of public boards by contrast need to be willing to scrutinize, to ask difficult questions; to promote ideas, and to act as a channel from the public to the management. In crisis they need to be able to forge coalitions with other board members to see through difficult decisions, including sacking the Chief Executive if necessary. Again, too much charisma and an over-personalized style can be counterproductive. Meanwhile the backroom strategists will need a different culture again— without ego, self-effacing but also both analytic and creative.

The Dimensions of Leadership

When John Kennedy made his famous speech committing the USA to land a man on the moon he didn't offer much reassurance. He said that the task would be difficult, uncertain, and very costly. But he also said that it would be ennobling—that taking on a great task, which would depend on the creative ingenuity of thousands of scientists, engineers, and officials, would make America a greater nation.

His speech was a good example of three-dimensional leadership. The first dimension of leadership is simply about getting from A to B, and in an instrumental view the question to be asked of leaders is whether they stick to the tasks they are prescribed by others—like a head teacher implementing a national curriculum. A two-dimensional view goes wider and includes the interests and capacities of the people in the organization. A good leader is one who leaves behind more capacity—supporting, coaching, and guiding, and sometimes setting stretching tasks. A three-dimensional view of leadership goes wider still, taking responsibility for the whole situation, including the interests of people who have no formal stake in or rights over the decisions being made.

These wider views of leadership emphasize the importance of sharing power and knowledge, in ways that leave behind more capacity to act, regardless of whether what's done follows a strategy. Kennedy's lunar ambitions were very much of this kind (and he, of course, had very little idea of how his ambition might be realized). These richer ideas of strategy and leadership are at odds with the classic models of management or performance management, with chains linking high-level strategies to dutiful deliverers. Instead, they recognize that bigger goals and ambitions can only be achieved with wider circles of engagement. If those engaged in a great strategic project take full responsibility for their situation and for the future, then that may entail them challenging the messages and commands coming from above them. Indeed they need to be willing to resist as well as to comply, to shape their 'authorizing environment' rather than just carrying out its orders. They need to be willing to change themselves, and they need to be willing to give their organization—and society—not just what it expects and wants but what it needs, even at personal risk.

One of Franklin Delano Roosevelt's aides memorably described how hard it is for leaders to impose their will:

> half of a President's suggestions...can be safely forgotten by a Cabinet member. And if the President asks about a suggestion a second time, he can be told that it is being investigated. If he asks a third time a wise Cabinet officer will give him at least part of what he suggests. But only occasionally, except about the most important matters, do Presidents ever get around to asking three times.[11]

One conclusion might be that leaders should assert their will more aggressively. Another is that they should appoint people who share their sense of mission. But I read this anecdote in a different way. Since leadership capital will always be scarce, it must be better to have many competent sources of leadership rather than just one.

It should be evident that leadership and strategy are not such easy bedfellows. A system full of leadership capacity will challenge, and often reject, formal strategies. It's sometimes said that the true benefit of rising to the top of a large organization is not money or perks, but never again having to listen to anyone who disagrees with you, and, for some, strategy is a way of reinforcing authority. But strategic systems depend on internal contradiction: it's precisely this that allows them to adapt to change.

In the past, states sat as thin layers outside and on top of society—a caste apart, made up of specialist administrators, priests, and warrior kings. The state was imagined—and still often is—as a single thing, a coherent bloc of power separate from daily life and from everyday hopes, fears, and passions. Yet today the state is increasingly integrated in society, sitting within a wider ecology of knowledge in which states can no longer so easily monopolize resources and in which their work is less about working on a passive society and more about working with it, from inside as well as outside to shape behaviours. States continue to be the most visible, self-conscious means by which societies adapt to change. But how they do this has changed.

These shifts make some of the older models of planning and strategy redundant. These imagined the knowledge that states used as entirely separate from the self-knowledge of the society. Instead in contemporary democratic states the job of being a politician or an official is becoming more about leadership from within than from without; about mobilizing others or being mobilized by them; about cooperation and collaboration more than diktat; and about intensive continuous communication. These are the skills necessary for states to reduce the risks of the external environment, and expand the room for enterprise and opportunity.

In Diderot's famous eighteenth-century encyclopedia the entry for kings ('rois') stands next to the entry for cooks ('rotissiers').[12] Both are presented as crafts which can be learned and perfected through practice and reflection. Strategy and leadership have this character too. They cannot be learned simply through pedagogy, or by following the book (including this one). But nor can they simply be improvised. Instead learning involves the acquisition of methods, and then their constant refinement and improvement through practice, repetition, and critical reflection. With experience some methods become almost second nature. But because the environment for strategy changes, in ways that the character of a piano keyboard, or of the materials used in carpentry, do not change, strategists have to invest much more in refreshing their knowledge and their understandings. Intuition built on experience can greatly assist in making complex decisions: but it should never be trusted uncritically.

What experienced strategic leaders build up is a skill not dissimilar to that of a cook, or a police officer. They become good at spotting patterns, making quick judgements as well as slower analyses. They gain a nose for opportunities and above all for cumulative gains. And they learn how to avoid mistakes. Plato recommended that no one should become a leader before the age of 50. In unchanging societies that makes sense. In fast-changing ones the benefits of wisdom and experience need to be matched with the benefits of grasping the uncertainties of what's new as well as what's unchanging.

Here we come to the nub of leadership and strategy. At its best leadership involves a higher order of service, a passionate immersion in the goals and means of strategy that is often risky, but also often exhilarating. Most people would rather not be leaders—indeed sometimes it looks like madness to want leadership. And many of the people who become leaders are ill-suited for it, either because of their own limitations (all tip and no iceberg) or because their lust for power obscures their moral sense.[13] But the willingness to engage deeply with an organization, or a community, and to grasp in full its problems and its potential, is part of what helps any society avoid stagnation.

PART III

15

Separating the Urgent and the Important: Strategy as a Public Good

STRATEGY fills the space between the wide, almost limitless avenues of what's possible in the far future, and the modest steps which appear to be on offer in the near future. At its best it helps societies face up to their true potential and their weaknesses, but for that very reason it's bound to be uncomfortable.

I argued earlier that modern governance has been shaped by the growing importance of three types of public good: democracy, knowledge, and connections. But public strategy is also itself a public good, and like many public goods one that tends to be under-produced because of inadequate incentives. These weak incentives to act responsibly combine with the optical distortion that affects most governments: the tendency to overestimate how much they can achieve in the short term (sometimes mistaking activity for impact) while underestimating how much they can achieve in the long run through consistently and persistently doing the right things. Strong structures, processes, and cultures that support long-term strategy can help to mitigate this distortion and give governments a more realistic view both of their limits and of their potential. So can formal methods which institutionalize lower discount rates than those which characterize electoral politics and the market.

But its own strategy is never inherently benign, in either its ends or its means. A strategic dictator is more dangerous than one who flits from project to project. A strategic strongman can ride roughshod over others' interests. Visiting Vladimir Putin's Kremlin a few weeks after his 2000 election victory, I was impressed by the clarity with which his staff explained how they would centralize power, marginalize independent media, set up their own hegemonic political parties, and see off the big business oligarchs (all of which they subsequently achieved). But I was also troubled at how easily democratization could lead to de-democratization.

The Russians turned out to have a fairly accurate understanding of their environment. But strategy can be full of deception and hubris. It can place too much faith in data, or analysis or models. It can underestimate implementers' power to subvert. Many strategies exist only on paper, floating in mid-air with no supporting pillars, or at such a level of abstraction that they stand little chance of being implemented. Big machines work only because of small screws and so it is with government: the big picture depends on the multitude of details, and often the screws which hold the whole together are skills, norms, or cultures which aren't immediately visible to the strategists and planners looking down from on high.

Every strategy is a gamble on the future. It may be better or worse grounded in analysis and understanding. But because the future is unknowable it involves a moral risk, an exposure to vulnerability that is greater than anything faced by the purely tactical pragmatist. Many such gambles foundered dramatically. Others ended ambivalently—like Lyndon Johnson's war on poverty or Ronald Reagan's and Margaret Thatcher's promise to restore traditional family values, or the USA's space programme. Today, the world has plenty of strategic gambles that remain in the balance, like Dubai's gamble on becoming a pre-eminent global economic entrepôt or Abu Dhabi's equally ambitious (and more environmentally sustainable) plans to invest its way into the front rank, or Turkey's bid to join the European Union, or China's race to ensure that growth can be kept at a sufficient pace to dampen social unrest.

Psychology tells us that people thrive when they set themselves, and then pursue, goals which are stretching but not impossible, and which reflect underlying values.[1] They also flourish when they are mindful of themselves and their place in the world.[2] What makes governments thrive is not so different. But, as with individuals, their ability to do these things depends not only on their character but also on the conditions in which they operate, and in particular the institutional structures which govern them. Economic historians have shown conclusively that institutions are decisive for economic growth. When the institutional context is right, with the right incentives for entrepreneurialism, investment, and honest trading, stagnant economies quickly turn into dynamic ones.[3] Much the same applies to governments. When institutions and attitudes reward attention to the future, to investment and innovation, societies become much more effective in navigating change. In part that depends on getting things right inside government. But just as important is an environment that rewards responsible and effective behaviour, through parliaments, media, international organizations, and NGOs (and one of the welcome developments of recent years is a far richer set of data sources on the effectiveness and accountability of governments—from the World Bank, Bertelsmann Stiftung, and others).

Even with these conditions in place, being strategic is not the natural tendency of public organizations in democracies. Pressures from the media and politics will point towards tactics, the avoidance of difficult issues, and pandering to vested interests. Politicians will often be frustrated if offered excessively complicated diagnoses and reflections (Mrs Thatcher was a rare example of a leader who said to some of her top advisers that she didn't only want better answers; she also wanted better questions). Moreover the specialists who oversee strategy in any public organization always face their own risks. They can become too analytical, too detached from practice, and, even more fatal, detached from leadership priorities, producing marvellous reports, but not about the issues that most concern their clients, or in ways that link long-term issues and possibilities to the short-term time horizons within which many politicians and officials have to operate. Then there are what British Prime Minister Harold Macmillan called 'events, dear boy, events', that can derail even the most carefully prepared plans. Volatility makes strategy much harder: it's much easier to think and act long-term against a backdrop of political and economic stability. Uncertainty drives the implicit and explicit discount rates up.

Rainbow Government

These problems encourage the sceptics who believe that strategy is neither possible (because of the day to day pressures of politics) nor desirable (because no one can know enough to steer a complex society). But such scepticism is at odds with history and the many counter-examples cited in this book and, at a deeper level, it is at odds with democracy. The public have a right to expect governments to be open about their longer-term goals and means, and they have reason to believe that they will be served better by governments that are driven less by events and more by goals.

That's why I have advocated the conscious and open pursuit of a better future. I've argued that all in a position of power should seek to clarify what they are trying to achieve and why, and share what results with the people they are trying to serve. I've argued that they should try to understand their environment, and challenge their own assumptions about it; that they should organise the available time, resources, and structures to ensure that this happens; that they should frame their plans in the light of the power and knowledge they have at their disposal; and that they should learn fast, and institutionalize fast learning, so as to be ready, if necessary, to change direction.

No one frame is adequate for understanding things as complicated as governments and public sectors. To see them solely through the lens of the latest management theories, or contracts, or consumer power, or risk, or innovation, is misleading. Good governments have to master a wide repertoire not only of tools but also of cultures of governing, from paranoid preparation for low-probability risks to attentive service. A good metaphor for the ideal twenty-first-century state might therefore be a rainbow, rather than a Leviathan or a marketplace. A rainbow combines many different colours which add up to a coherent whole. It is transparent. And it constantly pulls our attention to the horizon.

In a dense planet with getting on for seven billion people (and a likely nine billion by mid-century) the challenges facing public institutions are immense, from climate change to ageing, migration to regulating biotechnology. Their chances of success will be greatly improved if they follow some simple, if challenging, prescriptions which I advocate for any public leader:

- use power to bring about changes your society needs—don't just preside;
- focus on a few things that really matter and where you have the power to make a difference—and resist distractions;
- prepare and plan—don't just react;
- use what's already known about what works and what doesn't;
- don't be afraid to innovate—particularly where existing policies don't work;
- don't try to do everything at once (and remember that most governments overestimate what they can achieve short-term, but underestimate what they can achieve long-term);
- organise your time and staff with a rough balance between the short, medium, and long term—rather than being trapped in the present;
- favour strategies that are simple and give room for the implementers to collaborate and adapt, over ones that are elaborate and inflexible;
- build challenge into how you work, and resist complacency (and as in other areas of life, seek out your fiercest critics to sharpen your ideas); and

- never stop learning, since the world is full of surprises which can be used to make wiser decisions.

Why should anyone follow these prescriptions? Why not just hoard power, or enjoy the trappings of office? Here we come to the heart of the motivation to be strategic. Many of the most influential accounts of government analyse their actions as the predictable result of the self-interest of officials or politicians. That self-interest has generally been interpreted in the narrowest sense, as about maximizing power or money. Yet, as philosophers and psychologists throughout history have pointed out, for most people the critical feature of self-interest is recognition. It's not enough to be rich or powerful; human beings want to be recognized, respected, or even loved.

When today's officials and politicians imagine themselves at a ripe old age, sitting in a rocking chair overlooking the sea, and their granddaughter asks them what they did with their life, answers that mention the scale of the budget they oversaw, the tens of thousands of employees they were responsible for, or the important conferences they attended, will not impress her much. Nor will it be enough for the former officials to say that they were a competent hired hand for whatever political leaders came along. Instead their only plausible answers will be about legacy and values: about what they did to improve the lives of their fellow citizens, to prepare for future threats, and make the most of the opportunities they were given.

Notes

Chapter 1

1. See David Myers, Intuition: Its Powers and Perils (New Haven: Yale University Press, 2002) for an excellent overview of recent research on intuition.
2. James Tobin and Edward Elgar, *World Finance and Economic Stability: Selected Essays by James Tobin and Edward Elgar* (Cheltenham: Edward Elgar Publishers, 2003), 210.
3. Adam Smith, *Theory of Moral Sentiments*, pt IV.
4. Manutius is often credited as the founder of modern publishing.
5. Norway's legislation makes this a requirement; Spain's provides incentives but isn't mandatory.
6. For a good recent review of strategy in government see Thomas Fischer, Peter Gregor Schmitz, and Michael Seberich, *The Strategy of Politics* (Gütersloh: Bertelsmann Stiftung, 2007).
7. In business the fashion for wholly separate strategy teams using over-formalized methods has largely passed. The models of strategy developed in the 1990s and 2000s are rather less vulnerable to the hubris, inflexibility, and ultimate irrelevance that beset some of the more grandiose strategies in the 1960s and 1970.
8. Chapter 13 discusses the concept of public value in more detail. Its main intellectual pioneer has been Professor Mark Moore at Harvard.
9. That learning is primarily about actions and directions but it also includes 'double loop' learning, which reflects on underlying values.
10. A. Wildavsky, *Speaking the Truth to Power: The Art and Craft of Policy Analysis* (New Brunswick: Transaction, 1987).
11. The greatest contemporary thinker on experimental governance is Roberto Mangabeira Unger, professor of law at Harvard, political theorist, and in the late 2000s minister in the Brazilian government. He re-energized the traditions of American pragmatism to show how societies could be conceived as systems of experiment and innovation, constantly seeking new knowledge in the pursuit of well-being and democracy. See e.g. *The Self Awakened* (2007).
12. Daniel Yankelovich, *Coming to Public Judgment: Making Democracy Work in a Complex World* (New Haven: Yale University Press, 1992).
13. There have been many other attempts since the first, promoted by the Rockefeller Foundation in 1909, which aimed to eliminate hookworm: a billion people today still suffer from it.

14. Lawrence Brilliant, *The Management of Smallpox Eradication in India* (Ann Arbor: University of Michigan Press, 1985); Jack Hopkins, *The Eradication of Smallpox: Organizational Learning and Innovation in International Health* (Boulder, Colo.: Westview Press, 1989).

15. Some of these are being implemented by the Young Foundation in the UK including surveys of needs combining statistical and ethnographic research with tapping the insights of frontline staff across key sectors; collaboratives on well-being and neighbourhoods combining government departments, local authorities, academics, and NGOs; and social venture funds like the Health Launch pad. See www.youngfoundation.org

16. For more on these methods see G. Mulgan and T. Steinberg, *Wide Open: Open Source Methods and their Future Potential*, (London: Demos, 2006); C. R. Sunstein, *Infotopia: How Many Minds Produce Knowledge* (Oxford: Oxford University Press, 2006); Y. Benkler, *The Wealth of Networks: How Social Production Transforms Markets and Freedom*, (London: Yale University Press, 2006).

17. The London Cultural Industries Strategy, launched in 1984, was accompanied by a series of strategies for music, advertising, film, and other sectors. Some of its ideas were later published in the book *Saturday Night or Sunday Morning*, which I co-authored with Ken Worpole. Subsequently similar ideas were adopted by many other cities around the UK and elsewhere. A network of 'creative cities' was set up in the 1990s, and prompted a series of publications, notably by Charles Landry. In the 2000s similar ideas were successfully popularized by Richard Florida, who linked them to arguments about the rise of a creative class.

18. These can be found at http://interactive.cabinetoffice.gov.uk/strategy/survival-guide/index.htm

19. Gordon Brown in the UK and Kevin Rudd in Australia.

20. This was a substantial jump from a decade before. *British Social Attitudes*, 2008

21. Quite what counts as quality is not entirely objective, though attempts have been made to map and define it including the World Bank's league tables which draw on several hundred individual variables measuring perceptions of governance, put together from 25 separate data sources constructed by 18 different organizations.The World Bank authors come to rather pessimistic conclusions about the global trends they have analysed: 'we cautiously conclude that we certainly do not have any evidence of any significant improvement in governance worldwide, and if anything the evidence is suggestive of a deterioration, at the very least in key dimensions such as control of corruption, rule of law, political stability and government effectiveness.' http://siteresources.worldbank.org/INTWBIGOVANTCOR/Resources/govmatters3_wber.pdf

22. For an insightful view of what governments have done well and badly see D. Bok, 'Measuring the Performance of Government' in *Why People Don't Trust Government*, ed. J. Nye, S. Joseph, P. D. Zelikow, and D. C. King (Cambridge, Mass.: Harvard University Press, 1997), 55–77.

23. For a particularly outstanding example see Peter Lindert, *Growing Public: Social Spending and Economic Growth since the Eighteenth Century* (Cambridge: Cambridge University Press, 2004).

24. World Bank, *The Wealth of Nations: Measuring Capital for the 21st Century* (Washington, DC, 2007).

Chapter 2

1. The full quote is 'Why should I care about posterity? What's posterity ever done for me?' available at www.theotherpages.org/alpha-m1.html

2. See Loizos Heracleous, *Strategy and Organisation* (Cambridge: Cambridge University Press, 2003); Henry Mintzberg, *The Rise and Fall of Strategic Planning* (London: FT/Prentice Hall, 1994); Adrian Woods and Paul Joyce, *Strategic Management: A Fresh Approach to Developing Skills, Knowledge and Creativity* (London: Kogan Page, 2001).

3. http://www.quotationspage.com/quote/28685.html

4. Including e.g. Paul Joyce, *Strategic Management for the Public Services* (London: Open University Press, 1999); John M. Bryson, *Strategic Planning for Public and Nonprofit Organizations: A Guide to Strengthening and Sustaining Organizational Achievement*, 3rd edn (San Francisco: Jossey-Bass, 2004); and the various books written by Yehezkel Dror, such as *The Capacity to Govern* (London: Frank Cass, 2001).

5. Owen E. Hughes, *Public Management and Administration: An Introduction* (London: Palgrave Macmillan, 2003); Hal G. Rainey, *Understanding and Managing Public Organizations*, 3rd edn. (San Francisco: 2003); Daniel Jossey-Bass Lozeau et al., 'The Corruption of Managertal Techniques by Organizations', *Human Relations*, 5/5 (2002); Michael Barzelay, *The New Public Management: Improving Research and Policy Dialogue* (Berkeley and Los Angeles: University of California Press, 2001); Wayne Parsons, *Public Policy: An Introduction to the Theory and Practice of Policy Analysis* (London: Edward Elgar, 1995); Charles Lindblom, *The Policy-Making Process* (London: Pearson, 1994).

6. http://www.iun.edu/~bnwcls/j401/qspm.doc is an example of a quantitative strategic planning tool.

7. James Q. Wilson, *Bureaucracy: What Government Agencies Do and Why They Do It* (New York: Basic Books, 1989).

8. The major consultancies—PWC, KPMG, Booz Allen, BCG, and McKinsey—do much of their business with public clients. I'm sure that individual consultants have sophisticated understandings of the complexities of public strategy. But many attempts to uncover the underlying corporate view of public strategy have drawn a blank. Indeed in some cases it is an article of faith that the same methods can be used for any kind of organization or problem. As will be apparent I see this view as neither intellectually tenable nor very helpful for

their clients. Standard methods can work well for the tasks public agencies have which are similar to those facing businesses—such as better understanding consumers, or designing IT architectures. But the closer to the heart of government you go the less their methods turn out to be useful, even though exceptional individuals may have gained good insights across many fields that are useful.

9. I've seen far too many examples of this kind: the typical consultancy recommendation is for simple lines of accountability (often ignoring the complexities of politics), and taking seriously only what can be measured (when one of the marks of competent leadership is that it can cope with things that can't be measured as well as things that can).

10. Colin Price, *Time Discounting and Value* (Oxford: Blackwell, 1993). See also Avner Offer, *The Challenge of Affluence* (Oxford: Oxford University Press, 2006) for an imaginative application of thinking about preferences through time.

11. Herbert Simon, *The Sciences of the Artificial* (Cambridge, Mass.: MIT Press, 1996), 111–28.

12. E. Ostrom, 'Achieving Progress in Solving Collective Action Problems', in C. Leigh Anderson and J. W. Looney (eds), *Making Progress* (Lanham, Md.: Lexington Books, 2002). Also see W. Lidwell, K. Holden, and J. Butler, *Universal Principles of Design* (Gloucester, Mass.: Rockport, 2003).

13. P. Greenwood et al., *Diverting Children from a Life of Crime: Measuring Costs and Benefits*, RAND research brief, 1996.

14. Aaron Wildavsky, 'If Planning is Everything, Maybe it's Nothing', *Policy Sciences*, 4 (1973), 127–53.

15. Henry Mintzberg, *The Rise and Fall of Strategic Planning* (London: FT/Prentice Hall, 1994).

16. Charles Lindblom, 'The Science of Muddling Through', *Public Administration Review*, 19/3 (1979), 79–88, and its follow-up 'Still Muddling, Not Yet Through' *Public Administration Review*, 39/6 (1979), 517–26.

17. Robert Behn, 'Management by groping along', *Journal of Policy Analysis and Management*, 7/4 (1998), 643–63.

18. The science fiction writer Arthur C. Clarke stated that if an eminent expert said something was possible in the future we should believe him; if he said that something was impossible he was quite likely to be wrong.

19. D. Halberstam, *The Best and the Brightest* (New York: Ballantine, 1993).

20. H. Brooks, 'The Typology of Surprises in Technology, Institutions and Development', ch. 11 in W. C. Clark and R. E. Munn (eds), *Sustainable Development of the Biosphere* (Cambridge: International Institute for Applied Systems Analysis/Cambridge University Press, 1986), 325–50; D. Collingridge, *The Management of Scale: Big Organizations, Big Decisions, Big Mistakes* (London: Routledge, 1992).

21. Paul C. Nutt, *Why Decisions Fail: Avoiding the Blunders and Traps that Lead to Debacles* (San Francisco: Berrett-Koehlerr, 2002); Dietrich Dorner, *The Logic of Failure* (London: Perseus Books, 1996).

22. Christopher Hood, *The Art of the State: Culture, Rhetoric and Public Management* (Oxford: Clarendon Press, 1998), provides a good overview of the cultural perspectives that underpin many theories.

Chapter 3

1. Laar claimed that the only book on economics he'd ever read was Milton Friedman's *Free to Choose*.
2. Dickens later attributed this view to his character Mr Micawber.
3. This account was first set out in work by William Baumol and William Bowen in the early 1960s. For an interesting recent analysis of how some service industries were able to overcome cost disease see Barry P. Bosworth and Jack E. Triplett, *Productivity Measurement Issues in Service Industries: 'Baumol's Disease' Has been Cured* (Washington: Brookings Institution, 2003).
4. The government failure literature argued that politicians and public agencies could destroy value for a range of reasons including poor information about citizen preferences, the self-interest and rent-seeking behaviour of public officials, capture of public agencies by narrow interest groups, and a lack of incentives for public agencies to act efficiently or responsively to citizen needs.
5. Joseph E. Stiglitz, *Economics of the Public Sector*, 3rd edn. (New York: Norton, 2000).
6. I'm referring here to Mo Ibrahim's prize for African leaders.
7. Perhaps the most impressive example of changing behaviour is measured by the data on annual murder rates which in England fell from over 20 per 100,000 in the 13th and 14th centuries to around 1 by the end of the 20th century. See Manuel Eisner, 'Modernization, Self-Control and Lethal Violence', *British Journal of Criminology* 41 (2001), 618–38.
8. The percentage of overweight schoolchildren dropped from 14% in the early 1990s to about 10% in the mid-2000s. Overweight military recruits (for compulsory national service) face an additional six weeks of fitness work on top of the usual 10 weeks of basic training. For more information see the report on obesity by the Foresight Panel, UK, 2007.
9. The technical definition of a public good is something that is non-excludable and non-rival: that means when it is provided to one person it is also available to many others, and that person's consumption of the good doesn't diminish what's available for others. Democratic governance is a classic example; so is knowledge. Connections in networks have somewhat more complex characteristics.
10. The recent writings of Harvard's Daron Acemoglu provide a very useful economic analysis of democracy and the state. Another good source is Vito Tanzi and Ludger Schuknecht, *Public Spending in the 20th Century* (Cambridge: Cambridge University Press, 2000).

11. Robert T. Deacon, 'Dictatorship, Democracy and the Provision of Public Goods', Departmental Working Paper, Dept of Economics, University of California Santa Barbara.

12. David Stasavage, *Democracy and Education Spending in Africa*, Discussion Paper DEDPS/37, London School of Economics.

13. Around the edges of state power China has been experimenting with public engagement: from large-scale public consultations in Chongqing to deliberative democracy in the township of Zeguo in wealthy Zhejiang province.

14. *Everyday Democracy*, Demos, 2008.

15. The key figures included John Graunt, theorist of political arithmetic, and William Paterson, founder of the Bank of England in the 1690s. Prussia went even further—and Frederick William I and his successors created over twenty university chairs in public administration. Cameralism was a generally progressive movement to replace superstition and tradition with science and reason. Its later British equivalent was utilitarianism, articulated by Jeremy Bentham and John Stuart Mill and embodied in the figure of Edwin Chadwick, who was hugely influential in encouraging better public health, but also utterly hardnosed in applying utilitarian principles to social problems, and forcing the poor to work. Their work set the tone for much of the future of public administration, combining observation, measurement, incentives, and punishments to achieve what they saw as desirable ends.

16. http://www.wtec.org/ConvergingTechnologies/3/NBIC3_report.pdf

17. A useful overview of the changing roles of government is provided by the OECD paper *Governance in the 21st Century*, 2001.

18. Paul Miller and Niamh Gallagher, *The Collaborative State*, Demos, 2006.

19. G. Bertucci, and A. Alberti, 'Globalization and the Role of the State: Challenges and Perspectives', in D. A. Rondinelli and S. Cheema (eds), *Reinventing Government for the Twenty-First Century; State Capacity in a Globalizing Society.* (Bloomfield, Conn.: Kumarian Press, 2003), 17–33.

20. P. Hall, 'The World's Urban Systems: A European Perspective', *Global Urban Development*, 1 (2005).

21. *Everyday Democracy*, Demos, 2008, provides a comprehensive account of the links between well-being and democracy in all its forms across Europe

22. Wallace E. Oates, *Fiscal Federalism* (New York: Harcourt Brace Jovanovich, 1972), is the classic account.

23. In the old system state enterprises had to submit all their surpluses to the centre; the result of central control was a rollercoaster of incoherence as subsidies lurched up and down with no obvious rationale, whereas local control has proven much more stable (albeit during a period of huge redistribution from poor rural areas to richer urban ones).

24. See Francis Fukuyama, *State-Building: Governance and World Order in the Twenty First Century* (Ithaca, NY: Cornell University Press, 2004).

25. *Meeting Global Challenges*, report of the International Task Force on Global Public Goods, co-chaired by Ernesto Zedillo and Tidjane Thiam, Final Report (Stockholm: 2006), 4.

26. This issue was first brought to light in M. J. Molina and F. S. Rowland's 'Strato-spheric Sink for Chlorofluoromethanes: Chlorine Atom-Catalysed Destruction of Ozone', *Nature Journal*, 249 (28 June 1974).
27. See *Meeting Global Challenges* (n. 25 above).
28. See the Young Foundation pamphlet *Contentious Citizens* for an overview of the changing ways in which campaigns are organized both within nations and globally.
29. Like Lukashenka in Belarus who in 2006 repressed and marginalized the brave minority of protesters to 'win' his election with 82.6% of the vote.
30. Public management and administration were influenced by new global insti-tutions and networks that both reflected on experience and promoted their own answers. The PUMA group at the OECD was for a time particularly influential; the World Bank and European Commission also propagated their own ideas; while more academic networks like the International Institute for Administrative Sciences and national Institutes for Public Administration spread ideas amongst practitioners too.
31. William Kristol, for example, described the health plan developed by Hillary Clinton in her husband's first term as signalling 'the rebirth of centralized welfare-state policy', and argued that consequently it had to be stopped at all costs.
32. This was known as the 'Dob a Job' scheme.
33. Paul C. Light, *The True Size of Government* (Washington, DC: Brookings Institu-tion Press, 1999).
34. Oana Zabava, quoted in the *International Herald Tribune*, 25 November 2004.
35. J. March and J. P. Olsen, *Democratic Governance* (New York: Free Press, 1995).
36. Partnership for Solutions, *Chronic Conditions: Making the Case for Ongoing Care* (Baltimore: Johns Hopkins University, for the Robert Wood Johnson Founda-tion, 2002).
37. World Health Organization, The World Health Report 2001, *Mental Health: New Understanding, New Hope* (Geneva: World Health Organization, 2001).
38. www.iccs-isac.org/eng/default.asp
39. T. Tyler, *Why People Obey the Law* (Princeton: Princeton University Press, 2006).
40. The EPP has 12,000 participants with plans to raise this to 100,000 by 2012. It encourages patients to learn five management skills: problem-solving; deci-sion-making; resource utilization; developing effective partnerships with healthcare providers; and taking action. Early evaluation suggests it works better with already motivated patients and can be impeded by unenthusiastic doctors. An alternative model—Whole System Informing Self-Management Engagement (WISE) is now being tested out, with the aim of influencing power-brokers in the system, including doctors.
41. The writings of Ivan Illich on schooling and health can appear more at home in this century than when they were written.
42. See e.g. http://www.euro.who.int/observatory/Publications/20060915_2

43. C. Maller M. Townsend A. Ptyor P. Brown, and L. St Leger, *Healthy Nature Healthy People: 'Contact with Nature' as an Upstream Health Promotion Intervention for Populations* (Oxford: Oxford University Press, 2005).

44. F. Kuo, 'Coping with Poverty: Impacts of Environment and Attention in the Inner City', *Environment and behavior* (2001), 5–33.

45. Bert Klandermans, Marlene Reofs, and Johan Olivier, 'Grievance Formation in a Country in Transition: South Africa 1994–1998', *Social Psychology Quarterly*, 64/1 (March 2001), 41–54.

46. V. Chanley, T. J. Rudolph, and W. M. Rahn, 'The Origins and Consequences of Public Trust in Government: A Time-Series Analysis', *Public Opinion Quarterly*, 64 (2000), 239–56.

47. D. A Easton, *Systems Analysis of Political Life* (New York: Wiley, 1965).

48. *Everyday Democracy Index*, Demos, 2008. These figures are drawn from Euro-barometer.

49. This chapter draws on several publications: a series of articles I wrote in the early 1990s on the rising importance of happiness; the work of Demos on time and the good life (in the collections *Wellbeing and Time* and *The Good Life*); the work of a group of economists including Andrew Oswald and Richard Layard who have started to persuade the economics profession to think differently about happiness. I also commissioned the publication of a report by the UK Cabinet Office in 2001—*Life Satisfaction*—which was one of the first (perhaps the first) report from the heart of a major government on happiness as a goal of public policy.

50. World Values Survey (2007) World Database of Happiness.

51. Avner Offer, *The Challenge of Affluence* (Oxford: Oxford University Press, 2006).

52. For a time researchers claimed that as much as 50% of variations in happiness was caused by genetic dispositions, drawing mainly on studies by David Lykken. However, changing views on the nature of genetics, and gene–environment interactions, now make these claims suspect.

53. F. Huppert, N. Baylis, and B. Keverne (eds), *The Science of Well-being* (Oxford: Oxford University Press, 2005).

54. Sen, A, 'Capability and Well-being', in A. Sen and M. Nussbaum, *The Quality of Life* (Oxford: Clarendon Press, 1993).

55. M. Seligman, *Authentic Happiness* (New York: Free Press, 2002).

56. See e.g. J. Kagan, *What is Emotion? History, Measures and Meanings* (New Haven: Yale University Press, 2007).

57. Daniel Gilbert, *Stumbling into Happiness* (London: Penguin, 2007), is a brilliant account of the many misperceptions people suffer from, and how poor we are at formulating wise plans for ourselves, let alone for whole societies.

58. See A. Buonfino, and G. Mulgan, *Report on Positional Goods* (London: Young Foundation, 2006).

59. Tanzi and Schuknecht, *Public Spending in the 20th Century* (n. 10 above) also attempted an analysis of the relative value of spending by the state.

60. The full list of factors can be found on the UK Cabinet Office website, Strategic Audit 2003.

Chapter 4

1. Mary Helen Immordino-Yang and Antonio Damasio, 'We Feel Therefore We Learn: The Relevance of Affective and Social Neuroscience to Education', Journal Compilation *International Mind, Brain and Education* Society, 1 (2007), 1.
2. A good sourcebook on these is Stephen Cummings and David Wilson (eds) *Images of Strategy*. (Oxford: Blackwell, 2003).
3. From Herbert Simon and Charles E. Lindblom to Aaron Wildavsky, as well as more recent work such as Gary Klein, *Sources of Power: How People Make Decisions* (Cambridge, Mass.: MIT Press).
4. Like many bons mots this one is obviously wrong on close inspection—but it contains more than a grain of truth.
5. Peter Schwartz, *The Art of the Long View* (Hoboken, NJ: John Wiley, 1997); Peter Schwartz, *Inevitable Surprises* (New York: Free Press, 2003); R. Cooper and R. Layard, *What the Future Holds: Insights from Social Science* (Cambridge, Mass.: MIT Press, 2003).
6. For an overview of futures methods see the report commissioned by the UK Performance and Innovation Unit from the Henley Centre on best practice in futures methods—Henley Centre, *Benchmarking UK Strategic Futures Work* (Performance and Innovation Unit, 2001). Other useful sources include: Corporate Executive Board, *Scenario Planning* (Washington and London Corporate Strategy Board: 1999); Arie de Geus, *The Living Company* (London: Nicholas Brealey Books, 1999); Jerome C. Glenn, Theodore J. Gordon, and James Dator, 'Closing the Deal: How to Make Organisations Act on Futures Research', *Foresight Journal*, 3/3 (2001); Global Business Network/Nakamae International Economic Research, *The Future of Japan Project*,www.nier.co.jp/index-e.html.; Keith Grint, *Fuzzy Management* (Oxford: Oxford University Press, 1997); Kees van der Heijden, *Scenarios: The Art of Strategic Conversation* Chichester: John Wiley and Sons, 1996); Pekka Himanen, *The Hacker Ethic and the Spirit of the Information Age* (London: Secker and Warburg, 2001); Art Kleiner, *The Age of Heretics*, (London: Nicholas Brealey Books, 1996) Gill Ringland, *Scenario Planning: Managing for the Future*, Chichester: John Wiley and Sons, 1998); Peter Schwarz, *The Art of the Long View*, (Chichester: John Wiley and Sons, 1998).
7. Lester Salamon, *The Tools of Government: a guide to new governance* (Oxford: Oxford University Press, 2002).
8. Christopher Hood and Helen Margetts, *The Tools of Government in a Digital Age* (London: Palgrave Macmillan, 2007).
9. A good recent source is Patrick Dunleavy and Helen Margetts, *E Government and Policy Innovation in Seven Liberal Democracies* (2003), http://www.governmentontheweb.org/access_papers.asp

10. Good overviews include Christopher Pollitt, Janice Caulfield, Amanda Smullen, and Colin Talbot (eds) *How Governments Do Things Through Semi-autonomous Organizations*. (London: Palgrave Macmillan, 2004); Christopher Hood, Oliver James, B. Guy Peters, and Colin Scott (eds) *Controlling Modern Government: Variety, Commonality and Change* (London: Edward Elgar, 2004).

11. John Adams, *Risk* (London: Routledge, 2001), ch. 7.

12. R. Moss Kanter, *The Change Masters* (New York: Simon and Schuster, 1983); A. Pettigrew et al., *Shaping Strategic Change: Making Change in Large Organisations* (London: Sage, 1992); Neal Crasilneck Gross, Jospeh Giacquinta, and Marilyn Bernstein, *Implementing Organizational Innovations: A Sociological Analysis of Planned Educational Change* (New York: Basic Books, 1971).

13. S. Kelman, *Unleashing Change* (Washington: Brookings Institution Press, 2005).

14. Richard Rose, *Inheritance in Public Policy* (New Haven: Yale University Press, 1994).

15. Richard Musgrave, *Public Finance in Theory and Practice* (Columbus, oh.: McGraw-Hill College, 1973).

16. This is drawn from a talk by James M. Beggs, the former head of NASA.

17. Alfred Chandler, *The Dynamic Firm: The Role of Technology, Strategy, Organization, and Regions* (Oxford: Oxford University Press, 1998); Alfred Chandler, *Strategy & Structure: Chapters in the History of the Industrial Enterprise* (Cambridge, Mass.: MIT Press, 1962).

18. John Roberts, *The Modern Firm* (Oxford: Oxford University Press, 2004), 17.

19. B. Guy Peters, *The New Institutionalism* (London: Cassell, 1998), 96.

20. All legislation of this kind runs the risk of being used mainly by commercial lobbies—the same can be true of Freedom of Information laws that are used primarily by wealthy media organizations.

21. G. Klein, *Sources of Power: How People Make Decisions* (Cambridge, Mass.: MIT Press, 1998), 71.

22. D. Dorner, *The Logic of Failure* (New York: Basic Books, 1997).

23. For a positive assessment see the National Audit Office report *JobCentrePlus: Delivering Effective Services through Personal Advisors* (London: NAO, 2006).

Chapter 5

1. See e.g. the many biographies of Franklin Delano Roosevelt and F. Bailey, *Humbuggery and Manipulation: The Art of Leadership* (Ithaca, NY: Cornell University Press, 1988) or M. Edelman, *Constructing the Political Spectacle* (Chicago: University of Chicago Press, 1988).

2. Between 1997 and 2007 the British government was often riven by battles between Prime Minister Blair and Chancellor Gordon Brown. We involved both groups of political advisers and senior officials on the steering group which determined the Strategy Unit's work programme.

3. A good example is the toolkit developed by Rosabeth Moss Kanter for practitioners in education. http://www.reinventingeducation.org/RE3Web/

4. In *Wide Open: Open Source Methods and their Future Potential* (Demos, 2005), Tom Steinberg and I tried to provide a more rounded assessment of the potential for open source methods. The hype has, perhaps not surprisingly, continued. A recent book on the topic is *Wikinomics* by Don Tapscott.

5. Oliver MacDonagh *Early Victorian Government, 1830–1870* New York: Holmes and Meier, 1977), 6.

Chapter 6

1. See Academy of Medical Sciences *The Environmental Causes of Disease* (London, 2007), for an excellent overview of the state of the field, and the relative virtues of Randomized Control Trials, non-experimental survey data, and natural experiments.

2. G. Mulgan, 'Government and Knowledge', *Evidence and Policy Journal*, 1/2 (2005).

3. National Institute for Clinical Excellence: http://www.nice.org.uk; NHS Centre for Reviews and Dissemination: http://www.york.ac.uk/inst/crd; Cochrane Collaboration: http://www.cochrane.org/index0.htm; EPPI-Centre: http://eppi.ioe.ac.uk/EPPIWeb/home.aspx; ESRC Research Centre for Analysis of Social Exclusion: http://sticerd.lse.ac.uk/case; Social Care Institute for Excellence: http://www.scie.org.uk; Campbell Collaboration: http://www.campbellcollaboration.org; ESRC UK Centre for Evidence Based Policy and Practice: http://www.evidencenetwork.org

4. http://www.cochrane.org/

5. I became increasingly surprised in the UK government to find myself the only person at meetings who had been at the equivalent meeting five or six years previously. Often, all of the other officials and ministers had changed, leaving me as the corporate memory. Not surprisingly many mistakes risked being repeated. I proposed a fairly lean but comprehensive knowledge management system which would include lessons learned reports, directories of the officials who had led on previous programmes and projects, as well as more formal research and evaluations. The estimated cost was fairly low (under £3m) but it failed to secure support from the Treasury.

6. HMT (2006) Stern Review on the economics of climate change.

7. Karl Weick, *The Social Psychology of Organizing* (Reading, Mass: Addison Wesley, 1969).

8. See http://www.strategy.gov.uk

9. Lisa Anderson, *Pursuing Truth, Exercising Power: Social Science and Public Policy in the Twenty-First Century* (New York: Columbia University Press, 2003).

10. Terry Eagleton, *Ideology* (London: Longman, 1994), 212.

11. Larry Summers, former president of Harvard, once commented that the laws of economics are universal; I doubt Keynes would have ever claimed this.

Chapter 7

1. See Michael Barber, *Instruction to Deliver* (London: Methuen, 2007).
2. Christopher Hood, 'Gaming in Targetworld: The Targets Approach to Managing British Public Services', *Public Administration Review*, Jul/Aug (2006), 515.
3. National Consumer Council, *Customer Focus in Public Services* (London, 2006).
4. MORI, 2004, quoted in *Future Strategic Challenges for Britain*, Cabinet Office, February 2008.
5. A good recent example is Results Based Accountability, set out by Mark Friedman in his book *Trying Hard is Not Good Enough* (Crewe: Trafford Publishing, 2005), which shows how to link population accountability questions (outcomes) to performance accountability questions (which are usually about services to particular clients).
6. McKinsey & Co., *Consistently High Performance: Lessons from the World's Top-Performing School Systems* (London, 2007).
7. Simon Parker, 'Beyond Delivery', in *The Collaborative State*, Demos, 2006.
8. UK examples include Patient Opinion in health.
9. 'What the citizen wants', Henley Headlight Vision, London, 2008.
10. I made this argument in 'The Power of the Boot: Democratic Contestability in Public Services', *Oxford Review of Economic Policy* (1996).
11. See Chapter 8 for more on direct payments and 'In Control'.
12. See David Halpern, Clive Bates, Geoff Mulgan, Stephen Aldridge, Greg Beales, and Adam Heathfield, 'Personal Responsibility and Changing Behaviour: The State of Knowledge and its Implications for Public Policy', Prime Minister's Strategy Unit (2003), which set out many of the theoretical and practical issues that would arise as questions of behaviour change moved to the fore in public policy. David Boyle, Geoff Mulgan, and Rushanara Ali, *Life Begins at 60: What Kind of NHS after 2008?* (London: Young Foundation/New Economics Foundation, 2007), sets out the implications of these ideas in health policy.
13. Even the better ones apply manufacturing principles (of automation, modularization, and standardization) to services rather than the intensely personal care demanded at the high end of the market This was the theme of Shoshanna Zuboff and Jim Maxmin's book *The Support Economy: Why Corporations Are Failing Individuals and the Next Episode of Capitalism* (New York: Viking, 2002), and of a cluster of research institutes in Scandinavia in the 1970s and 1980s whose investigations of the practical meaning of service now look very prescient.
14. In principle wherever possible, multiple funding sources should be integrated into a single funding stream before reaching the delivery unit, and ideally there should be a 'single conversation' with those responsible for delivery.
15. This section draws on literature including Michael Hill and Peter L. Hupe, *Implementing Public Policy* (London: Sage, 2003); Paul R. Niven, *Balanced Scorecard Step-by-step for Government and Nonprofit Agencies* (Hoboken, NJ: John Wiley, 2003); R. Sanchez, offers a framework for thinking about how to scale up new ideas through 'architectural rules' and high degrees of 'modularity' in

Modularity, Strategic Flexibility, and Knowledge Management (Oxford: Oxford University Press, 2000); Sandford Borins, 'The Challenge of Innovating in Government', *Canadian Public Administration*, 38 (spring 2001).

Chapter 8

1. DARPA is the Defense Advanced Research Projects Agency, which is the central research and development organization for the US Department of Defense. CERN is the European Organization for Nuclear Research, which is the world's largest particle physics centre.
2. William J. Baumol, *The Free-Market Innovation Machine: Analyzing the Growth Miracle of Capitalism* (Princeton: Princeton University Press, 2002).
3. The Harvard programme of awards for innovation has confirmed over twenty years how creative public services can be. See Sandford Borins (ed.), *Innovations in Government: Research, Recognition and Replication* (Washington: Brookings Institution, 2008).
4. OECD, *OECD Science, Technology and Industry (STI) Scoreboard 2005* (Paris: OECD, 2005).
5. For further information on the World Bank's 'Government Effectiveness' rating see http://info.worldbank.org/governance/kkz/worldmap.asp#map
6. OECD *OECD Factbook 2006: Economic, Environmental and Social Statistics*, available at http://lysander.sourceoecd.org/vl=1451893/cl=16/nw=1/rpsv/factbook/
7. B. Nooteboom, *Learning and Innovation in Organizations and Economies* (Oxford: Oxford University Press, 2000).
8. Rogers, Everett *Combatting AIDS: Communication Strategies in Action* (London: Sage, 2003).
9. For further information on the PUBLIN network of researchers, see www.step.no/publin/
10. Philip Davies et al., 'The Relevance of Systematic Reviews to Educational Policy and Practice', *Oxford Review of Education*, 26/3–4 (2000).
11. T. Greenhalgh et al., *How to Spread Good Ideas: A Systematic Review of the Literature on Diffusion, Dissemination and Sustainability of Innovations in Health Service Delivery and Organisation*. Report for the National Coordinating Centre for NHS Service Delivery and Organisation R&D (NCCSDO), 2004 (available at http://www.sdo.lshtm.ac.uk/files/project/38-final-report.pdf).
12. Sandford Borins, 'The Challenge of Innovating in Government', *Canadian Public Administration*, 38 (spring 2001).
13. Jean Hartley, (2006) 'Knowledge Transfer and the UK Beacon Scheme: Improvements in Public Services', in S. Martin (ed.), *Public Service Improvement: Policies, Progress and Prospects* (London: Taylor and Francis, 2006).
14. HEFCE, 'The National Student Survey', Higher Education Funding Council for England (2006), available at www.hefce.ac.uk/news/hefce/2006/survey.htm
15. www.quotationsbook.com/quote/7252/

16. Jaime Lerner, *Cities Climate Change Summit* (2005), available at www.london.gov.uk/mayor/environment/climate-summit/docs/plenary4oct-jaimelerner.rtf. Further background on Lerner's work is available at www.worldchanging.com/archives/005940.html

17. Further information is available at www.news.harvard.edu/gazette/2004/03.11/01-mockus.html

18. Eleanor Glor, 'Impacts of a Prenatal Program for Native Indian Women', *Canadian Journal of Public Health*, 78/4 (July/Aug 1987).

19. For a critique of Bratton's policies see Bernard E. Harcourt and David E. Thacher, 'Is Broken Windows Policing Broken?' *Legal Affairs: The Magazine at the Intersection of Law and Life* (2005), 1–27.

20. E. Schall, 'Notes from a Reflective Practitioner of Innovation', in A. A. Altshuler and R. D. Behn (eds), *Innovation in American Government: Challenges, Opportunities, and Dilemmas* (Washington: Brookings Institution Press, 1997).

21. Borins, 'The Challenge of Innovating in Government'.

22. Harvard University's John F. Kennedy School of Government has run an Innovations in American Government award scheme since 1986, which has become a significant force in recognizing and promoting excellence and creativity in the public sector in the United States. South Africa set up the Centre for Public Service Innovation (CPSI) in 2002, and now runs regular awards. There are also now, under NEPAD, all-Africa public service innovation awards. Brazil has a variety of awards including one for innovators in education.

23. For a more extensive account of the role of civil society see G. Mulgan et al. *Social Innovation: What is it, Why it Matters, How it can be Accelerated* (London: Young Foundation, 2006).

24. www.cleanindia.org.

25. Denmark has created the Danish Innovation Council to identify potential areas for the government to support innovative projects (Mandag Morgen, 2006). Finland has a national Fund for Research and Development, which has published reports into future innovation strategies (Finnish National Fund for Research and Development, 2005). Sweden has introduced Framtidens Naringsliv, a cross-political forum bringing business, politicians, and academia together to discuss innovation strategies. Ireland introduced widespread educational, economic, and political reforms since the 1960s which have done much to transform the prospects of the country as a whole (T. Hämäläinen and R. Heiskala (eds), *Social Innovations, Institutional Change and Economic Performance: Making Sense of Structural Adjustment Processes in Industrial Sectors, Regions and Societies* (Cheltenham: Edward Elgar, 2007).

26. National Audit Office, 2006.

27. Finnish National Fund for Research and Development, 2005.

28. J. Smith, 'Institutionalising Public Sector Innovation', *Public Sector Technology & Management*, 2/5 (Sept. / Oct. 2005), available at www.tec.gov.sg/TEC%20News/2005/News2005_PSTM.htm

29. I co-authored a report on public innovation for the Cabinet Office in 2002/3; we were disappointed that no ministers or senior officials showed much interest in this agenda.

30. For further information on the 'Invest to Save Budget' see www.isb.gov.uk

31. Joseph Rowntree Foundation, *The Impact of External Inspection on Local Government* (London: Joseph Rowntree Foundation, 2001).

32. Clayton Christensen, *The Innovators Dilemma: The Revolutionary Book that Will Change the Way You Do Business* (New York: HarperCollins, 1997).

33. http://www.sitra.fi/en/News/release_2006-09-07.htm

34. Robert L. Savage, 'Policy Innovativeness as a Trait of American States,' *Journal of Politics*, 40 (1978), 212–24.

35. Robert B. Denhardt and Janet V. Denhardt, 'Leadership for Change', in Mark Abrahamson and Ian Littman (eds), *Leaders* (Lanham, Md.: Rowman and Littlefield, 2002), 143–73.

36. Barcelona, Helsinki, Amsterdam, and Phoenix exemplify the 'organizational variance model' in innovation studies which focused on how receptive organizations were to new ideas (see e.g. L. B. Mohr, 'Determinants of Innovation in Organizations', *Political Science Review*, 63/1 (1969), 111–26; V. Gray, 'Innovation in the States': A Diffusion Study', *American Political Science Association*, 67/4 (1973), 1174–85).

37. The City of St Paul, Minnesota, was a pioneer in this area. For further information on the 'Block Nurse' programme in St Paul see www.blocknurse.org/

38. For further information on these processes, see papers on campaigning and on how civil society responds to changing needs—from the Young Foundation for the Carnegie Inquiry into the future of civil society (www.youngfoundation.org).

39. Netmums is a local network for mothers that has a wide range of information and advice on being a mum. For further information see www.netmums.com

40. The Expert Patients Programme is an NHS-based training programme that provides opportunities to people who live with long-term chronic conditions to develop new skills to manage their condition better on a day-to-day basis. For further information see www.expertpatients.nhs.uk/public/default.aspx

41. For further information on 'In Control' see www.in-control.org.uk

42. See e.g. *Innovation Nation*, the UK government's science and technology white paper published in March 2008.

43. Mihaly Czikszentmihalyi, *Flow: The Psychology of Optimal Experience* (New York: Harper and Row, 1990).

44. For example, E. de Bono, *Lateral Thinking: Creativity Step by Step* (London: Perennial Library, 1970).

45. Teresa Amabile, *The Social Psychology of Creativity* (New York: Springer Verlag, 1983), is a good overview.

46. This was Richard Sennett's characterization of Michael Young's method—in *Porcupines in Winter* (London: Young Foundation, 2006).

47. Further information is available at www.firstscience.com/home/poems-and-quotes/quotes/linus-pauling-quote_2399.html

48. Rosabeth Moss Kanter, *Rosabeth Moss Kanter on the Frontiers of Management* (Boston: Harvard Business School, 1997).

49. Stephen R. G. Jones, 'Was There a Hawthorne Effect?', *American Journal of Sociology*, 98/3 (Nov 1992), 451–68.

50. Orley Ashenfelter, 'Estimating the Effect of Training Programs on Earnings', *Review of Economics and Statistics*. 60/1 (1978), 47–57.

51. Lawrence J. Schweinhart, *The High/Scope Perry Preschool Study: A Case Study in Random Assignment* (Ypsilanti, Mich. 2000). Available at www.multilingual-matters.net/erie/014/0136/erie0140136.pdf

52. D. Allnock, J. Tunstill, S. Akhurst, C. Garbers, and P. Meadows, 'Facilitating Access to Services for Children and Families: Lessons from Sure Start Local Programmes', *Child and Family Social Work*, 11/4 (2005), 287–96.

53. See Kevin Lang, *Poverty and Discrimination* (Princeton: Princeton University Press, 2007), for a good discussion of this and many other examples where evidence has been ambiguous.

54. Ibid. 134

55. A good survey of recent experiences in knowledge management and networks in the public sector is provided by *Public Finance and Management* (April 2006). See also J. Benington and J. Hartley *Inter-organizational Collaboration for Knowledge Generation and Application between Academics, Policymakers and Practitioners*, Warwick Business School, Apr 1999.

56. J. Kao, *Jamming: The Art and Discipline of Corporate Creativity* (New York: Harper Business, 1996).

57. Constantinos C. Markides and Paul A. Geroski, *Fast Second: How Smart Companies Bypass Radical Innovation to Enter and Dominate New Markets* (San Francisco: Jossey Bass, 2005).

58. 'Skunk works' refers to a semi-independent group set up to innovate within an organization which is less restricted by bureaucracy

59. C. Leadbeater, *The Man in the Caravan and Other Stories* (London: Improvement and Development Agency, 2003). This book contains many illuminating case studies of innovation in local services.

60. The importance of strong informal networks is being investigated by the current NESTA–Young Foundation research on innovative localities making use of network analysis models to compare more and less innovative sectors.

61. S. Sambrook and J. Stewart, *Human Resource Development in the Public Sector: The Case of Health and Social Care* (London: Routledge, 2007).

Chapter 9

1. Benjamin Friedman, *Moral Consequences of Economic Growth* (London: Knopf, 2005).

2. The UK government introduced non-executives into many departments during the 1990s and 2000s. Their constitutional position was often ambiguous—but oversight of risk is an example of a constructive role they can play.

3. For a thoughtful overview of the cultural aspects of risk, commissioned by a public regulator, see http://www.hse.gov.uk/research/rrpdf/rr035.pdf

4. Christopher Hood, Henry Rothstein, and Robert Baldwin, *The Government of Risk: Understanding Risk Regulation Regimes* (Oxford: Oxford University Press, 2001); Carlo C. Jaeger, Ortwin Renn, Eugene A, Rosa, and Thomas Webler, *Risk, Uncertainty, and Rational Action* (London: Earthscan, 2001).

Chapter 10

1. Sources in this area include Vernon Bogdanor (ed.) *Joined-Up Government*, British Academy Occasinal Papers (Oxford: Oxford University Press, 2005); Mark Sproule-Jones 'Horizontal Management: Implementing Programs across Interdependent Organisations' *Canadian Public Administration*, 43 (2000); the work of Vincent Ostrom on the virtues of weak hierarchies and polycentricity; the OECD paper on Policy Coherence, 2003.

2. The speech was made in late 1997 and was to launch the Social Exclusion Unit. Various other people subsequently claimed to have coined the phrase 'joined-up government', but I've yet to find an example which predates this.

3. *Governing Partnerships: Bridging the Accountability Gap* (London: Audit Commission, 2005).

4. Some of the underlying analysis and prescription was set out in a programme of work at the think tank Demos: *The British Spring* (1997) by Geoff Mulgan et al.; *Holistic Government* (1997) by Perri 6; *Governing in the Round* (1998) by Perri 6 and Gerry Stoker.

5. Quoted by Don Kettl, see also Don Kettl, Patricia Ingraham, Ronald Sanders, and Constance Horner, *Civil Service Reform: Building a Government that Works* (Washington: Brookings Institution, 1996).

6. See http://www.nao.gov.uk/publications/workinprogress/joinedup1.htm

7. PIU, *Wiring it Up*, Cabinet Office, 2000.

8. Charles Sabel, 'Beyond Principal–Agent Governance: Experimentalist Organizations, learning and Accountability', WRR discussion paper, 2004.

9. The Young Foundation report *Transformers: How Localities Innovate* (London: NESTA, 2008) shows a series of social network analyses of localities.

10. See Jake Chapman, *Systems Failure* (London: Demos, 2002); and the presentation prepared by Mulgan, Mabey, and Laing for the 2004 International Systems Dynamics Conference.

11. Broadly, organizations fall into one of five (strongly overlapping) categories—though, over time and especially through changes in leadership or major external pressures, they can change their category: first movers or pioneers; early adopters; followers laggards; resisters. Further discussion of this typology and related issues can be found in F. Damanpour, et al. 'The Relationship between Types of Innovation and Organisational Performance', *Journal of*

Management Studies, 26 (1989), 587–601; E. Rogers, *Diffusion of Innovations* (London: Free Press, 1995); A. van de Ven et al., *The Innovation Journey* (Oxford: Oxford University Press, 1999).

Chapter 11

1. These are the fuller figures: smoking cessation programmes—counselling and nicotine replacement, £503–692/QALY (Source: NE Derbyshire PCT), £817-1,040/ QALY (Source: 2005 Netherlands study). Tamoxifen for breast cancer prevention in high-risk groups: £21,7367/QALY (Source: S. Cybert, *Obstetrics & Gynecology*, Sept 2004). Beta Interferon for Multiple Sclerosis £39,972–810,481 (Source: NICE/ MS Research Trust).

2. This chapter draws on several sources. My ESRC lecture in 1996, 'Coproduction and Personal Responsibility'; the 1997 Demos collection *Missionary Government*, which drew attention to the rising importance of culture and behaviour change in public policy; and the Strategy Unit paper *Personal Responsibility and Changing Behaviour*, published in 2003, which was followed up by another paper on culture change in late 2007.

3. D. Wanless, *Securing Our Future Health: Taking a Long-Term View*, HM Treasury, 2002.

4. *Curbing the Epidemic: Governments and the Economics of Tobacco Control* (Washington: World Bank, 1999).

5. 'The Effect of a Snack Tax on Household Soft Drink Expenditure', University of Wisconsin working paper (2006).

6. C. S. Sunstein and R. H. Thaler, 'Libertarian Paternalism is not an Oxymoron' AEI-Brookings working paper (2003).

7. For more information see www.irwellvalleyha.co.uk

8. One of the most useful recent books is R. B. Cialdini, *Influence: Science and Practice*, 4th edn (Boston: Allyn and Bacon, 2001). Other sources include K. Glanz, B. Rimer, F. M. Lewis (eds.) *Health Behavior and Health Education: Theory Research and Practice*, 4th edn (San Francisco: Jossey-Bass, 2002); A. Tversky and D. Kahneman, 'Judgment under Uncertainty: Heuristics and Biases', *Science*, NS 185 (1974) 1124–31; I. P. Pavlov, *Conditioned Reflexes* (Oxford: Oxford University Press, 1927); B. F. Skinner, *Science and Human Behavior* (New York: Macmillan, 1953).

9. K. R. McLeroy, D. Bibeau, A. Steckler, and K. Glanz, 'An Ecological Perspective on Health Promotion Programs,' *Health Education Quarterly* 14/4 (1988), 351–77; E. S. Reed, *Encountering the World: Toward an Ecological Psychology* (New York: Oxford University Press, 1996); R. G. Barker, *Ecological Psychology: Concepts and Methods for Studying the Environment of Human Behavior* (Stanford, Calif.: Stanford University Press, 1968).

10. O. Dudley Duncan, A. O. Haller, and A. Portes 'Peer Influences on Aspirations: A Reinterpretation', *American Journal of Sociology*, 74/2 (1978).

11. L. Festinger, *A Theory of Cognitive Dissonance* (Stanford, Calif.: Stanford University Press, 1957).

12. Tversky and Kahneman, 'Judgment under Uncertainty': (a. 8 above).

13. D. Kahneman, L. Knetsch, and R. H. Thaler, 'Experimental Tests of the Endowment Effect and the Coase Theorem', *Journal of Political Economy*, 98/6 (1990), 1325–48.

14. P. Salovey and A. J. Rothman (eds), *The Social Psychology of Health: Key Readings* (Philadelphia: Psychology Press, 2003).

15. A. Bandura, *Social Foundations of Thought and Action: A Social Cognitive Theory* (Englewood Cliffs, NJ: Prentice Hall, 1986).

16. A. S. Gerber and D. P. Green, 'The Effects of Canvassing, Telephone Calls, and Direct Mail on Voter Turnout: A Field Experiment' *American Political Science Review*, 94/3 (2000), 653–63.

17. Ibid.

18. David P. Farrington and Brandon C. Welsh *Effects of Improved Street Lighting on Crime: A Systematic Review*, Home Office Research Study 251 (2002).

19. See Robert J. Sampson, Stephen Raudenbush, and Felton Earls, 'Neighborhoods and Violent Crime: A Multilevel Study of Collective Efficacy', *Science*, 277 (1997), 918–24.

20. P. Crewson, 'Public Service Motivation: Building Empirical Evidence of Incidence and Effect', *Journal of Public Adminsitration Research and Theory*, 7/4 (1997), 499–518.

21. G. A. Brewer, S. C. Selden, and R. L. Facer, 'Individual Conceptions of Public Service Motivation', *Public Administration Review*, 60 (2000), 254–64.

22. Jane Steele, *Wasted Values: Harnessing the Commitment of Public Managers* (London: Public Management Foundation, 1999).

23. A survey of 125 NHS staff—65 managers, 24 hospital doctors, 20 medical managers, and 16 GPs. Among thirteen possible motivating factors, the desire to provide a good quality service to users was ranked the highest by all groups, except GPs. None of the groups was especially motivated by prospect of personal gain. The work undertaken by Graham and Steele is consistent with earlier work done by Shaw, Mitchell, and Dawson in 1995. A BMA survey in 1995 of doctor's attitudes towards health found that only 2% felt that 'medicine was a job like any other and that doctors had a right to work normal hours and forget about work when they get home', though over half of the respondents (58%) agreed with the statement that 'medicine is a major commitment, but doctors also deserve a decent family life and leisure time', while a further 29% felt that 'the practice of medicine must be organized in a way which allowed doctors to balance their career with family and other interests'. Crilly and Le Grand (forthcoming) explored the motivation and goals of NHS trusts, using a survey of 1,500 hospital consultants and managers and a statistical analysis of 100 acute trusts over three years. Consultants considered service goals (quality and quantity) more important than financial break-even. With managers the primary goal was financial break-even. Managers were, however, heterogeneous: quality mattered most to the managers whose jobs were closest to service delivery. The results showed that consultants and significant groups of managers have relatively little commitment to the financial health of

institutions. A similar study was done by Peter Taylor-Gooby looking at the motivations of dentists deciding whether to treat patients privately or publicly. Those deciding to leave the NHS were motivated by belief that there would be an increase in personal benefit and they felt they would be able to give more time and attention to patients.

24. Jeremy Kendall, 'Of Knights, Knaves and Merchants: The Case of Residential Care for Older People in England in the Late 1990s', *Social Policy & Administration*, 35/4 (2001), 360–75.

25. Julien Forder, 'Mental Health: Market Power and Governance,' *Journal of Health Economics* 19/6 (2000).

26. Simon Burgess, Carol Propper, and Deborah Wilson, *Does Performance Monitoring Work? A Review of the Evidence from the UK Public Sector, Excluding Health Care*, Centre for Market and Public Organisation 02/049, Department of Economics, University of Bristol. (2002).

27. Ibid.

28. It was found that financial incentives affected health care resources with a direct impact on admission rates to and length of stays in hospital. They also found evidence that incentives affected compliance with clinical practice guidelines and the achievement of immunization targets.

29. Peter Doltom, Stephen McIntosh, and Arnaud Chevalier, *Recruiting and Retaining Teachers in the UK: An Analysis of Graduate Occupation Choice from the 1960s to the 1990s*, CEP Paper CEEDP0021, (2002).

30. Diana Leat, *For Love or Money* (York: Joseph Rowntree Foundation, 1990).

31. See e.g. Teresa Amabile's paper on intrinsic and extrinsic motivation. http://hbswk.hbs.edu/item/0543.html

32. These figures are taken from the ISSP Work Orientations Module for OECD countries.

33. Michael Thompson, and Marco Verweij, (eds) *Clumsy Solutions for a Complex World* (New York: Palgrave Macmillan, 2006).

34. Though this was also George Orwell's definition of Doublethink in his novel *1984*.

Chapter 12

1. Peri K. Blind, 'Building Trust in Government in the 21st Century', *Review of Literature and Emerging Issues*, (UNDESA, 2006).

2. In the UK, for example, sentencing is broadly in line with public attitudes. But because of media coverage of crime and punishment the public believe that sentencing is much more lenient, and therefore demand stiffer penalties. This then influences the actions of ministers and judges.

3. C. Crouch, *Post-Democracy* (Cambridge: Polity, 2004); R. Dalton, *Democratic Challenges, Democratic Choices, The Erosion of Political Support in Advanced Industrial Democracies.* (Oxford: Oxford University Press, 2004); I. Marsh, 'Neoliberal-

ism and the Decline of Democratic Governance: A Problem of Institutional Design?', *Political Studies*, 53 (2005), 22–42. All provide acute analyses of the travails of modern democracy.

4. John Lloyd, *What the Media are Doing to our Politics* (London: Constable, 2004).

5. Two books with the title *The Modern Prince*—by Carnes Lord and Dick Morris— offer some useful insights into contemporary politics. Dennis C. Mueller *Public Choice III* (Cambridge: Cambridge University Press, 2003), provides a survey of the various theories of the state and politics including voting rules, federalism, the theory of clubs, two-party and multiparty electoral systems, rent-seeking, bureaucracy, interest groups, dictatorship, the size of government, voter participation, and political business cycles.

6. In Milton's writings Satan was sometimes represented as a mist.

7. The best recent survey of the whole field of trust is B. A Mistzal, *Trust in Modern Societies: The Search for the Bases of Social Order* (Cambridge: Polity, 1996).

8. Russell J. Dalton, 'The Social Transformation of Trust in Government,' *International Review of Sociology*, 15/1 (March 2005), 133–54.

9. D. Kaufman, *Myths and Realities of Governance and Corruption*, World Economic Forum (Nov 2005). Accessible at http://www.worldbank.org/wbi/governance/pubs/gcr2005.html

10. Organization of Economic Cooperation and Development (OECD) Public Management, *Building Trust: Ethics Measures in OECD Countries*, Puma Policy Brief 7 (Sept 2000), 1–6.

11. Janet and Robert Denhardt, *Creating a Culture of Innovation* (London: Price Waterhouse Coopers, 2001).

12. J. M. Kauzya, 'Strengthening Local Governance Capacity for Participation', in D. A. Rondinelli and S. Cheema (eds), *Reinventing Government for the Twenty-First Century: State Capacity in a Globalizing Society* (Bloomfield, Conn.: Kumarian Press, 2003), 181–95.

13. Jakob Nielsen, who is a commentator on use patterns in networks, refers to 'participation inequality' and argues that participation follows a 90-9-1 rule: '90% of users are lurkers; 9% of users contribute from time to time; and 1% of users participate a lot and account for most contributions.'

14. Colin Crouch, *Capitalist Diversity and Change* (Oxford: Oxford University Press, 2005), 92.

15. Pippa Norris, *A Virtuous Circle* (Cambridge: Cambridge University Press, 2000).

16. E. Ostrom and J. Walker (eds), *Trust and Reciprocity: Interdisciplinary Lessons from Experimental Research* (New York: Russell Sage Foundation, 2003).

Chapter 13

1. This piece draws on two main sources: G. Mulgan, G. Kelly and S. Muers, *Creating Public Value*, published by the Cabinet Office in 2002, and a report for the Commission on Architecture and the Built Environment by Geoff Mulgan,

Gareth Potts, Matthew Carmona, Claudio de Magalhaes, and Louie Sieh, published in 2006. Other relevant recent reports include the major study by Sir Tony Atkinson, *Measurement of Government Output and Productivity for the National Accounts*, which has begun a major programme of more detailed assessment of public service productivity. The full Atkinson report is at: www.statistics.gov.uk/about/data/methodology/specific/PublicSector/Atkinson/final_report.asp

2. Paul Dolan and Robert Metcalfe, 'The Impact of Subjective Wellbeing on Local Authority Interventions' Imperial College London, Feb 2008.

3. Paul Dolan and Robert Metcalfe, 'Valuing Non-market Goods: A Comparison of Preference-Based and Experience-Based Approaches', Imperial College London, 2008.

4. Thomas H. Johnson *Relevance Lost: The Rise and Fall of Management Accounting* (Boston: Harvard Business School Press, 1991).

5. Bent Flyvbjerg, Nils Bruzelius, and Werner Rothengatter, *Megaprojects and Risk: An Anatomy of Ambition* (Cambridge: Cambridge University Press, 2003).

6. The following books provide a good overview: C. J. Barrow, *Social Impact Assessment: An Introduction*. (London: Arnold, 2000); H. Becker and F. Vanclay, The International Handbook of SIA (Cheltenham: E. Elgar, 2003); H. A. Becker, *Social Impact Assessment: Method and Experience in Europe, North America and the Developing World* (London: UCL Press, 1997); Scholten, P. J. Nicholls, S. Olsen, and B. Galimidi, *SROI: A Guide to Social Return on Investment* (Amsterdam: Lenthe Publishers, 2006).

7. http://www.matrixknowledge.co.uk/wp-content/uploads/economic-case-for-and-against-prison.pdf

8. We sought to draw on the work done by Mark Moore in the 1990s. The 'strategic triangle' he developed provides a useful heuristic device for managers to think about their roles in creating value. The triangle links together the 'authorizing environment'—where power and legitimacy come from: the 'operating capacity' of the organization or agency, and the public value being created which is ultimately defined by the public. For managers in the middle this model serves as a reminder that they need to pay attention to what the public really wants—whether through polls and surveys, consultations or focus groups—and that at times they may need to work as hard to influence their authorizing environment as they do to carry out instructions.

9. This section draws on work that began at the Cabinet Office in the early 2000s, which was published as *Creating Public Value* by the Cabinet Office in 2002.

10. We drew on what was then an emerging literature making use of the concept of public value. See M. Moore, *Creating Public Value: Strategic Management in Government* (Cambridge, Mass.: Harvard University Press); Barry Bozeman, 'Public-Value Failure: When Efficient Markets May Not Do', *Public Administration Review*, 62/2 (2002).

11. For example, an opinion poll that suggests that citizens would like government to spend more money on services but fails to indicate public willingness to pay

for this course of action does not constitute evidence that higher spending will increase public value.

12. Public Management Foundation, *The Glue that Binds: Public Value of Public Services* (1996).

13. Institute of Fiscal Studies, (1997). *What Drives Support for Higher Public Spending?* (1997).

14. *The Glue that Binds.*

15. Arthur H. Miller and Ola Listhaug, 'Political Performance and Institutional Trust', in Pippa Norris (ed.), *Critical Citizens: Global Support for Democratic Government* (Oxford: Oxford University Press, 1999).

16. L. Demery et al., *Understanding the Social Effects of Policy Reform* (Washington: World Bank, 1993) *The Development Effectiveness Record: Learning from Experience* (Washington: World Bank, 2002).

17. For a useful analysis of the economic arguments that surround the Stern Review's discount rates see http://johnquiggin.com/wp-content/uploads/2006/12/sternrevwedo6121.pdf

18. Colin Price, *Time Discounting and Value* (Oxford: Oxford University Press, 1993). See also Avner Offer, *The Challenge of Affluence* (Oxford: Oxford University Press, 2006), for an imaginative application of thinking about preferences through time.

19. These include 'multi-criteria' analysis methods such as VALID or DQI; 'stated preference' models and an array of choice modelling and hedonic methods, quality of life metrics, Environmental Impact Assessments, environmental footprints, Placecheck, Local Environmental Quality Survey (LEQS), and Landscape Area Characterization methods. These and others are described in *Value Maps Literature Survey* (2006), Young Foundation and CABE (available on youngfoundation.org).

Chapter 14

1. Tony Blair once said to his rather baffled senior civil servants that he wanted them to think of themselves as 'social entrepreneurs'.

2. Jim Collins, *Good to Great* (New York, Random House, 2001).

3. This was the list developed by the late Dan Gowler at Templeton College Oxford.

4. J. Arquilla and D. Ronfeldt, *Swarming and the Future of Conflict*, Rand Corporation, 2005, http://www.rand.org/publications/DB/DB311/

5. K. C. Beardsley, D. M. Quinn, B. Biswas, and J. Wilkenfeld, 'Mediation Style and Crisis Outcomes,' *Journal of Conflict Resolution*, 50/1 (Feb 2006), 58–86.

6. See e.g. R. T. Hogan, G. J. Curphy, and J. Hogan, 'What Do We Know about Leadership?', *American Psychologist*, 49 (1994), 493–504.

7. Some recent developments and disputes are covered in the special issue of the *Leadership Quarterly*, 10/4 (1999).

8. R. A. Heifetz, *Leadership without Easy Answers* (Cambridge, Mass.: Belknap Press, 1994).
9. Though sceptics would point out that the arguments around EQ are little different from some of the ideals of the Human Relations school of the 1930s and in that guise they were only marginally successful in developing or distinguishing leaders. See e.g. Keith Grint, *The Sociology of Work* (Cambridge: Polity, 1998).
10. From *Sustaining the Leading Edge*, a report on leadership training and development by the Modernising Defence People Group, April 2000.
11. In G. Allison and P. Zelikow, *Essence of Decision: Explaining the Cuban Missile Crisis* (New York: Longman, 1999), 303–4.
12. See Richard Sennett's excellent book on craft, *The Craftsman* (London: Allen Lane, 2007).
13. I discuss the history of thinking about the morality of leadership, and why the wrong people so often become leaders, in *Good and Bad Power* (London: Allen Lane, 2006).

Chapter 15

1. T. Kasser and R. M. Ryan, 'Further Examining the American Dream: Differential Correlates of Intrinsic and Extrinsic Goals', *Personality and Social Psychology Bulletin*, 22 (1996), 280–7; J. Brunstein, O. Schultheiss, and R. Grassman, 'Personal Goals and Emotional Wellbeing: The Moderating Role of Motive Dispositions', *Journal of Personality and Social Psychology*, 75 (1998), 494–508.
2. This is the insight of many traditions, including Buddhism. More recently it's been confirmed by the strongly evidence-based work of John Kabat-Zinn and others on mindfulness.
3. Douglass North's work has been particularly influential in this area; see e.g. *Institutions, Institutional Change and Economic Performance* (Cambridge. Cambridge University Press, 1990). Attitudes also play a decisive role in ensuring that institutions are fully utilized.

Name Index

Includes all referenced authors.

Subject Index